BRAVE NEW WORLD

FOREWORD

To celebrate the turn of the century and the new millennium, **THE EVENTFUL CENTURY** series presents the vast panorama of the last hundred years—a century which has witnessed the transition from horse-drawn transport to space travel, and from the first telephones to the information superhighway.

THE EVENTFUL CENTURY chronicles epoch-making events like the outbreak of the two world wars, the Russian Revolution and the rise and fall of communism. But major events are only part of the glittering kaleidoscope. It also describes the everyday background—the way people lived, how they worked, what they ate and drank, how much they earned, the way they spent their leisure time, the books they read, and the crimes, scandals and unsolved mysteries that set them talking. Here are fads and crazes like the Hula-Hoop and Rubik's Cube . . . fashions like the New Look and the miniskirt . . . breakthroughs in entertainment, such as the birth of the movies . . . medical milestones such as the discovery of penicillin . . . and marvels of modern architecture and engineering.

BRAVE NEW WORLD tells what became of the high hopes and noble dreams of the generation that came through the shattering experience of the Second World War and vowed to make a better world. Western Europe made a miraculous recovery, helped by the Marshall Plan. But the Soviet satellites in Eastern Europe were not allowed to benefit, for the Cold War was at its height. Looming over the Superpower rivalry between the U.S. and the U.S.S.R., and opening up the terrifying possibility of mankind's self-destruction, was the mushroom-shaped shadow of the atomic bomb. The new world that emerged in these perilous years had no place for the old empires. Some, like Britain in India, recognized that the day of Imperialism was over; others tried fruitlessly to resist the "Wind of Change." Power shifted between social groups, as well as between nations. The civil rights movement in America, the rise of feminism, and the challenge thrown down by the next generation in the "Youth Explosion" were all part of the Brave New World.

BRAVE NEW WORLD
—— 1945-70 ——

 Reader's Digest

The Reader's Digest Association, Inc.
Pleasantville, New York/Montreal

BRAVE NEW WORLD
Edited and designed by Toucan Books Limited
Written by Robin Hosie
Edited by Robert Sackville West
Designed by Bradbury and Williams
Picture research by Wendy Brown

FOR THE AMERICAN EDITION
Produced by The Reference Works
Director Harold Rabinowitz
Editor Rachel Soltis
Production Antler Design Works
Director Bob Antler

FOR READER'S DIGEST
Group Editorial Director Fred DuBose
Senior Editor Susan Randol
Senior Designers Carol Nehring, Judith Carmel
Production Technology Manager Douglas A. Croll
Associate Designer Jennifer R. Tokarski
Editorial Manager Christine R. Guido

READER'S DIGEST ILLUSTRATED REFERENCE BOOKS
Editor-in-Chief Christopher Cavanaugh
Art Director Joan Mazzeo
Operations Manager William J. Cassidy

First English edition copyright © 1999
The Reader's Digest Association Limited,
11 Westferry Circus, Canary Wharf,
London E14 4HE

Copyright © 2001
Reader's Digest Association, Inc.
Reader's Digest Road
Pleasantville, NY 10570

Copyright © 2001
The Reader's Digest Association (Canada) Ltd.
Copyright © 2001
Reader's Digest Association Far East Limited
Philippine copyright © 2001
Reader's Digest Association Far East Limited

Printed in the United States of America

Library of Congress
Cataloging in Publication Data
Brave new world 1945-70.
      p. cm.—(The Eventful 20th century)
Includes index.
ISBN 0-7621-0290-X
    1. History, Modern—1945- 2. Cold War.
3. Reconstruction (1939-1951)—Europe. 4. Asia—
Politics and government—1945- I. Reader's Digest
Association. II. Series.

D840 .B67 2000
909.82'5—dc21

                                        00-028608

FRONT COVER
From Top: Martin Luther King, Jr.; Marshall Plan
poster; teen idol Marlon Brando.

BACK COVER
Crowd showing support for Mao in China;
Nikita Khrushchev in a forceful mood; youth
counter-culture poster in Vietnam era.

Page 3 (from left to right): Marlon Brando;
Volkswagen advertisement; anti-apartheid protesters;
United Nations poster.

Background pictures:
Page 15: Neon lights in West Berlin.
Page 45: Japanese shipyard.
Page 87: Red Guards in Beijing.
Page 125: Beatles fans.

Address any comments about Brave New World to:
Reader's Digest
Editor-in-Chief, U.S. Illustrated Reference Books
Reader's Digest Road, Pleasantville, NY 10570

To order additional copies of Brave New World, call
1-800-846-2100

You can also visit us on the World Wide Web at:
www.readersdigest.com

CONTENTS

FIRST AID FOR EUROPE   6

1 A TENSE RECOVERY IN EUROPE   15
THE COLD WAR SETS IN   16
BRAVE NEW BRITAIN   24
FRANCE: THE ROAD BACK   32
THE GERMAN MIRACLE   38
TOWARD EUROPEAN UNION   42

2 WHEN EMPIRES VANISH   45
FREEDOM AT MIDNIGHT   46
NEW NATIONS FROM OLD   53
A NEW WIND IN AFRICA   64
THE AGONY OF ALGERIA   74
MIDDLE EAST IN TURMOIL   77

3 IN THE SUPERPOWER ERA   87
INSIDE THE U.S.   88
BEHIND THE CURTAIN   99
COLD WAR CLASHES   107
IN THE VIETNAM QUICKSANDS   113
RED DAWN IN THE EAST   118

4 CHANGING TIMES   125
THE YOUTH EXPLOSION   126
A NEW DEAL FOR WOMEN   133
DREAMS AND DIVERSIONS   137

TIMECHART   144

INDEX   156

ACKNOWLEDGMENTS   160

FIRST AID FOR EUROPE

RAVAGED AND EXHAUSTED BY SIX YEARS OF WAR, EUROPE TURNED TO THE ONE COUNTRY WITH THE RESOURCES AND THE WILL TO HELP

The war in Europe ended on May 7, 1945, when Hitler's successor as Führer of the Third Reich, Grand Admiral Dönitz, surrendered unconditionally to the Allies. Victory in Japan followed on August 14. As the guns fell silent, and millions of people dreamed of building a better world, two formidable challenges faced the Allied leaders: to make sure that defeated Germany would never again threaten world peace, and to repair the ravages of the war.

Among the victors, America emerged rich and confident. Its industries were booming, its cities and landscapes unscarred by bombing. Its greatest challenge would be to bring home its millions of soldiers and reintegrate them into society. The number of active mili-

tary troops shrank from 12 million in 1945 to 3 million in 1946—and all of these soldiers needed to find housing, education, and jobs. With the country's growing prosperity, most of them did.

America's leaders were determined that there would be no retreat into isolationism as there had been at the end of the First World War. They were committed to playing their part in world affairs—the first step of which was helping Europe rebuild from the destruction of the past decade.

Britain ended the war triumphant but exhausted. The nation that had just lived through what Winston Churchill described as its "finest hour" was on the brink of bankruptcy. The war had cost the country £7.5 billion ($30 billion), and overseas assets had been largely sold off to meet the bill. Britain's factories had been almost totally devoted to winning the war, and the holds of its merchant ships had been crammed with war materials. As a result, the value of exports had shrunk to below half the 1938 figure. Nevertheless, Britain still looked upon itself—and was accepted by the world—as a great power, the mother country of a mighty empire, with a policing role in many of the trouble spots of the world. But the country was living beyond its means.

The newly liberated countries of Western Europe were, with one exception, in perilous conditions. That exception was Denmark, which had been lucky enough to

TRIUMPH AND TRAGEDY Right, U.S. soldiers celebrate the end of the war and anticipate the return home. Left, a bombed-out mother trudges barefoot through Berlin streets, looking for a night's shelter.

TALES OF THE GI BRIDES

Between 1942 and 1945, around 1.5 million American soldiers and airmen landed in Britain in the build-up to the liberation of Europe. With their easy confidence, generous pay packets and glamorous image, they were a revelation to a nation hardened to the deprivations of war. Some 60,000 British girls married their "Yank" sweethearts, and early in 1946 the U.S. government brought the GI brides to their new homes. Pamela Winfield, herself a GI bride, collected their stories. The first impression for many was the sheer size of the country:

"I had no idea of how big America was and how lonely all those hundreds of miles of absolutely nothing looked. I was dressed very prim-like with my black suit, black gloves and my Deanna Durbin hat. Florida, that land of sunshine, and I was dressed for a winter day!"

Some found the American dream exactly as they had expected it to be:

"The family home, though far from pretentious, was an attractive picture of chintz and bright white-painted staircases and window sills. It had the kind of look we had seen in the Andy Hardy pictures."

For others, the reality fell some considerable way short of the dream:

"When he took me to his home in the woods I found his two sisters running in bare feet. I thought I had come to a gypsy camp. Believe me, it was more like 1846 than 1946. They had a coal stove, fetched water from a spring and had an outside toilet. I was shocked and started to cry."

HUNGER PROTEST With Paris liberated but starving in March 1945, women demand milk for their children and better food for their husbands, "to finish the war quickly."

escape the general devastation of the war and whose abundant farm produce was now in great demand. Elsewhere, shortages of food and goods of all descriptions led to inflation and a thriving black market.

Norway and Belgium tackled inflation with drastic currency devaluations. But both of these countries had plenty of other problems. Norway, which made its living from the sea, had lost half its merchant navy. Tiny Belgium had lost half a million workers, deported to German concentration camps. In the Netherlands, sheets of water covered what ought to have been fertile low-lying land: the retreating Germans, out of spite and to delay the Allied advance, had opened the dikes.

France, humiliated by defeat in 1940 and by the Vichy government's collaboration, looked to the Resistance and to General de

REVOLUTION IN A RUSH Communist peasants, hungry for land, and hoping that liberation will change their lives, march on a big estate near Palermo, Sicily.

SIMPLE PLEASURES Just having something to cook brings a smile to the faces of these refugees in the bleak Europe of 1945.

borders more than 100 miles westward, and German nationals were expelled from the lost provinces of East Prussia, Pomerania and Lower Silesia. In Danzig, German families were given half an hour to leave. Czechoslovakia solved the problem of the Sudetenland Germans by forcing them at bayonet point across the border. All told, there were between 12 and 14 million refugees, of whom it has been estimated that more than 2 million died.

The defeated land was split into four zones, controlled by the Soviets, the Americans, the British and the French. Germany faced a reparations bill of $20 billion, half of it to go to the U.S.S.R. Trainloads of goods and machinery trundled east, as the Soviets scoured their zone. Giant firms like Krupps of Essen and I.G. Farben, the biggest chemical trust in the world, were taken over. The Western Allies soon realized that there was a point beyond which Germany could not pay, and in May 1946 the British and Americans announced an end to the dismantling of factories beyond those already earmarked for the Soviets.

People were starving. In effect, the British and American taxpayers were feeding the Germans. It was as much as they could do (and sometimes beyond them) to provide starvation rations of 1,500 calories a day. As Field Marshal Montgomery, in charge of the British zone, put it: "It is not part of my plan to pamper the Germans . . . They brought this disaster upon themselves. However, I am not prepared to see widespread famine and

continued on page 12

Gaulle, leader of the Free French, for a new start. One-fifth of the nation's houses had been destroyed, and its factories were running at well below 50 percent of their prewar output. Wheat production was down by half, vegetable production by two-thirds. With rations set at 3½ ounces of bread a day and just over 3 ounces of meat a week, the black market flourished.

In Italy there were 4 million unemployed and 5 million homeless. Malnutrition was so widespread that 30 percent of babies died within 24 hours of birth. Those lucky enough to have a job could earn 100-150 lira a day, at a time when a pair of leather shoes cost 3,500-4,500 lira. A fact-finding mission of American and British trade unionists found "corruption, looting and black marketing activities on a large scale."

Refugees and famine in Germany

Germany, the nation that had been the root

THE QUARTERED REICH The Allies divided Germany into four occupation zones, with Berlin an island under joint control, marooned in the Soviet zone.

cause of so many refugees streaming across stricken countrysides, now had millions of refugees of its own. As the victors redrew the map of Eastern Europe, Germany lost 30 percent of its territory. Poland shifted its

JUDGMENT AT NUREMBERG

IN THE MALIGNANT HIGH NOON OF THEIR POWER, THE NAZI LEADERS HAD BROUGHT UNTOLD SUFFERING TO OCCUPIED EUROPE, BUT RETRIBUTION WAS ON ITS WAY

In the years before the war, Nuremberg won a special place in the hearts of the Nazi faithful. It was the setting for the Nuremberg rallies, brilliantly stage-managed by Hitler's architect, Albert Speer, when the city's medieval watchtowers would be silhouetted against the glow of torchlight processions, and "Sieg Heil" would burst from a quarter of a million throats to greet Hitler in the vast Zeppelin Field stadium. It was also the city where the Nuremberg Laws were proclaimed in 1935 —laws that stripped Jews of their rights to citizenship and forbade them to marry non-Jews. It could be seen as poetic justice, then, that although pulverized by the time the war ended, the city still had, standing above the rubble, a jail, where the Nazi leaders could be kept under guard, and a courthouse, where they could be put on trial.

There was some heart-searching among the victors about what the actual charges should be; some of the Nazi crimes were so unprecedented in enormity that new laws had to be framed to encompass them. The prosecution finally decided on four charges: conspiracy to wage aggressive war; crimes against peace (that is, the actual waging of war); war crimes (violation of the rules of war); and crimes against humanity—including genocide.

Highest-ranking of the 22 men in the dock was Reichsmarschall Hermann Göring, the swaggering, overweight, pill-addicted chief of the Luftwaffe and founder of the Gestapo. He was to lose 55 pounds in weight during the trial. "The victor will always be the judge, and the vanquished the accused," he responded when he was indicted. Among those accused with him were Rudolf Hess, Joachim von Ribbentrop, Field Marshal Wilhelm Keitel, Albert Speer, Ernst Kaltenbrunner, Julius Streicher, Robert Ley, and Martin Bormann, Hitler's secretary, who had not been captured and was tried in his absence.

Those found guilty were convicted largely on the evidence of their own carefully preserved records. The prosecution labored through papers by the ton, and selected 4,000 documents for translation and use in evidence. There was film evidence, too—scenes of executions and of the death camps. This harrowing evidence caused mixed reactions in the dock. Keitel wiped his brow and shook his head. Göring yawned. The Allies decided early on that the defense of *tu quoque* ("You did it too") would not be permitted. Most of the accused put forward the defense that Hitler's

will was supreme, and that they had been trained to obey orders without question. In fact, every German soldier carried in his paybook an instruction that an illegal order was not to be obeyed; when Field Marshal Rommel was ordered to shoot captured British commandos, he had thrown the official order into the fire.

HITLER'S HENCHMAN Ernst Kaltenbrunner, former SS and Gestapo chief, in the dock at Nuremberg. Kaltenbrunner had run the Nazi concentration camps for Hitler; he was sentenced to death by hanging.

Verdicts and sentences were pronounced on October 1, 1946, in a courthouse protected by 1,000 troops. The judges—American, Soviet, British and French—handed down death sentences to 11 of the Nazi leaders, including Ribbentrop, Keitel, Kaltenbrunner and Streicher. Göring, sentenced to hang, escaped the gallows by taking

DAY OF RECKONING Nazi leaders on trial at Nuremberg, for war crimes, crimes against peace and genocide. Ten were hanged, but the highest-ranking defendant, Reichsmarschall Hermann Göring (inset), escaped the gallows by committing suicide.

cyanide the night before the executions. Hess received a life sentence and Speer 20 years. Martin Bormann was sentenced to death in his absence. Three of the accused were acquitted, and the rest were given sentences ranging from ten years to life.

History's verdict on Nuremberg is that although it was justice dispensed by the victors, it was still justice. The trial revealed to the world the full documented horror of the Final Solution, and putting the Nazi leaders on trial, rather than shooting them on capture, left no doubt: these men were criminals, not martyrs.

A postscript to the Nuremberg trials was written on May 31, 1962, when Adolf Eichmann, the organizer of the Final Solution, was tried, found guilty, and hanged in Israel. He had fled to South America, where he was hunted down by Israeli agents.

ROUND-UP AT THE REICHSTAG Only one economic activity flourished in Berlin in 1946: the black market. Police round up suspects in the Reichstag gardens.

was beheading by the public executioner.

During the war, Henry Morgenthau, Secretary of the U.S. Treasury, had put forward a plan to strip Germany of its industries and reduce the nation to a land of small farms—"a potato patch." In any event, the plan was dropped, but for a time reality fell not too far short of what Morgenthau had intended. The Ruhr was desperately short of miners, yet it had to supply coal as reparations to France, Belgium and other countries. The firm of Siemens, which had once employed 50,000 workers and supplied 80 percent of Germany's electrical equipment, was down to 250 men producing rakes, wheelbarrows and wooden buckets.

A ravaged Europe

To the east, Poland's cities lay in ruins. The Jewish population, 3.5 million before the war, had been reduced by Nazi persecution to 80,000, and even the survivors

THE RUBBLE MOUNTAIN

By the end of the war, many of Germany's towns and cities had been pounded into little more than heaps of rubble, and the task of clearing and rebuilding them was daunting. A British military observer calculated that if the rubble in Essen were removed at the rate of 1,000 tons a day, it would take 30 years to clear.

disease sweep through Europe." He put forward a plan to send 1.5 million tons of wheat to Germany.

Famine was not the only threat. At the war's end, there were more than 5 million slave laborers inside Germany. Three million were swiftly repatriated, but that still left 2 million, most of them Poles and Russians. These men had little pity in their hearts for the nation that had enslaved them. A menacing army of the uprooted roamed the land looting, raping and murdering. One of the worst incidents happened in the village of Fürstenau near the Dutch border. An armed gang of more than 40 Poles set fire to houses in the village, and left

behind them seven corpses in retaliation for the killing of one of their number by a German policeman.

Rumors spread like wildfire in the general chaos: one of the most alarming was of the Werewolves, a group of fanatical Nazis pledged to fight a guerrilla war. Orders were issued to hand in all weapons on pain of death. In the British zone, six German soldiers found with weapons were handed over to the civil authorities for the sentence to be carried out. In a chilling hangover from Nazi times, the punishment

PASSPORTS TO SURVIVAL
In their defeated and devastated land, the Germans needed ration cards and money issued by the Allies to survive.

THE RIDDLE OF THE AMBER ROOM

Of all the art treasures plundered from conquered Europe by the Nazis, none was more valuable than the Amber Room, and none met a more mysterious fate.

Amber is a fossilized resin, golden-brown and translucent, found chiefly along the shores of the Baltic Sea. The room was created from great panels of solid amber, six tons in all, exquisitely carved and decorated with gold leaf. Peter the Great, Tsar of Russia, saw it on a visit to Prussia in 1716, and was so entranced that he persuaded the Prussian king, Frederick William I, to give it to him. For almost 200 years, the room's resting place was to be the Winter Palace of the tsars, near St. Petersburg.

In June 1941, Hitler launched Operation Barbarossa, his attack on the U.S.S.R., and at first achieved stunning success. The Soviets, in headlong retreat, had no time to think about moving the Amber Room to safety, and it fell into German hands. A special detail, reporting to Erich Koch, Gauleiter of East Prussia, packed it into 24 crates for shipping to SS headquarters in the East Prussian capital of Königsberg (now Kaliningrad). Following an RAF raid in 1944, the panels were moved for safety to the cellars of Königsberg castle. But when the Red Army, now on the advance, arrived at Königsberg, there was no sign of the Amber Room. With panic-stricken refugees swarming through the city, it looked as though Koch, who escaped in the confusion, had taken the priceless panels with him.

Theories abound. One is that the Amber Room is still in Königsberg, buried beneath its streets. Another is that it lies at the bottom of a salt mine, near Göttingen in central Germany, that was flooded following an explosion. A third is that it lies at the bottom of the Baltic Sea. A German cruise ship, the *Wilhelm Gustloff*, set out from Königsberg on January 30, 1945, carrying 8,000 refugees and soldiers. She was sunk by a Soviet submarine, with the loss of at least 5,400 lives—the worst single disaster in the history of the sea. People at the dockside reported seeing crates being taken aboard the *Wilhelm Gustloff* before she pulled away.

Koch was picked up in Hamburg in 1949 and handed over to the Soviets. After lengthy interrogation, he was put on trial in 1958 for war crimes and sentenced to death, but later reprieved. One final, tenuous clue to the mystery turned up in May 1997, when a picture composed of gemstones was offered for sale in Germany. It was from the Amber Room, but nobody knows how or when it became detached; and the fate of the rest of the room remains shrouded in mystery.

LOST TREASURE Once described as "the eighth wonder of the world," the Amber Room vanished after being stolen from a Russian palace by retreating Germans.

than in any other country, even the U.S.S.R. Nearly one-third of Poland's houses and more than half its cattle were destroyed. The same sorry tale of destruction was repeated in Hungary, Bulgaria and Romania: road and rail bridges wrecked, towns and cities reduced to rubble, livestock decimated. Czechoslovakia had escaped the worst of the fighting during the war, but the country was liberated by the Red Army and was soon to discover what that meant.

Greece was a ravaged land. More than 6,000 schools and well over 1,000 towns and villages were in ruins. Some 1.5 million were homeless. When the Red Cross moved into newly liberated Athens, late in 1944, they found people dying of starvation in the streets at the rate of 300 a day. Inflation was running wild. Even after a currency reform meant to stabilize the drachma at 600 to the gold sovereign, the drachma's price on the black market continued to plummet, reaching 39,000 to the sovereign by October 1945. Furthermore, Greece was in the grip of a vicious civil war between government troops and communist guerrillas.

Yugoslavia bore all the marks of a country first brutally occupied, then fought over by the dogs of war. Marshal Tito's partisans had fought not only against the Germans,

AND WAR GOES ON In Greece, as one war ended, a new one began—a bitter civil war. Their possessions on their backs, a peasant family flees communist guerrillas.

were not safe. On July 4, 1946, the town of Kielce suffered a pogrom of medieval ferocity. A nine-year-old boy claimed he had seen the bodies of 15 Christian children, ritually murdered by Jews. He retracted his story later, but by then 42 Jews had been killed and dozens of Jewish homes plundered.

Ironically—since Britain and France had gone to war to protect them—Poland's frontiers were radically altered after the war. A thick slice of Polish territory in the east, more than 100 miles wide, became part of the U.S.S.R. In compensation, Poland was given part of East Prussia and a 100 mile slice of Germany. Six million Poles had lost their lives during the war—a higher proportion of the population (around 18 percent)

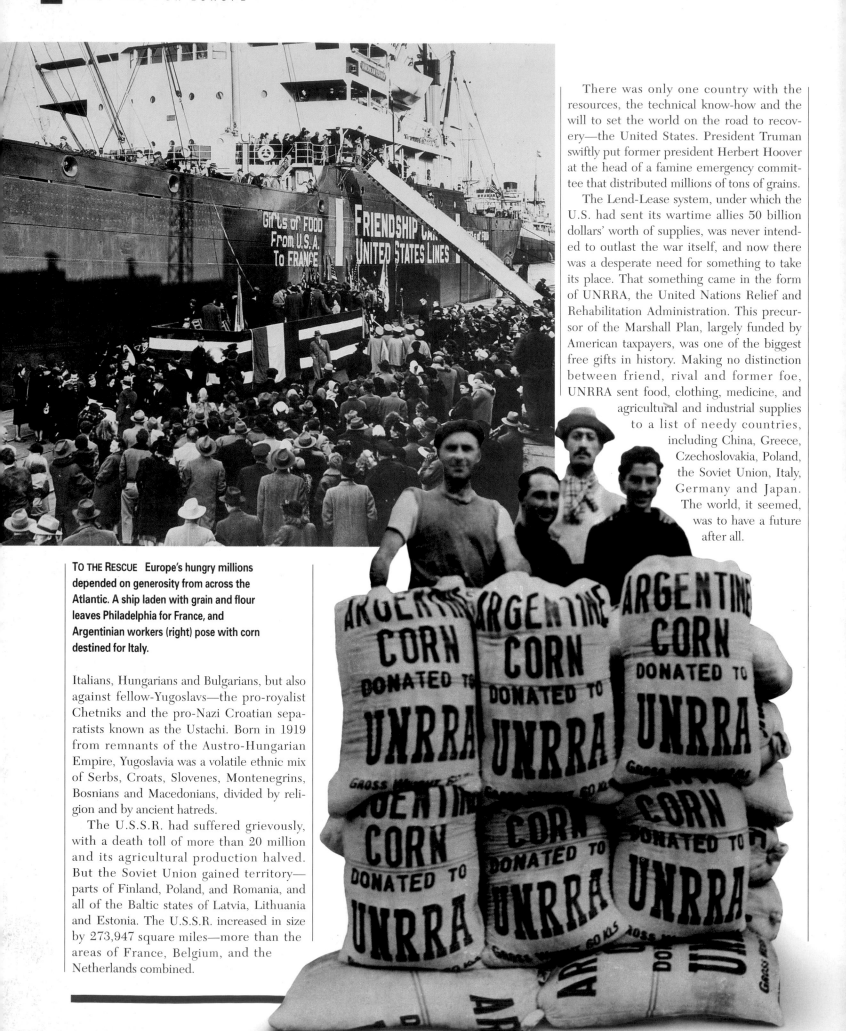

There was only one country with the resources, the technical know-how and the will to set the world on the road to recovery—the United States. President Truman swiftly put former president Herbert Hoover at the head of a famine emergency committee that distributed millions of tons of grains.

The Lend-Lease system, under which the U.S. had sent its wartime allies 50 billion dollars' worth of supplies, was never intended to outlast the war itself, and now there was a desperate need for something to take its place. That something came in the form of UNRRA, the United Nations Relief and Rehabilitation Administration. This precursor of the Marshall Plan, largely funded by American taxpayers, was one of the biggest free gifts in history. Making no distinction between friend, rival and former foe, UNRRA sent food, clothing, medicine, and agricultural and industrial supplies to a list of needy countries, including China, Greece, Czechoslovakia, Poland, the Soviet Union, Italy, Germany and Japan. The world, it seemed, was to have a future after all.

TO THE RESCUE Europe's hungry millions depended on generosity from across the Atlantic. A ship laden with grain and flour leaves Philadelphia for France, and Argentinian workers (right) pose with corn destined for Italy.

Italians, Hungarians and Bulgarians, but also against fellow-Yugoslavs—the pro-royalist Chetniks and the pro-Nazi Croatian separatists known as the Ustachi. Born in 1919 from remnants of the Austro-Hungarian Empire, Yugoslavia was a volatile ethnic mix of Serbs, Croats, Slovenes, Montenegrins, Bosnians and Macedonians, divided by religion and by ancient hatreds.

The U.S.S.R. had suffered grievously, with a death toll of more than 20 million and its agricultural production halved. But the Soviet Union gained territory— parts of Finland, Poland, and Romania, and all of the Baltic states of Latvia, Lithuania and Estonia. The U.S.S.R. increased in size by 273,947 square miles—more than the areas of France, Belgium, and the Netherlands combined.

A TENSE RECOVERY IN EUROPE

WITH GERMANY AND JAPAN DEFEATED, DEEP-SEATED SUSPICIONS BETWEEN FORMER ALLIES LED TO THE COLD WAR, AND AN "IRON CURTAIN" FELL ACROSS EUROPE. LOOMING OVER EVERY CRISIS BETWEEN THE NEW SUPERPOWERS, THE UNITED STATES AND THE SOVIET UNION, WAS THE MUSHROOM-SHAPED SHADOW OF THE ATOM BOMB. YET IN A WORLD FULL OF PERIL, NEW HOPE WAS BORN. THE U.S.-FUNDED MARSHALL PLAN KICK-STARTED A RETURN TO PROSPERITY.

THE COLD WAR SETS IN

IT DID NOT TAKE LONG AFTER VICTORY OVER HITLER'S GERMANY FOR WARTIME ALLIES TO BECOME PEACETIME RIVALS AND FOES

Shortly after midday on April 26, 1945, men of the U.S. 69th Infantry Division, identifying themselves with cries of "Amerikansky!", crossed the River Elbe near Torgau to link up with the Red Army's 175th Rifle Regiment. This first encounter of ordinary GIs and Soviet fighting men, in the heart of Germany, was a back-slapping session, with toasts drunk in beer and vodka. It meant that Germany was cut in two, and the end of the war was in sight. But it also meant

more than that: there could be no more dramatic symbol of the fact that Europe's future, and that of the entire world, was no longer mainly Europe's to decide. The Day of the Superpowers had dawned.

The Red Army had fought its way from Stalingrad on the Volga to Berlin and beyond. And wherever the Red Army went, the Red Flag followed. The Americans were even farther from home, for their journey had begun on the other side of the Atlantic.

The most urgent strategic question facing Western democracy was: could America be kept in Europe as a barrier against Soviet expansion? Ironically, it was the Soviet leader, Stalin himself, who made certain that the answer would be "Yes."

For Stalin set about turning the newly liberated nations of Eastern Europe into Soviet satellites. The U.S.S.R. had been an ally of the West; now it became a threat. The Soviet obsession with security was not hard to understand, given their savage losses in the Second World War. Hitler's invasion, in June 1941, had punched a path through Poland and the other countries on Russia's western borders. "What can there be surprising,"

SETTLING THE WORLD'S FUTURE Germany headed the agenda when Attlee, Truman and Stalin (seated, left to right), the leaders of the "Big Three," met at Potsdam in July 1945.

1946 Churchill makes "Iron Curtain" speech

1947 Truman Doctrine pledges U.S. to fight communism; Marshall Plan introduced

1948 Communist coup in Czechoslovakia; Berlin Airlift begins

1949 NATO founded; Berlin Blockade lifted; U.S.S.R. tests A-bomb

1955 Warsaw Pact signed

TITO IN TRIUMPH Surrounded by the tough communist partisans he had led against the Germans, Yugoslavia's Marshal Tito makes a victory speech in Belgrade in May 1945.

asked Stalin, "in the fact that the Soviet Union, anxious for its future safety, is trying to see to it that governments loyal in their attitude to the Soviet Union should exist in these countries?"

To ensure that loyalty, the Baltic states of Latvia, Lithuania and Estonia were simply annexed. Yugoslavia and Albania could be counted on, it seemed, because in both countries the communist partisans were in power. Elsewhere in Eastern Europe, the general pattern was for the communists to gain a foothold by joining a coalition government and insisting on key ministries that gave them control of the police and security. The complete takeover was then only a matter of time, and with it came the full panoply of purges, show trials and executions.

In conventional military terms, the Soviet Union and its satellites far outmatched the Western powers. "Bring the boys home" was a popular slogan in America, and in September 1945 the U.S. announced plans to demobilize 8.8 million men from its armed forces in the next ten months. By the end of 1946, Britain's armed forces had also been reduced dramatically—from 5 million to 1 million. Demobilization in the U.S.S.R., from a peak of 20 million under arms, was on nothing like

the same scale. However, as long as America had the atomic bomb and the U.S.S.R. did not, Stalin was playing chess without the queen. The next few years would show that the Soviet leader was prepared to provoke the West, and test its resolve, especially in Germany, but that he would always withdraw from the brink of open conflict.

The Iron Curtain falls

An early warning that the two superpowers could be on a collision course came in February 1946 from the U.S. diplomat George Kennan. In an 8,000-word message, known as the "long telegram," he told his chiefs in Washington that the Soviet leaders had a "neurotic" attitude, shaped by the history of their land. The Russians had never known a friendly neighbor. Theirs was the insecurity of an agricultural people living on a plain, at the mercy of fierce nomads. Russian nationalism, in its new guise of international Marxism, was now "more dangerous and insidious than ever before."

Kennan's message was for private ears only. It was

CHURCHILL'S WARNING Winston Churchill making his prophetic "Iron Curtain" speech at Fulton, Missouri, in March 1946.

Churchill, no longer prime minister but still a statesman of world renown, who put the entire Western world on the alert. Speaking at Fulton, Missouri, he drew on all his powers of rhetoric: "From Stettin in the Baltic to Trieste in the Adriatic an iron curtain has descended across the continent. Behind that line lie all the capitals and all the ancient States of Central and Eastern Europe— Warsaw, Berlin, Prague, Vienna, Budapest, Belgrade, Bucharest and Sofia . . . The communist parties, which were very small in all these Eastern States of Europe, have been raised to a pre-eminence and power far beyond their numbers and are seeking everywhere to obtain totalitarian control."

Calling for a permanent alliance between the United States and the British Empire, and for the United Nations to have its own armed forces, Churchill warned: "The Dark Ages may return. The Stone Age may return on the gleaming wings of science . . . Beware, I say. Time may be short."

This opening shot in the Cold War provoked a response from Stalin: "I regard it as a dangerous act, calculated to sow the seeds of dissension among the Allied States. There can be no doubt that Mr. Churchill's position is a war position, a call for war on the U.S.S.R." Initially, the leaders of the U.S. had been more suspicious of

imperial powers, like the British and the French, than they were of the U.S.S.R. "I had the kindliest feelings for Russia and the Russian people, and I liked Stalin," President Harry S Truman wrote. "But I found after a very patient year that Russian agreements are made to be broken." Plain-spokenness was one of Truman's virtues. "Molotov called on me at the Executive Office and began to tell me how I could cooperate with Russia by doing what Russia wanted. I explained to him in words of one syllable and in language he could understand that cooperation required agreement and concessions on both sides and that coopera-tion is not a one-way street. He remarked that he'd not been so bluntly addressed since he'd been a foreign minister." Truman had responded: "Keep your agreements, and you won't get talked to in that way."

Among the unkept agreements was one made at the wartime Yalta conference to hold free elections in Poland and the other satellite countries. Another was a pledge that Soviet troops would withdraw from northern Iran within six months of the end of the war. They finally left in March 1946, but only under American pressure and with the car-rot of valuable oil concessions.

One promise that Stalin did keep was over Greece. At a meeting in Moscow during the war, Churchill had produced what he called a "naughty document." He scribbled some figures on a piece of paper, suggesting that Hungary, Romania, Bulgaria, Yugoslavia and Greece should be divided up into Soviet and British spheres of influence, and that Britain should have 90 percent of the influence in Greece. In effect, this meant that the U.S.S.R. would stay out of Greece and out of the Mediterranean region. When civil war broke out in Greece, Stalin kept to this unofficial agreement.

Civil war in Greece

This savagely fought war, in which 80,000 died, began during the Greek struggle for liberation from German occupation. The fight was between two rival groups of partisans: the communist-dominated ELAS, whose political wing was the National Liberation Front, EAM; and the anti-communist EDES, or National Republican Greek League, backed by Britain. After the Germans had been driven out of Greece in 1944, British troops helped to suppress an EAM rising in Athens. EAM boycotted a general election,

MOMENTS FROM DEATH Both sides in the Greek civil war were capable of extremes of heroism and savagery. Captured guerrillas hear their death sentences being read out, and respond with a revolutionary song.

CHECKPOINT IN THE HILLS Greek soldiers searching villagers in the Macedonian mountains, to make sure they are not smuggling arms to communist rebels.

held in March 1946, and a right-wing coali-tion government came to power. The swing to the right continued in September, with a vote in favor of the return of the Greek monarchy in the person of King George II. In the rugged mountains of the northwest, the ELAS partisans, led by General Markos, fought on, supplied from Yugoslavia and Albania across the border.

Britain was spending £135 million ($540 million) a year on aid to Greece, and the nation's ambitions were proving big-ger than its purse. Apart from aid to Greece, Britain was stretch-

THE GULF BETWEEN TWO WORLDS

Superpower rivalry was not all that divided East from West in the era of the Cold War. The ideological chasm between them seemed unbridgeable. Marxist-Leninists believed with an almost religious fervor that history was on their side, and that the West would collapse under its own contradictions. Capitalism, lurching between booms and slumps, and creating an unequal distribution of wealth, was a system that exploited the mass of workers in the interests of the few. Its inevitable outcome was class struggle—a struggle that could be resolved only by revolution. The natural leaders of the revolution were the class-conscious minority who would establish a "dictatorship of the proletariat." Once this had been achieved, there would be no need for government, and the State would wither away. The final stage of capitalism, in its search for new markets, was imperialism, the exploitation not only of workers but of one nation by another. The appeal of communism lay in its promise to the dispossessed, the landless, the underprivileged.

The Western view was that this promise was a sham. Communism in practice meant totalitarian rule and a police state. The "dictatorship of the proletariat" meant simply that the communists became the new ruling class. Marxist-Leninism, with its emphasis on State planning, was not good at giving people what they really wanted. Capitalism, for all its imperfections, held out the best hope for the happiness and prosperity of the human race: representative government and free elections, the rule of law, free speech, freedom of religion and of conscience, free enterprise and free choice in a competitive market.

ing its meager resources to feed the British zone of Germany, to keep an uneasy peace in Palestine, and to help support Turkey, with troops and economic aid, in its resistance to Soviet demands for a foothold in the Dardanelles.

The British government told President Truman that it could no longer afford to help Greece and Turkey. Truman's response, in March 1947, was to have momentous consequences. He persuaded Congress to vote $400 million to aid Greece and, in what became known as the Truman Doctrine, pledged that the U.S. would always support "free peoples who are resisting attempted subjugation by armed minorities or by outside pressures." America had turned its back on isolationism and taken the first step against communism.

Soon, the Greek army was being trained by U.S. advisers, and U.S. supplies were pouring in, turning the tide against ELAS. Both sides committed atrocities in Greece's civil war, but the act that truly shocked the West was the abduction of thousands of children by ELAS. Western observers were convinced that the children had been kidnapped, to be trained across the border as the next generation of guerrilla fighters. The communists claimed that they had been evacuated from war zones for their own protection. Whatever the truth of that

claim, the rebels could not be defeated as long as they had a refuge and supply base in Yugoslavia. This came to an end when the Greek communists supported Stalin in his quarrel with Tito, and Tito closed the border to them. Markos was defeated in a battle in the rugged Vitsi mountains in August 1949. By October, the civil war was over.

Behind the Curtain

Stalin may have kept out of Greece, but he was more aggressive elsewhere in Eastern Europe. In Poland, the U.S.S.R. had set up a puppet government of Moscow-trained Poles in Lublin during the war, as a rival to the London-based government in exile. In a

civil war from April to July 1945, it crushed remnants of the Polish Home Army, which had led the resistance against the Nazis.

In Romania, the pro-Nazi dictator Ion Antonescu had been ousted in August 1944 by a coup led by King Michael. The Romanian Communist Party had fewer than 1,000 members, but they were highly active. When government troops opened fire on a communist demonstration in Bucharest, the Red Army disarmed loyal troops in the capital, and the king was ordered to take communists into a coalition government. They soon came to dominate it. Newspapers critical of the new regime were closed down.

There was little popular backing for the Communist Party in Hungary. When free elections were held in the autumn of 1945, the communists were trounced, and the Smallholders Party took 57 percent of the vote. But the Red Army was ever-present, and the Smallholders' leaders were forced to take a communist into their government, as Minister of the Interior. Mass demonstrations were organized against right-wingers, and following violent clashes, bans were issued against Catholic Youth organizations and even against the Boy Scouts.

In Czechoslovakia, where communists had played a major role in the Resistance,

CHEERS BEFORE TEARS A jubilant crowd in Bucharest welcomes the abdication of Romania's King Michael in 1947. A harsh communist dictatorship was to follow.

they had more support. In May 1946, they won 38 percent of the vote in free elections. The Czechs were mindful of recent history: if they had to be dominated by the U.S.S.R. or Germany, the choice was clear.

The Marshall Plan

In Western Europe, the winter of 1946-7 was the most vicious of the century, and the misery caused by the weather was matched by economic gloom. Industrial stagnation, austerity, strikes, and shortages of food and fuel meant that postwar Europe was beginning to look like a breeding ground for communism—indeed, the communist parties of

France and Italy were ominously strong. Europe was in need of a kick-start.

This came from the U.S. in the form of the Marshall Plan. General George C. Marshall, Secretary of State, launched the plan in a speech at Harvard University on June 5, 1947. Officially called the European Recovery Program, it aimed to build long-term revival, rather than offer short-term relief. Europe had to help itself, said Marshall. "It would be neither fitting nor efficacious for this country to draw up unilaterally a program designed to place Europe on its feet economically. This is the business of Europeans." The offer was open to any nation in Europe, including the U.S.S.R. and her satellites. "Our policy is directed not against any country or doctrine," Marshall explained, "but against hunger, poverty, desperation and chaos."

British Foreign Secretary Ernest Bevin responded swiftly to Marshall's proposals. "I grabbed them with both hands," he told Parliament. With his French counterpart, Georges Bidault, he organized a conference in Paris to work out a recovery program. The Paris Conference was attended in its early days by the Soviet Foreign Minister, Vyacheslav Molotov, but he soon walked

A HELPING HAND   A U.S. factory worker finishes stencilling the emblem of the Marshall Plan onto a crated tractor bound for France. U.S. aid was welcomed in many European countries, including West Germany (left).

out, denouncing the plan as an attempt by the United States to dominate Europe's economy. "The nations of Europe would become controlled countries," he warned. Czechoslovakia, Poland, Hungary and Bulgaria showed interest in applying for aid, but after a word from Moscow hastily withdrew their applications. The result of Stalin's rejection of the Marshall Plan

Shaken by the readiness of some of the satellite states to apply for American aid, Stalin tightened his grip. September 1947 saw the formation of the Cominform, the Communist Information Bureau, which fed Moscow's party line to communists in France and Italy, as well as Eastern Europe.

In February 1948 came a move that sent the temperature of the Cold War plummeting: the Czech coup. The uneasy coalition government in Prague began to totter when the communist Minister of the Interior dismissed several high-ranking police officials in preparation for show trials. The noncommunists resigned in protest, thinking they would win support in new elections. They were mistaken. With the Red Army conducting maneuvers on the border, Prime Minister Klement Gottwald formed a government in which all posts went to communists or their supporters. The former foreign secretary, Jan Masaryk, either committed suicide or was murdered, falling from a window of the Foreign Ministry.

WINNER AND LOSER Klement Gottwald's supporters carry his portrait through Prague in a communist takeover. Jan Masaryk (left) died mysteriously after the coup.

was to deepen the division of Europe into two camps. Truman won the approval of Congress to allocate $17 billion to the plan, spread over 4½ years, and by 1950 Western Europe was on its way back to prosperity. Factories were pulsing with activity; trains were moving grain, coal, steel and machinery. West Germany, in particular, was beginning to emerge as an economic powerhouse.

The next trial of strength came in Germany. The British and American zones had been merged in January 1947, and in June of the following year the three Western powers announced a currency reform in their zones, replacing the Reichsmark with the Deutschmark. It was the first step in a process that Stalin feared: the creation of a powerful and prosperous West Germany, loyal to the West. In Berlin, 110 miles inside East Germany, the Soviets were already harassing

Western military traffic. When, on June 23, 1948, Britain, France and the U.S. introduced the Deutschmark to their sectors of Berlin, the Soviets closed all road, rail and canal links from the West. Claiming "technical difficulties," they cut off power and coal supplies to West Berlin. By brandishing the threat of mass starvation, they hoped to force the Western powers to quit Berlin and to reverse their plans to build a West German state.

The Berlin airlift

Some U.S. military men urged sending an armed convoy up the autobahn to investigate the difficulties and ram its way through to Berlin if necessary. In Washington, calmer views prevailed. General Lucius D. Clay, the U.S. military commander in Berlin, was ordered to organize the most massive airlift in history. "Curt, can you transport coal?" he asked Air Force General Curtis Lemay. Over the next 10½ months he got his answer.

DAYS OF TENSION . . . AND OF JOY
Anxious Berliners watch as an American plane comes in to land with supplies for their blockaded city. Above: Children cheer the end of the blockade.

GEORGE ORWELL, PROPHET OF THE LEFT

It was during the Spanish Civil War that George Orwell became disenchanted with Stalin's version of communism. He and other left-wing idealists who were fighting for the Republican cause came face to face in Spain with Stalinism in all its brutality. Orwell was to put his experiences into two of the most thought-provoking political novels of the century—*Animal Farm* and *1984*.

The first is a satirical fable in which the farm animals rise in revolt against their treatment by Farmer Jones. Napoleon the pig, who emerges as their leader, turns out to have an agenda of his own. One of his first actions is to introduce a pack of fierce dogs that will always enforce his will. And he uses propaganda to control minds. The gullible animals see all the apples and milk going to the pigs, but they are told that pigs, being brainworkers, are entitled to special food. All is made clear in the slogan, "All animals are equal, but some animals are more equal than others."

EVER-WATCHING EYES
Big Brother watches from the cover of a 1950 German edition of *1984*.

Written in 1945, the book is a work of prophecy based on bitter experience. One of the pigs is the Trotsky-like figure Snowball, a potential rival to Napoleon, who is chased off the farm by the snarling dog pack. Events in the book bear a striking resemblance to what was about to happen behind the Iron Curtain. Some of the animals begin to have doubts about Napoleon after he introduces a 60-hour workweek and orders the hens to surrender all their eggs. There is a show trial of a group of hens and pigs, who confess to being agents of Snowball and are torn to pieces by the dogs. In Eastern Europe, Stalin made sure that communist parties in the satellite states would always control the police, internal security and the organs of propaganda. He, too, had his show trials, his bogus confessions and his executions.

George Orwell was the pen name of Eric Blair (1903-50), who was born in India and educated at Eton. In *1984*, published in 1948, he returned to the theme of thought control. "Who controls the past controls the future. Who controls the present controls the past," he wrote. His hero, Winston Smith, lives in a world in which Big Brother is constantly watching over the actions and supervising the thoughts of every citizen. Again, there are clear parallels with Stalin's Soviet Union. Orwell, however, became angry if critics took *1984* to be simply an anti-communist tract. He meant it as a warning against totalitarianism of any sort, whether from the Left or from the Right.

60 B29 bombers, capable of carrying nuclear bombs, to bases in the U.K. They were to stay. Even worse, the blockade brought about what it had been intended to prevent —the creation of an independent West Germany. The Federal Republic was proclaimed in May 1949, and its first parliament, the Bundestag, was elected in August. The Soviets responded by transforming their zone into the German Democratic Republic in October 1949.

The scare over Berlin, the Soviet subjugation of Eastern Europe and, especially, the Czech coup underlined to the West the need for collective security. In April 1949, NATO, the North Atlantic Treaty Organization, came into being. The U.S., Canada and ten nations of Western Europe, including Britain and France, agreed to come to one another's aid to resist armed aggression. An attack on one was an attack on all. Now the battle lines were drawn.

As the troubled 1940s came to a close, the world woke up to a new peril. In August 1949, the U.S.S.R. caught up with the U.S. and tested its first atomic bomb. The days of American nuclear monopoly were over, and if the Cold War should become a hot war, the two superpowers were capable of destroying the entire world.

DRAWING THE LINE NATO delegates meet in Brussels in April 1949. The NATO alliance was the West's response to Stalin's takeover of Eastern Europe and to the Berlin blockade.

Flying around the clock and in all kinds of weather, the U.S. Air Force and the RAF delivered 1.4 million tons of coal, food, clothing and medical supplies to the 2.4 million citizens of West Berlin. The coal would stretch only to schools, hospitals and special warming centers, so Berlin's mayor, Ernst Reuter, organized a tree-cutting program to chop down alternate trees in the city's streets. By the spring of 1949, the airlift was landing an average of 8,000 tons a day at Tempelhof and Gatow airfields. A makeshift runway had been hastily constructed at Tempelhof of rubble and metal strips, and as planes took off, German laborers would rush in to repair it for the next landing.

On May 12, 1949, the Soviets called off the blockade. From their point of view, it had proved a costly blunder. When the tension was at its height, the U.S. had moved

BRAVE NEW BRITAIN

THE WAR LEFT BRITAIN IMPOVERISHED BUT UNBOWED, AND IN THE YEARS OF AUSTERITY IT BUILT A NEW SOCIETY

The normally reserved British danced with strangers in the streets and public parks on VE Day, May 8, 1945, celebrating Victory in Europe. But as the celebrations ended, and the cheers of victory parades faded into memory, another mood took over. It had been a people's war, and now it was to be a people's peace. For too many of them, prewar Britain held memories of poverty, unemployment, poor housing and poor health.

Led by the unassuming Clement Attlee, Churchill's deputy in the wartime cabinet,

LINES FOR EVERYTHING Lines were a fact of life in an era of shortages. Shoppers in London line up to exchange their bread coupons for "points" for other goods.

VOTERS IN UNIFORM A 1945 Labor Party poster spells out a vision of Britain's future that was important to the men in the fighting forces.

and helped by the Armed Forces' vote, the Labor Party won the election of July 1945 in a landslide—393 seats in the House of Commons to 213 for the Conservatives. Churchill commented: "All our enemies having surrendered unconditionally, or being about to do so, I was instantly dismissed by the British electorate from all further conduct of their affairs."

The style of the new government was set from the start. Churchill left Buckingham Palace, after tendering his resignation to King George VI, in a large chauffeur-driven Rolls-Royce. Within half an hour, Mr. Attlee arrived at the palace in a Standard 10, driven by his wife, Vi.

An "economic Dunkirk"

At the end of the war, Britain's earnings from exports were only enough to cover a quarter of its imports. Overseas debts amounted to £3.3 billion ($15 billion), and there were serious shortages of coal, food and manpower. To make matters worse, America ended the

1945 Labor wins General Election

1946 Coal mines nationalized

1947 Independence for India and Pakistan

1948 National Health Service begins

1949 The pound is devalued by 30 percent

1956 Suez Canal Crisis

CLEMENT ATTLEE: A MAN OF DEEDS, NOT WORDS

When Clement Attlee was an undergraduate at Oxford, his tutor summed him up as "a level-headed, industrious, dependable man with no brilliance of style or literary gifts, but with excellent sound judgement." Winston Churchill described him as "a modest man who has much to be modest about." The tutor's description was the more accurate, as well as being kinder, but both missed an essential element in Attlee's character: the quality of decisiveness that made him such an effective leader.

Clement Attlee (1883-1967) came from an unspectacular middle-class Victorian background—his father was a lawyer, and he went to Haileybury public school, then Oxford. He became a socialist as a young man when he volunteered to help in a boys' club in London's dockland neighborhood. During the First World War, he rose to the rank of major and was wounded. After the war, he returned to London, and became Mayor of Stepney. There followed a long, steady climb up the political ladder. In the Second World War, Attlee was deputy prime minister in Churchill's coalition government.

This was the man who was to transform British society. Somewhat to its surprise, Labor won a landslide victory in the first postwar election. In a torrent of legislation, Attlee's government introduced the welfare state, with its crowning achievement, the National Health Service; it nationalized key industries, including coal and the railways; and granted independence to India, Pakistan, Burma and other lands in what had once been the British Empire. Attlee stood firm against Soviet aggression, and his foreign secretary, Ernest Bevin, played a major role in the formation of NATO, Western Europe's shield against the Soviet threat.

Attlee was a man of few words, but they could be biting. When the left-wing Member of Parliament Konni Zilliacus presumed to advise him on foreign policy, Attlee sent him a note: "My dear Zilly, Thank you for sending me your memorandum, which seems to be based on an astonishing lack of understanding of the facts." One junior minister discovered how tough and straightforward Attlee could be when he was summoned to 10 Downing Street and told: "I want your job." When the shaken minister asked why, the reply came: "Afraid you're not up to it."

Attlee survived several attempts from within his own party to unseat him, including one in August 1947, in the thick of yet another foreign exchange crisis. Stafford Cripps went to Attlee, to tell him that he should resign and make way for Ernest Bevin. The story goes that Attlee picked up the phone and called his foreign secretary: "Ernie, Stafford's here. He says you want my job." Bevin, a pillar of loyalty, denied any such ambition. "Thought not," said Attlee. The rebellion was over.

Clement Attlee was indeed a modest man. Perhaps this was because his achievements spoke for themselves.

SMILING THROUGH Britain has a surfeit of economic worries. But Clement Attlee still manages a cheerful wave in August 1947.

compared with the old days, who have a guaranteed minimum wage of £4 8s 6d [$18] a week whether you work or not?" The dockers went back to work.

Labor's reforms

The government set about its program with great energy: within 2½ years, the airlines, railways, coal mines, gas, electricity and other key industries were nationalized. Labor's other major promise was to create a cradle-to-grave welfare state, and for this it drew heavily on the vision presented in 1943 in the Beveridge Report. The National Insurance Act covered loss of earnings due to sickness or unemployment, and the Industrial Injuries Act gave similar protection to people who had been injured at work. A family allowance of 5 shillings ($1) a week for all children after the first was inherited from the previous government. Old age pensions were improved, and for those who fell through the gaps, there was a safety net

Lend-Lease arrangement on August 21, just seven days after VJ (Victory in Japan) Day.

Britain's new government had to find from somewhere the money to carry out a radical political program of nationalization, to set up a welfare state, and to meet international commitments ranging from Europe to east of Suez. The economist Lord Keynes warned that the country could be facing an "economic Dunkirk."

"Export or Die" became the slogan. New furniture was available only to newlyweds or families who had been bombed out of their homes. Clothes and gas were rationed, and rents and prices controlled. Housewives stood in line for hours, and learned to make 2 ounces of butter, 4 ounces of margarine, and 25 cents' worth of meat per person last all week. "Scrape it on, scrape it off" was the rule when buttering bread. Lord Keynes

was sent to the U.S. to raise a loan, and he negotiated one of $3.75 billion, with an additional $1.25 billion from Canada.

Trade union leaders supported the Labor Party and urged wage restraint, which explains why when strikes happened they were often unofficial. During a strike by London dockers in June 1948, the prime minister made a personal appeal. "This strike is not a strike against capitalism or employers. It is a strike against your mates, a strike against the housewife . . . And why should you men strike, who are well paid

1958 CND begins ban-the-bomb marches

1962 Open door policy for Commonwealth immigrants ends

1969 Army moves into Northern Ireland

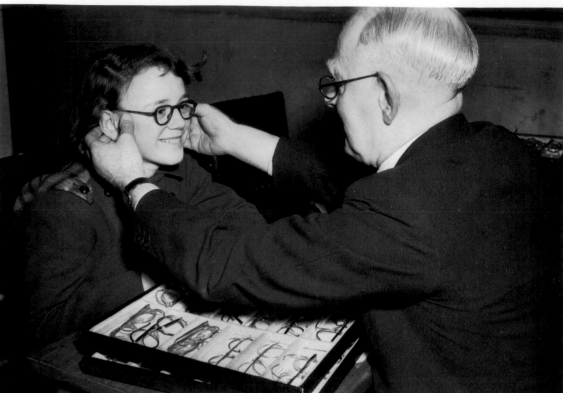

A NATIONAL GIFT A girl at Moorfields Eye Hospital, London, is fitted with her first pair of free National Health Service glasses.

in National Assistance.

The reform that gave Labor its greatest sense of achievement was the creation of the National Health Service (NHS), which began operating on July 5, 1948. Aneurin Bevan, the minister of health, had no easy task persuading the nation's doctors to accept it. "Mass murder of the hospitals," said one of their spokesmen. But Bevan won the doctors over. He agreed, among other concessions, that consultants could treat fee-paying patients in National Health hospitals—"stuffing their mouths with gold," as he put it.

The Beveridge Report predicted that a national health service would cost £170 million ($680 million) a year. In fact, the NHS cost £249 million ($996 million) in its first full year, during which more than 200 million prescriptions were written, 8.5 million people received free dental treatment, and 4.5 million pairs of glasses were issued.

The welfare state was a triumph for Attlee's government, but there was trouble ahead. It began in the atrocious winter of 1946-7. With roads blocked by snowdrifts, and railway points frozen, coal could not be moved to the power stations, and factories were forced to shut down. Unemployment reached 2.5 million. Emmanuel Shinwell, the minister of fuel and power, was blamed for not foreseeing the crisis. "Shiver with Shinwell" was the Tory slogan, and it was soon joined by "Starve with Strachey" when food minister John Strachey rationed bread—a low point not reached even during the darkest days of the Second World War.

Stafford Cripps—"Mr. Austerity"

In 1947, Sir Stafford Cripps was appointed Chancellor of the Exchequer. A man whose very appearance suggested austerity, Cripps was a vegetarian who rose every morning at four o'clock and put in three hours' work before a cold bath and breakfast. His priorities were the export drive and the needs of industry. Whalemeat, horsemeat and a strange, fibrous canned fish called snoek were introduced to the British diet. The black market flourished and the figure of the "spiv" came into the national consciousness: a shady figure who could find all manner of scarce goods—at a price.

At an exchange rate of $4.03 to the pound, British exports were hard to sell in America, and in 1949 Cripps was forced to announce a devaluation to $2.80. This helped exports, but hopes of easier times were dashed by the outbreak of the Korean War in June 1950. Economies were called

FUN . . . FANTASY . . . FESTIVAL

In May 1951, visitors by the tens of thousands swarmed to London's South Bank, on the opposite side of the Thames from the Houses of Parliament, to gaze on such marvels as the Dome of Discovery and the Skylon, a thin, cigar-shaped obelisk that rose into the sky. This was the Festival of Britain, the country's way of giving itself a pat on the back after surviving the war and enduring six years of continued austerity.

The festival, with a budget of $33 million, had an eye on the past, for it marked the anniversary of the Great Exhibition of 1851. But mainly it looked to the future, offering, in the words of its director, Sir Gerald Barry, "fun, fantasy and color." There were murals by artists Graham Sutherland and John Piper, and sculptures by Henry Moore. The design style known as "contemporary," all bright colors and abstract geometrical shapes, set the tone. There was also an affectionate look at the kind of Britain portrayed in the film comedies of the day coming out of Ealing studios—a land peopled by amiable eccentrics and dotty geniuses. One of the most popular exhibits was the Far Tottering Railway, designed by *Punch* cartoonist Roland Emmett.

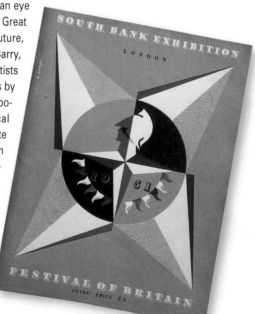

STYLISH GUIDE The Festival catalogue, designed in the "contemporary" style.

for across the board—even in the NHS, where charges were introduced for glasses and false teeth. This caused Aneurin Bevan, champion of the free health service, to resign from the government.

The Conservatives won the general election in October 1951 on a promise to "set the people free" and to build 300,000 houses a year. When Winston Churchill, back as prime minister, was shown the rations on which people were supposed to exist, he pronounced them "not a bad meal" for a day. Then somebody told him that what he had seen was meant to last for a week. From 1952 onward, rationing ended for tea, sweets, eggs, sugar, butter and cheese, until at last, in July 1954, meat and bacon joined the list, and the ration books could be thrown away.

Churchill retired in 1955, and Sir Anthony Eden became prime minister. He lasted only until 1956, when the Suez crisis marked the end of Britain's claims to be a leading world power. Following Egypt's nationalization of the Suez Canal, Britain and France invaded Egypt but were forced by U.S. pressure to withdraw. Eden, humiliated and in poor health, resigned, and was succeeded by Harold Macmillan.

The Fifties and Sixties were Britain's "Stop-Go" years—a phase that began in January 1952, when the Chancellor of the Exchequer R.A. ("Rab") Butler introduced a credit squeeze to cool down an economy that was beginning to overheat because of the Korean War. "Stop-Go" meant that in times of boom the chancellor's foot moved to the accelerator. Restrictions on credit and hire purchase

A PLACE TO LIVE

One of the most formidable social problems facing Britain in 1945 was a shortage of housing. About 700,000 houses had been either destroyed or badly damaged by enemy action, and no new houses had been built during the war. Building materials were scarce, and much of the timber used had to be imported. The minister of health and housing, Aneurin Bevan, ruled that public housing should have priority, with four public housing projects built for every private home.

But thousands of newlyweds and people with young families could not wait. The first solution to the housing problem was direct action by the homeless. All over the country there beckoned the empty Nissen huts of abandoned army camps and hangars. In a movement that began in Scunthorpe, Lincolnshire, and soon gathered pace, some 40,000 people moved into more than 1,000 camps as squatters. In some camps they had to evict "sitting tenants" in the shape of sheep or cattle. Many local councils turned a blind eye to the fact that the law had been broken and provided water and electricity.

A more official solution, though it was intended as a stopgap, was the prefab house. The parts were mass-produced in factories, then transported to their sites, bolted together and levelled. Bevan called the single-story prefabs "rabbit hutches," but with their high standard of bathroom and kitchen fittings, and their neat little cottage gardens, they became popular with their tenants. By 1951, around 160,000 had been erected. They were only expected to last for ten years or so, but some were still in use as the 20th century approached its end.

What the planners regarded as the best long-term solution came with the development of New Towns, following a proposal by the country's most eminent urban planner, Professor Sir Patrick Abercrombie. His idea was to relieve pressure on congested cities, especially London, and he found his inspiration in the garden cities, such as Welwyn and Letchworth, built in the Twenties and Thirties.

The first of the new towns was Stevenage, 25 miles north of London. The population grew later, but the town was originally planned to house 60,000 people, divided into six neighborhoods. Each neighborhood had its schools and shopping centers, with sites for churches and pubs. The principal roads ran between the neighborhoods, so that young children would not need to cross busy roads to get to school. Industrial and residential areas were kept well apart. Stevenage's town center was the first in the country to have a traffic-free pedestrian precinct.

The houses were mainly three-bedroomed and two-story, and the developers reported: "Almost every person coming to live in a new house at Stevenage . . . wants at least a small garden to make the country seem yet a little closer . . . Few wish to have a flat as a home and fewer still to live in a high building." The decision to build at Stevenage was taken in 1946, but it was almost three years before work started on the first house—a delay due mainly to objections raised by local farmers and inhabitants of the original small town that stood on the site. More than 100 existing houses had to be demolished because they stood on the site of the intended industrial area. In Labor's six years of office, more than a million new houses were built, many of them in the new towns. In places like Hatfield, Crawley, Peterlee, Basildon and East Kilbride, young families made new friends and began their new lives.

UP SHE GOES   Another prefab is erected, as part of what was meant to be a temporary solution to Britain's housing crisis. In fact, some prefabs lasted more than 50 years.

A WHOLE TOWN IN HIS HANDS   A planner checks the layout of Stevenage, Britain's first new town.

> ## " ON THE MARCH
>
> CND, the Campaign for Nuclear Disarmament, organized Easter Day marches in protest against Britain's possession of atomic weapons. The first, in 1958, was from London to the Atomic Research Establishment at Aldermaston; later marches began at Aldermaston and ended with a rally in Trafalgar Square. Ron Angel, a former paratrooper from Billingham, in the north of England, who was a lab technician at the time of the early marches, recalls those days:
>
> "We came down in a coach from Teesside, about 30 of us, singing Blaydon Races—I suppose to affirm our solidarity. Everyone was in wonderful spirits. We stayed in schools, council offices, anywhere that would have us. We took our own food and sleeping bags, and slept in classrooms and corridors.
>
> "We marched because we felt it was an obscene thing to do, to deliberately develop a weapon that could atomise whole cities and was a threat to generations unborn. They simply didn't know enough about what they were playing around with.
>
> "The spirit of camaraderie was wonderful. It was a stirring sight to look back from a hill and see the march winding away for miles. When we got back home, we read the Sunday papers for reports and pictures of the march, but it wasn't the march we had been on. They were trying to create the impression that the march was full of loonies and anarchists. In fact, there were all sorts and shades of opinion—I met Quakers for the first time. There were people with prams, people of all ages. I don't think I will ever forget it." "

(widely known as the "never-never") would be relaxed, employment would rise, and people would spend more freely. The result was always the same: soaring imports, leading to a new balance of payments crisis. The foot would then switch to the brake pedal, with a rise in the bank rate and tighter controls on credit, imports and hire purchase.

"Never had it so good"

Despite "Stop-Go," wages were increasing faster than prices. Unemployment was low, and drop-outs and graduates could walk straight into a job. It was no idle boast when, in July 1957, Macmillan claimed: "Let us be frank about it. Most of our people have never had it so good. Go around the country. Go to the industrial towns. Go to the farms, and you will see a state of prosperity such as we have never had in my lifetime—nor indeed, ever in the history of this country."

People were better housed. Car ownership stood at only 2.25 million in 1950, but

TV CHOICE   A leaflet from the early 1950s advertising a range of television sets. As Britain prospered, the number of sets rose to 10 million by 1960.

prosperity put the nation on wheels: by 1970 the figure had risen to 11.5 million. More people were taking vacations abroad. In the home, what had once been luxury items, like washing machines and refrigerators, were becoming everyday necessities.

Perhaps the biggest impact on daily life came with television. Ownership of TV sets began to soar in 1953, when the coronation of Queen Elizabeth II was televised. It was boosted further by the introduction of commercial television in 1955. One result of television was a sharp decline in movie audiences. In the Forties, it had not been unusual for people to go to the movies two or three times a week—attendances peaked in 1946 at 1.6 billion. But television was able to bring dreams and adventures into the home, with no need to stand in lines. Between 1956 and 1959, the J. Arthur Rank organization alone closed 91 theaters. Throughout the land, Ritzes and Alhambras, Tivolis, Essoldos and Odeons became bingo halls.

In 1964 the Conservatives lost the election to Labor, and Harold Wilson became prime minister on a pledge to forge a new Britain in the "white heat" of the scientific revolution. Wilson's government attempted to put an end to "Stop-Go." In September 1965, George Brown, in charge of the new Department of Economic Affairs, announced a National Plan to increase output by 25 percent in the next five years. But in November 1967, the country faced another balance of payments crisis—one so serious that the

A QUEEN FOR THE TELEVISION AGE   Television brought the coronation of Queen Elizabeth II from Westminster Abbey into the nation's homes, and sales of TV sets soared.

pound had to be devalued, from $2.80 to $2.40. Wilson told the nation: "It does not mean, of course, that the pound here in Britain, in your pocket or purse or in your bank has been devalued." The National Plan faded, and industrial unrest grew.

One of the problems was that salary demands by different unions leapfrogged as the old craft unions fought to protect their pay "differentials." Another was rivalry

AGAINST THE LAW

Until 1951, strikes were illegal in Britain, under a wartime Order in Council—Order No. 1305. In practice, invoking the order would have provoked more industrial trouble than it would have solved, so it was left unused.

between unions. In 1968, at the Girling brake factory in Cheshire, for instance, 22 machine setters came out on strike because a charge-hand from another union had attempted to give them instructions. The strike caused 5,000 workers in other plants to be laid off.

The new Britons

The benefits and drawbacks of "Stop-Go" were shared during the Fifties and Sixties by increasing numbers of new Britons. The first

A NEW LIFE IN AN OLD LAND West Indian immigrants just off the boat at Southampton in 1954, hoping to find work in a land with a labor shortage. Many found jobs in the new health service (right).

West Indian immigrants had arrived as early as 1948, when the *Empire Windrush* docked at Tilbury with 492 passengers from Kingston, Jamaica. It was not until 1954 that immigrants from the West Indies, India and Pakistan began arriving in large numbers.

The West Indians were recruited to ease Britain's labor shortage. They tended to fill low-paid jobs on the railways and in hospitals—jobs that many British workers were reluctant to take. The Asian immigrants tended to open restaurants or stores, and a number of them also joined the NHS, often as doctors or surgeons.

The concentration of immigrants in particular areas, such as Birmingham, Bradford and parts of London, sometimes led to racial tension, and in the summer of 1958 this tension erupted in race riots in London's Notting Hill and in Nottingham. Mobs of white youths chanted racist slogans, and gas bombs were thrown.

Entry to Britain was open to all Commonwealth citizens until 1962, when the Conservative government introduced work permits in the Commonwealth Immigration Act. No primary immigrant was allowed in without a permit, and family members needed visas to enter Britain. Hugh Gaitskell, leader of the Labor Opposition, said that the Act was directed against Asian and West Indian immigrants and described it as "miserable, shameful and shabby."

In 1968 Labor, back in government, rushed through a second Commonwealth Immigration Act in response to fears of a massive influx from Kenya of Asians holding

THE SCANDAL THAT ROCKED "SUPERMAC"

THE SORRY TALE OF A CABINET MINISTER, A CALL GIRL, A SOVIET ATTACHÉ AND A LIE TO PARLIAMENT SHOOK THE CONSERVATIVE GOVERNMENT AND THE COUNTRY TO ITS CORE

Despite the sexual revolution that came in the Sixties, there were still some bounds that could not be over-stepped. John Profumo, secretary of state for war, discovered this when he lied to his own party and to Parliament about his relationship with call girl Christine Keeler.

Profumo told the Commons, on March 22, 1963, that there was "no impropriety whatever" in the friendship. But outside the House, Dr. Stephen Ward, a West End osteopath who had introduced the pair and had made his apartment available to them, had a different story to tell. With the newspapers in hot pursuit, Profumo had to admit that he had lied both to members of parliament and to leading Tories sent to question him by Prime Minister Harold Macmillan. He had no choice but to resign.

As the scandal unfolded, it was revealed that, at the same time as she was the mistress of the man in charge of Britain's defense, Christine Keeler was also having an affair with a Soviet naval attaché in London, Eugene Ivanov. It was later established that there had been no risk to national security, but there was still plenty for the media to work on. Christine Keeler was exceptionally pretty, and she and Profumo moved in upper-class circles—they had met at Cliveden, the country seat of Lord Astor. The combination of decadence, high society, glamour, politics and sex made a potent brew.

Profumo was not the scandal's only victim. Dr. Ward, arrested and convicted of living off immoral earnings, committed suicide. Christine Keeler was jailed for perjury. But the most prominent victim was the prime minister himself. Macmillan's political dexterity had earned him the nickname "Supermac," but he had accepted Profumo's earlier denials, and overnight he became a figure of fun, portrayed as naive, bewildered, Edwardian in his attitudes, and out of touch.

Macmillan did not plan on being forced out of office by the scandal—indeed, he brought off another political coup in August 1963, when he signed a nuclear test-ban treaty with the U.S. and U.S.S.R. But there is no question that the scandal shook his authority. When, in October, he fell ill with an inflamed prostate, he resigned without delay, to be succeeded by Alec Douglas-Home.

DOOMED PLAYBOY West End osteopath and playboy Dr. Stephen Ward, who introduced Profumo to Christine Keeler. Ward was arrested and killed himself.

PRIVATE PASSION John Profumo, in his uniform as a privy councillor, and Christine Keeler (right).

NIGHTS OF VIOLENCE Race riots erupted in Nottingham and London in the autumn of 1958. Police in London's Notting Hill drag a rioter to their van.

British passports. Most were small businessmen, and a campaign to "Africanize" their businesses had led to a panic: in three months, 70,000 arrived in Britain. A bill aimed at restricting the further entry of Kenyan Asians became law on March 1, 1968.

Emotions, already high, were fanned yet higher in April 1968, when Enoch Powell, the Conservative shadow minister of defense, made what became known as the "rivers of blood" speech.

He told a Birmingham audience: "As I look ahead, I am filled with foreboding. Like the Roman, I see the River Tiber foaming with much blood." Powell was instantly dismissed from his post by Tory leader Edward Heath, but his views found some echoes in the country. London dockers and Smithfield meat porters marched in his support.

The controversy grumbled on, calmed to an extent by Race Relations Acts in 1965 and 1968 that outlawed discrimination based on race, color or origin in such matters as housing and jobs.

As the Sixties drew to a close, there were signs from Northern Ireland that matters were far from well. Roman Catholics, a minority in the community, had long faced discrimination when they applied for jobs or for public housing. The police reservists and auxiliaries known as B-specials were openly anti-Catholic, and elections were often gerrymandered to ensure Protestant control of local councils.

In January 1969, a march from Belfast to Londonderry demanding civil rights for Catholics flared into a battle between Catholics and Loyalist extremists. A 21-year-old psychology student, Bernadette Devlin, emerged as a leader in the civil rights protest, and she gave the movement a voice in Westminster when she was elected as a Member of Parliament for Mid-Ulster.

Trouble in Ulster

Despite promises of reforms, the marches and the violence continued. But the traditional Protestant marching season was approaching. In August 1969, the annual Apprentice Boys' march through Belfast ended in a pitched battle. Firebombs were thrown and guns used. Five people were killed and hundreds injured. On August 15, units of the British army were sent in to restore peace. The troops were greeted with flowers and cheers as they laid a protective barbed wire fence around the Catholic Bogside district but the welcome did not last long. A resolution was still many years away.

DAYS OF TURMOIL Ulster police in riot gear prepare to seize civil rights protesters in Londonderry in April 1969.

FRANCE: THE ROAD BACK

GENERAL DE GAULLE RESTORED FRANCE'S PRIDE, THEN GAVE HIS BACKING TO JEAN MONNET TO REBUILD ITS PROSPERITY

For France, recovery after the Liberation was more than a question of restoring the nation's economic health. It was a question, too, of restoring national pride. The collapse of 1940, the greatest military defeat in French history, had been followed by the misery of occupation and the shame of the Vichy years.

For General de Gaulle, who became head of France's Provisional Government in 1944, this was a moment of destiny. "All my life I have had a certain idea of France," he was to write in his memoirs. "France is not really herself except in the front rank. France cannot be France without greatness."

CONQUERING HERO Smiling French citizens greet their liberator, General de Gaulle, in 1944. Below: The ballot paper for the 1945 referendum, in which the French voted to end the discredited Third Republic.

The road back to the front rank seemed a long one, with inflation rampant, industrial output running at well below half the pre-war level, and the nation needing to go through *l'épuration*—purging the guilt of collaboration and punishing the collaborators.

Girls who had taken German soldiers as sweethearts had their heads publicly shaved in retribution. For others, there was a harsher fate, at the hands of the courts or of a vengeful Resistance. Some 4,500 executions were recorded, but the real figure may be several times higher, since the Resistance in many cases administered its own form of justice. Marshal Pétain, head of the Vichy government, and his henchman, Pierre Laval, were put on trial and sentenced to death. De Gaulle commuted the Marshal's sentence to

REFERENDUM DU 21 OCTOBRE 1945

1ʳᵉ Question :

Voulez-vous que l'Assemblée élue ce jour soit constituante?   OUI   NON

Rayez la réponse que vous n'acceptez pas

Si la majorité du corps électoral répond "NON" à cette première question, l'Assemblée élue ce jour formera la Chambre des Députés, prévue par les lois constitutionnelles de 1875, et un Sénat sera élu dans les deux mois.

2ᵉ Question :   Si le corps électoral a répondu "OUI" à la première question,

Approuvez-vous que les pouvoirs publics soient jusqu'à la mise en vigueur de la nouvelle Constitution organisés conformément aux dispositions du projet de loi dont le texte figure au verso de ce bulletin?   OUI   NON

Rayez la réponse que vous n'acceptez pas

Si la majorité du corps électoral répond "OUI" à cette deuxième question, le projet qui figure au verso de ce bulletin, devenu loi, sera immédiatement promulgué. Si elle répond "NON", c'est à l'Assemblée elle-même qu'il appartiendra de fixer à son gré l'organisation provisoire des pouvoirs publics.

1945 Third Republic abolished   1946 De Gaulle resigns as president   1947 Monnet plan for economic revival   1954 Geneva Agreement ends Indochina War

life imprisonment, but Laval, after a botched attempt at suicide, was dragged before a firing squad. "Pierre Laval no longer belongs to us," said de Gaulle. "Let the officer commanding the platoon do his duty."

The communists had been prominent in the Resistance. They were armed, and there were fears that they might attempt a takeover. But their leader, Maurice Thorez, was a Frenchman as well as a communist. Back from his wartime exile in Moscow, he declared that there could be only one government in France and disbanded the communist militias.

EDITH PIAF, SPARROW OF THE STREETS

Jean Cocteau wrote a play for her. The young Yves Montand and the middleweight champion of the world, Marcel Cerdan, fell in love with her. Everywhere she went, Edith Piaf captivated men. And when she stood on a stage and sang, even toward the end, when she was hunched with rheumatism, audiences adored her. She had an astonishing voice—far too powerful, it seemed, to come from such a tiny body.

Edith Piaf was born in Paris in 1915, the daughter of a street acrobat, Jean Gassion. Her mother walked out when she was seven, the first tragedy in a tragic life. She began singing on the streets of Paris in the Twenties, and then graduated to the bars and clubs of Montmartre. This was when she picked up the name Piaf, Parisian slang for "little sparrow." Piaf had a baby when she was 17, but tragedy struck again when the little girl, Marcelle, died of meningitis.

Through the Twenties and Thirties, through the Occupation years and after the Liberation, Piaf sang of love lost and love found, of loyalty and betrayal, of life lived for its moments of intensity. Her songs

THE VOICE OF PARIS To France, and to the world, the unmistakable voice of Edith Piaf came to stand for everything that was most romantic about Paris.

were the poetry of the streets, and she wrote the words of about 30 of them herself, including the bittersweet *La Vie en Rose*. The best popular composers and lyricists in France gave her a string of hits, based on real-life events and characters, among them *Mon Légionnaire*, *Milord*, *l'Accordioniste*, and the defiant *Non, je ne regrette rien*.

The third great tragedy of her life was the death of Marcel Cerdan in an air crash. She had other lovers, and in 1962 she married Theo Sarapo, a Greek hairdresser 20 years her junior. Years of drink and drug abuse took their toll, and Piaf died on October 11, 1963. She was only 47. Jean Cocteau, poet, film director and playwright, who had written *Le Bel Indifférent* for Piaf when she was in her prime, died the same day.

It rankled with many French, not least de Gaulle, that France was excluded from the Yalta conference in 1945, when the "Big Three"—Britain, the U.S. and the U.S.S.R. —re-drew the map of eastern Europe. But de Gaulle lobbied successfully for France to have a permanent seat—and a veto—in the Security Council of the United Nations. With British support, he secured for France a zone of occupation in Germany.

In a referendum held in October 1945, the nation voted to end the discredited Third Republic. De Gaulle wanted to replace it with a republic in which power would be in the hands of the president, but his time had not yet come. In January 1946, provoked by squabbling between the parties, he resigned as Head of State. "Before a week is up they'll be sending me a delegation asking me to

come back," he told one of his ministers. In fact, he was to wait 12 years for the call— years he spent in the village of Colombey-les-deux-Eglises in Burgundy.

The Fourth Republic

The constitution of the Fourth Republic, approved after another referendum in October 1946, gave power not to the president but to the National Assembly. Its deputies were elected by proportional representation, a system that tended to produce short-lived coalition governments. In the 12 years of its life, the Fourth Republic was to have 26 governments, and its longest-serving prime minister, Pierre Mendès France, held the office for well under a year.

A socialist prime minister, Paul Ramadier, dismissed the communists from his coalition

Cabinet in May 1947, and for the next five years France was governed by the "Third Force"—a loose partnership of Socialists, Christian Democrats, and Radicals. Outside the government were the Communists on the Left and de Gaulle's *Rassemblement du Peuple Français* (RPF) on the Right. De Gaulle maintained that the RPF was a movement, not a political party, but he allowed it to take part in elections.

From June 1954 to February 1955, Mendès France, a Radical, gave the Fourth Republic a short spell of decisive government. He ended a colonial war in Indochina and promised internal self-rule to Tunisia. He also antagonized France's powerful wine interests by attempting to persuade the French to drink more milk instead of wine.

A plan for prosperity

While coalitions were forming, coming apart and regrouping, France was living through a transformation. She was turning herself into a modern industrial power. The National Plan on which the recovery was based was largely the work of the economist Jean Monnet, who had spent the war in Washington, working on supply problems. Monnet showed how France could plan its way from near penury to prosperity through *dirigisme*—the State direction of investment and other national resources, in partnership with business and the unions. De Gaulle championed Monnet's plan, and put him in charge of France's economic miracle.

The Bank of France was nationalized, as were a number of other major banks, so that the State would be able to control credit.

STATE-OWNED CARS Officials inspect the Renault factory at Boulogne-Billancourt in December 1945, after nationalization.

Coal mines were nationalized, the Renault car factories taken over by the State, and the steel industry modernized. New industries, such as chemicals and engineering, provided jobs. Electricity production doubled in the

THE NEW WAVE HITS THE SCREEN

For French cinema, the late Forties and Fifties were a classic age. Audiences could laugh at the antics of Jacques Tati in *Jour de Fête* (1948) and *M. Hulot's Holiday* (1953), thrill to Yves Montand and his companions driving a cargo of explosives over a spectacularly dangerous mountain road in *The Wages of Fear* (1953), or gaze on Roger Vadim's new discovery, Brigitte Bardot, in *And God Created Woman* (1956).

But for one group of young critics and film directors, this success was not enough. They admired the B-movies of Alfred Hitchcock and John Ford, and in the pages of the influential magazine *Cahiers du Cinéma* they argued the case for making films that would be marked by the style, or "signature," of the director as plainly as a novel carries the style of its author. This was the theory of the *caméra-stylo*, the "camera-pen."

Jean-Luc Godard's *A Bout de Souffle* (1959), known to English-speaking audiences as *Breathless*, put many of the New Wave ideas into practice. It follows the fortunes of a petty crook, played by Jean-Paul Belmondo, who is betrayed to the police by his American girlfriend. It was a low-budget movie, shot on location rather than in the studio, drawing on such television techniques as hand-held cameras. It did not have a script: Godard relied on improvisation.

François Truffaut's *Les Quatre Cents Coups* (1959), the story of a delinquent working-class boy, also showed how improvisation, in the hands of a gifted director, could heighten realism in a movie.

FRENCH CINEMA A publicity poster for Jacques Tati's *Mon Oncle*, released in 1958.

The New Wave directors reacted against conventional films, with their emphasis on craftsmanship, a well-honed plot, and star names. Alain Resnais even questioned such basic concepts as time, sequence and memory in *Last Year at Marienbad* (1961). The biggest tribute to their work, perhaps, is that many of their theories have been absorbed into the mainstream of moviemaking.

SCREEN SENSATION Brigitte Bardot in a scene from Roger Vadim's controversial film, *And God Created Woman*.

MINERS' VICTORY A poster proudly proclaims the importance of the miners—and of coal—to France's economic recovery.

1950s, and the SNCF, the State-run railway, became the envy of Europe. Changes of such magnitude brought unrest in the form of strikes and high wage demands, but in a period of rising prosperity, governments were able to spend heavily on pensions, workers' insurance and social reforms. Guided by the plan, French exports had overtaken those of the U.K. by 1958.

Monnet's vision did not end at the frontiers of France. He worked out a plan, put forward by Robert Schuman, the French foreign minister, to pool the coal and steel resources of France and Germany through the European Coal and Steel Community (ECSC). This was not only an economic triumph—it was a way of overcoming centuries of enmity between the two countries, and it was to prove an important step toward the European Economic Community (EEC).

Funds to kick-start France's recovery came from America, first as a $650 million loan, and then with $2.5 billion through the

1946
les mineurs achèveront
la victoire du charbon...

...et le peuple gagnera
la bataille de la
Renaissance française

Marshall Plan.

One condition of the loan was that French movie theaters were allowed to show French films for only 13 weeks of the year, exposing audiences to a steady diet of Hollywood movies.

De Gaulle comes back

Events in Algeria brought de Gaulle back to power. The army had been sent there to quell an Arab rebellion, but a group of army chiefs threw in their lot with disgruntled colonists, the *pieds noirs*, and the revolt

threatened to spill over into France itself. Only one man had the authority to call the army to their duty. The long-awaited summons went out to Colombey on May 28, 1958, and de Gaulle returned on his own conditions—a Fifth Republic, with real power in the hands of the president. His new constitution was endorsed by a resounding "Yes" vote in a referendum, and de Gaulle took over as president in January 1959. In the Fifth Republic, the president had charge of foreign policy and defense and could dismiss the prime minister. So dominant was de Gaulle that the announcer on the State-run TV station once told viewers: "In the absence of General de Gaulle there is no political news today."

De Gaulle was fiercely insistent on France's right to be treated as a great power. He did not believe that America would risk a nuclear war in order to defend Europe. "It is intolerable that a great State should confide

COLONIAL COMBAT Some of the 500,000 French troops who were dispatched to Algeria in an attempt to suppress the nationalist rebellion there.

THE TALL TARGET

From the moment he decided that granting independence was the only way to end France's bloody war in Algeria, General Charles de Gaulle was a marked man—marked for assassination by the OAS, or Secret Army. This was a group of die-hard officers who, having seen the French army defeated by a peasant force in Indochina, regarded a retreat from Algeria as a disastrous and unacceptable blow to France's honor.

With his towering height and a disdain for danger, de Gaulle must have looked like an easy target. But his luck was as legendary as his courage. At least 18, and possibly as many as 30, attempts were made on his life. All failed, but some by the tiniest of margins.

ESCAPE VEHICLE   Bullet holes, and a flattened back tire, mark the car in which de Gaulle and his wife narrowly avoided being assassinated in 1962.

On September 8, 1961, an OAS commando unit under Colonel Jean-Marie Bastien-Thiry, code-named "Germain," lay in wait for de Gaulle's car near Nogent-sur-Seine on Route Nationale 19. De Gaulle was returning from Paris with his wife Yvonne to their home at Colombey. The OAS had spread the road with gasoline and hidden 66 pounds of plastic explosives beneath a pile of sand. As de Gaulle's car approached, they set fire to the gas. There was a blinding flash, and the car was hurled sideways, but the plastic failed to explode. The general's chauffeur drove to safety through the flames.

Mme. de Gaulle was again a passenger on August 22, 1962, when 12 men armed with automatic rifles were waiting at a crossroads on the Avenue de la Libération. De Gaulle's car, with an escort vehicle and two motorcycle outriders, was on its way out of Paris to Villacoublay airport. Bastien-Thiry gave the signal to open fire by raising his newspaper, and 14 bullets tore through the car. All told, 187 bullets were later picked up off the pavement. De Gaulle and his wife were showered with broken glass, but they calmly brushed it away and the general went on to Villacoublay, where he inspected a guard of honor. His comment on the would-be killers was: "They shot like pigs." Bastien-Thiry was tracked down and arrested in less than two weeks. He was executed by firing squad, de Gaulle refusing mercy because the commando had opened fire on a woman and because the colonel had taken no personal risks.

ALERTE!

BOMBES H SURVOLENT LA FRANCE EN PERMANENCE

LE PARTI COMMUNISTE FRANÇAIS

its destiny to the decisions and actions of another State, however friendly it may be," he said, ordering France to develop its own nuclear deterrent.

France exploded its first nuclear bomb in 1960, and in 1966 it refused to join Britain, the U.S. and the U.S.S.R. in signing a treaty banning nuclear tests in the atmosphere. In the same year, while remaining in NATO, de Gaulle withdrew French forces from NATO's command structure and told the Americans to remove their bases and troops from French soil. In January 1963 and again in November 1967, he vetoed applications by Britain to join the European Economic Community.

DEADLY DANGER   A poster produced by the French Communist Party in 1955, in protest against American planes carrying atomic bombs over France.

De Gaulle was a realist and came to the conclusion that independence was the only solution to the Algerian problem. This was granted in July 1962, and de Gaulle became the target of assassination attempts by the OAS, the "Secret Army" in Algeria. He came through all of them unscathed, but another crisis was brewing.

The events of May

The crisis began at Nanterre University, a bleak campus dominated by concrete tower blocks on the outskirts of Paris. The students found a mouthpiece for their discontent in a red-haired Trotskyite named Daniel Cohn-Bendit. Noisy protests against American policy in Vietnam became part of student life, and following the arrest of a student, riots broke out and the authorities closed the campus. Students at the Sorbonne in central Paris took to the streets in support of

Nanterre, and on May 3, as the demonstrators tore up paving stones, the riot police were ordered in. They used batons and teargas, injuring some 500 students. So began the "Days" of May, 1968—days during which TV audiences around the world saw cars overturned and set alight, Molotov cocktails thrown, and students beaten up. The students were joined by working-class marchers, angered by low pay, rising unemployment, and the lack of any say in their working conditions. A general strike was called to support their demands.

For a time it looked as if a full-scale revolution might topple the Fifth Republic. De Gaulle left the country to confer with

MAY '68 Cheery demonstrators march through Paris, unaware of the response awaiting them. Left: An injured protester left lying in the gutter after clashing with police.

General Massu, commander in chief of French troops in Germany, and there were rumors that he had lost his nerve. However, the threat of revolution vanished when the prime minister, Georges Pompidou, drove a wedge between the students and their allies by granting the workers wage increases, a reduced workweek, and better benefits. De Gaulle returned to France, and on May 30 made a television appeal to the nation. That day, 250,000 Parisians marched—in support of the Republic.

De Gaulle won a landslide victory in the election of 1968, and student protests were stopped by the allocation of funds to universities and promises of reform. But de Gaulle's paternalistic style was no longer in tune with the times, and the triumph was more Pompidou's than his. When he lost a referendum in April 1969, on two fairly minor constitutional issues, de Gaulle resigned.

THE GERMAN MIRACLE

CRUSHED AND CURSED IN 1945, GERMANY ASTONISHED THE WORLD WITH THE SPEED OF ITS RETURN TO THE FAMILY OF NATIONS

The collapse of Germany in May 1945 was total. In the eerie, lunar landscapes of its ruined cities, where a Leica camera could be bought for 25 cigarettes, the only market that flourished was the black market. The nation whose military machine had made Europe tremble was now near starvation. Where once Germany had demanded great tracts of land—*leben-sraum*—in the East, it now saw entire provinces lopped away by Poland and the U.S.S.R., and the rest of its territory divided into zones of occupation by the Allies. Reparations were being demanded on a colossal scale, and the Soviets showed every sign of exacting their share to the full.

Only ten years later, West Germany was a prosperous and trusted partner in the Western alliance. Two men led the way in this remarkable transformation: Chancellor Konrad Adenauer and his economics minister, Professor Ludwig Erhard.

Whatever its plight in 1945, history and geography combined to make Germany a force to be reckoned with: a nation of 70 million energetic, inventive and disciplined people in the heart of Europe, with no natural frontiers to the East. Originally, the Allies had expected Germany to emerge as a single country after a period of occupation, but neither of the two superpowers could accept a united Germany that was aligned

COUNTING THE COST The 1948 currency reform in the Allied zones of Germany left shoppers like these wondering if they had enough new Deutschmarks to feed their families.

1945 Allies confirm division of Germany into four zones

1948 Berlin Blockade begins; Erhard reforms revive economy

1949 Federal Republic of West Germany born; Adenauer becomes Chancellor of West Germany; German Democratic Republic (East Germany) created

1955 West Germany joins NATO

with its ideological rival. The two Germanies, the Federal Republic in the West and the Democratic Republic in the East, owed their existence to the Cold War. The Iron Curtain, with its blockhouses, its barbed wire and its guard dogs, was the ultimate symbol of their division.

The Federal Republic was proclaimed in September 1949, and Konrad Adenauer, leader of the Christian Democrats (CDU), became West Germany's first chancellor, at the age of 73. He faced a stark choice: alliance with the West seemed to rule out any possibility of Germany's reunification. Adenauer chose the West. Under his leadership, West Germany accepted the Marshall Plan, became a partner in NATO, re-armed, and ended a quarrel with France that had led to three wars within living memory.

Professor Erhard had already shown the way forward when he was economics director for Bizonia (the joint British and American zones). He turned away from the tight state controls that had been a feature of the Nazi era, reduced taxation and ended rationing. This was the strategy that was to produce West Germany's "economic miracle." In Erhard's "social market economy," businessmen were not hampered, but the workers were looked after generously with family allowances, pensions, and sickness and unemployment benefits.

Four billion dollars from the Marshall Plan primed the economy; the Korean War brought a mini-boom; and the country did

BUST TO BOOM Sacks of coal being distributed to needy families in Berlin in 1952 (above). Within ten years, West Germany's manufacturing industry was booming—as at the Krupps' train-making factory in Essen (below).

ADENAUER, THE "OLD FOX"

The year was 1933, and Adolf Hitler, the new chancellor of Germany, planned to make a rousing speech in Cologne. Up went the swastika flags in readiness, but the Führer was in for a surprise. Konrad Adenauer, the Mayor of Cologne, ordered the swastikas to be taken down from public property. This was enough to put him on the Nazis' list of suspects. It cost his dismissal and two jail sentences—one after the "night of the long knives," when Hitler purged the leadership of his SA stormtroopers, the other in 1944, after the failure of the July plot to assassinate the Führer. Both stays in jail were short, for no evidence was found against the man who came to be called the "old fox" for his wiliness and skill at surviving.

After the war, he became mayor of Cologne again, but he disagreed with the British military government and was dismissed a second time. He returned on a bigger stage when he became West Germany's first chancellor. When running a city, Adenauer had shown that he could get things done. He brought the same efficiency to running the country.

Konrad Adenauer (1876-1967) was a Roman Catholic Rhinelander with the cool, impassive look of a Native American chief. This was partly the result of a car crash before the war, which had left him needing reconstructive surgery to both cheekbones, and partly the product of his own innate dignity.

He had a short way with dissent. "If God had made men more intelligent they would know what to do," he was fond of saying. "If He had made them more stupid they would be easier to govern." Adenauer usually knew exactly what to do. He took West Germany into the European Coal and Steel Community and into the Common Market as a founder-member. He placed his country firmly on the side of the West in the Cold War, and his key principle when dealing with the Soviets was: "No concessions without concessions in return."

Adenauer built up a close understanding with General de Gaulle, and shared the Frenchman's somewhat dismissive view of the islanders across the Channel. "England," he said, "is like a rich man who has lost all his property but doesn't realize it."

He did not retire until October 1963, when he was 87 years old.

1961 Berlin
Wall goes up

TV AND A DRINK   A German magazine cover of 1952 reflects the country's new affluence and a new, more informal outlook.

not need money for defense until it joined NATO in 1955. But perhaps the most important factor in the economic miracle was that West German goods had a competitive edge in price and quality. The world quickly became aware that "Made in Germany" was a guarantee of reliability. Sales of cars, cameras, chemicals, machinery and electrical goods helped exports to increase eightfold during Erhard's years as economics minister, and the Deutschmark to become one of the world's strongest currencies.

Unemployment fell from 1,900,000 in 1950 to 200,000 in 1961. Indeed, the problem was not finding jobs for the workers but finding workers to fill the jobs. Some 3 million refugees were absorbed from East Germany before the Berlin Wall went up in

VW RISES FROM THE ASHES

In May 1945, the Volkswagen plant at Wolfsburg in the British zone of Germany was a picture of desolation. What the bombers had left standing was largely demolished by newly liberated slave laborers on a rampage of destruction. It seemed that Adolf Hitler's dream of a people's car that would do 40 miles to the gallon and sell for less than 1,000 marks (then the equivalent of $200) had gone the way of his many other dreams. However, the British army had vehicles that urgently needed repairs. When a handful of local workers turned up, hesitant and fearful, and offered to work in return, not for money, but for a mid-day meal and a handful of cigarettes, they were welcomed.

Some British officers at Wolfsburg, fascinated by the design ideas that Ferdinand Porsche had built into his "people's car," had a few VWs built as an experiment, and soon the car's fame was spreading by word of mouth. By the end of 1945, Wolfsburg had more than 6,000 employees, working by then for money, and

had turned out more than 700 cars for the military. The army invited British car manufacturers to see for themselves why the little beetle-shaped car was making such an impact. The reaction they got was a classic error of judgment: the VW's air-cooled engine was far too noisy; the design was ugly, and in any case it would be out of date in two or three years' time.

What the British car-makers overlooked was the VW's convenience, its reliability and its low running costs. Inside Germany, it found a growing market—and outside too, as VW's export drive flickered into life in 1947, with 57 cars exported, mainly to Holland and Switzerland. The following January, the British appointed a

FAMILY FAVORITES   One of the world's best-loved cars, the Beetle was still in production in Mexico at the end of the millennium.

German manager at Wolfsburg, Dr. Heinz Nordhoff, a refugee from Brandenburg, where he had managed an Opel plant. It was an inspired choice. Nordhoff, who arrived penniless in the West and had worked as a manual laborer for two years to feed his family, told his workforce: "The future begins when you cut every tie with the past." In September 1949, when the British handed Wolfsburg over to the Federal German Government, Nordhoff became VW's managing director. He always insisted that before a single car was exported to a new market, VW should set up a full service organization in that country. And for years he kept the Beetle's shape. The strategy was a spectacular success. Dr. Nordhoff saw the millionth Beetle roll off the assembly line in August 1955. He died in April 1968—seven months too soon to celebrate the completion of the 15 millionth model of the car Britain had resurrected—and then rejected.

MADE IN GERMANY   Leica cameras, which in 1945 changed hands for 25 cigarettes, were part of Germany's export drive by 1954.

1961, then came an influx of workers from Yugoslavia, Turkey, Italy and Spain—the *Gästarbeiter*, or guest workers.

Buildings in West Germany went up almost overnight. The autobahn system was extended, the railways electrified, canals widened. The newly prosperous West Germans became world tourists.

Adenauer retired in 1963, at age 87, making way for Erhard, who turned out to be less successful as chancellor

than he had been as economics minister. The boom took a downturn, and Erhard resigned. Twenty years of Christian Democrat government came to an end in 1969, when the Social Democrat Willi Brandt, mayor of Berlin during the dangerous years when the Wall was built, became chancellor. Adenauer had set West Germany firmly in the Western camp, and Erhard had been the architect of economic recovery. Now, from a position of strength, Brandt set out on his *Ostpolitik* (Eastern policy)—a bid to improve relations with Eastern Europe. Behind it lay the hope of Germany's reunification. But it was to be a long journey, with many stumbles on the way.

BUILDING BOOM   Neon lights in West Berlin (right) and brand-new blocks of apartments in Munich (below) testify to consumer confidence and to West Germany's economic miracle of the 1950s and 1960s.

TOWARD EUROPEAN UNION

RIVALRIES, WHICH TWICE IN 25 YEARS HAD PLUNGED THE WORLD INTO WAR, WERE PUT ASIDE IN WESTERN EUROPE'S NEW DRIVE FOR UNITY

Nationalism was born in Europe a thousand years ago, when nation-states began to emerge from a profusion of dukedoms, principalities and petty kingdoms. Following the catastrophe of two world wars in a single generation, both sparked by nationalism, the countries of Europe began a search for a way to overcome the limitations of the nation-state.

The European Economic Community (EEC), brought into existence by the Treaty of Rome in 1957, was a grouping of six nations, all of which had been victims of those limitations. France, Belgium, the Netherlands and Luxembourg had all suffered German occupation. Italy, a reluctant partner in aggression, had been ravaged by war. Germany, the original aggressor, had been the biggest loser of all.

The drive to unite Western Europe was powered by both economics and politics. Winston Churchill, ever alert to the need for security, called for a United Europe in a speech made in Zurich in 1946. But Churchill was out of office, and Britain's Labor government did not share his enthusiasm. Britain's emotional ties and trading links with the Commonwealth and the U.S. were stronger than anything Continental Europe had to offer.

Britain did, however, become a member of the Council of Europe that had arisen partly from Churchill's initiative. This body, which held its first session at Strasbourg in August 1949, echoed to the oratory of such committed Europeans as Belgium's Paul-Henri Spaak and Italy's Alcide de Gasperi. It published a Convention on Human Rights, but it had no authority to enforce decisions.

A more practical step toward European unity had already been taken, however. In October 1947, Belgium, the Netherlands and Luxembourg established Benelux, an economic union of their three countries. One of the first acts of the new group was to abolish customs duties between its members and to establish a common tariff against goods coming from outside. In a world dom-

THE "TROJAN HORSE" DOLLAR A cartoon in the Soviet magazine *Krokodil* explains why the U.S.S.R. rejected American aid for itself and for the East European satellites.

inated by the two superpowers, here was a Common Market in miniature.

The U.S. saw European unity as a bulwark against communism, and one of the conditions of the Marshall Plan, announced in 1947, was that countries benefiting from it should set up a plan and an organization to channel the aid. As well as distributing $23 billion of American money, the Organization for European Co-operation (OEEC) also gave Europe a valuable lesson in the mechanics of working together.

The French and the Germans, traditional enemies, had most to gain from new thinking about Europe. If France could not draw in Britain as a counterbalance to any potential threat from revived German ambitions, it would have to remove that threat by making a friend of Germany.

This was the political strategy that lay behind French Foreign

MAKING HISTORY IN ROME Statesmen from six European nations sign two Treaties of Rome in March 1957, one founding the Common Market, the other pooling their atomic power projects.

1945

1946 Churchill proposes Council of Europe

1947 Benelux Customs Union

1948 OEEC set up to channel Marshall Plan money

1952 Treaty for European Coal and Steel Community ratified

1957 Treaty of Rome sets up Common Market

1959 "The Seven" set up EFTA

1963 De Gaulle vetoes U.K. bid to join EEC

1968 Common Market members remove last customs barriers

1970

UNITED FOR PEACE

IN THE AGE OF SUPERPOWER POLITICS, THE UNITED NATIONS STRUGGLED TO CURB THE SCOURGE OF WAR— AND SOMETIMES IT SUCCEEDED

The United Nations, born in June 1945, in San Francisco, was always a balance between idealism and the realities of power politics. The idealism lay in the objective set out in its charter: to remove the scourge of war from succeeding generations. Its predecessor, the League of Nations, had held the same lofty aim, but it had failed between the wars to halt acts of aggression by Japan, Italy, and Germany. One reason for the weakness of the League was that the U.S., in an isolationist mood, had not joined. One reason for optimism about the UN was that this time the U.S., with all its strength, was an enthusiastic founder.

Reality dictated that none of the 51 founder-members of the UN was likely, in any dispute, to act against its own vital interests or those of its friends; and among them were some states too powerful to be ignored.

In the General Assembly of the United Nations, meeting in New York, every member state was given one vote, regardless of size. The Assembly's power was moral rather than political: it could make recommendations, but had no authority to enforce them. That authority was vested in the Security Council, also meeting in New York.

The UN has no armed forces of its own, but the 15 members of the Security Council—five of them permanent, the others elected for two years at a time—can call on member states to provide troops to take action when peace is threatened. In recognition of what were the perceived realities of world power in 1945, the "Big Five"—the U.S., U.S.S.R., Britain, France and Nationalist China—were allocated the permanent seats in the Security Council, and each was given the right of veto over any call for action.

In the early days of the UN, the Soviet Union used its veto so often that

TREE OF HARMONY A French poster of 1947 expresses the world's hopes for the future of the United Nations.

NATIONS UNIES

the other Security Council members lodged an official complaint. In response, the Soviet delegation boycotted the council—a tactic that backfired on them. When, in June 1950, North Korean troops swarmed across the border to attack South Korea, the Soviets were not in the chamber to veto the Security Council's call for action against communist aggression.

New nations emerged in the post-war world as former colonies, mainly in Africa and Asia, won their freedom. One result was that membership of the General Assembly rapidly grew. The powers of the Assembly were extended in 1950 through a resolution dubbed Uniting for Peace, sponsored by the United States. This gave the Assembly the right, in an emergency, to bypass the Security Council and to give a ruling on whether or not world peace was in danger. This resolution was used in 1956 when a UN Emergency Force was sent to Suez, following an attack on Egypt by Britain, France and Israel.

After the defeat of Chiang Kai-shek's nationalist forces in 1949 and their retreat to the island of Taiwan, it was clear that power in China lay with Mao Zedong's communists. For many years, however, America opposed Communist China's admission to the UN, and it was not until 1971 that Nationalist China was expelled, and mainland China became a member of the United Nations.

The UN has its own civil service, the Secretariat, headed by a Secretary General who can be of enormous influence in world affairs. Trygve Lie, a Norwegian lawyer, was the first to fill the post, and he was followed by the Swede Dag Hammarskjöld. In its first 15 years, the UN had a mixed record on peacekeeping. Its activities ranged from full-scale military intervention, as in Korea (1950) and the Congo (1960), to maintaining ceasefires, as in Indonesia (1946) and Cyprus (1964), and sending observers, as in the Lebanon (1958).

As well as having a peacekeeping role, the UN is responsible for the International Court of Justice in The Hague. It helps refugees, brings relief to disaster areas, and carries out other humanitarian activities. Among its specialized agencies are the Educational, Scientific and Cultural Organization (UNESCO), the World Health Organization (WHO), the International Monetary Fund (IMF) and the General Agreement on Tariffs and Trade (GATT). The UN's Relief and Rehabilitation Agency (UNRRA) was dissolved in 1948, its work done.

ARMED PEACEKEEPER A member of the UN peacekeeping force arriving at Port Said in response to the Suez Crisis.

Minister Robert Schuman's proposal for a European Coal and Steel Community (ECSC). It was a bold proposal, based on the ideas of French economist Jean Monnet, the man behind France's National Plan for recovery. Germany, France and other invited countries would pool the coalfields, steelworks and iron ore resources of some of the richest industrial areas in Europe. Decisions about output and investment would be taken from a European rather than a national point of view, by a body so important that it bore the title of the High Authority. Italy and the Benelux countries joined France and Germany in the ECSC when it was established in April 1952. Jean Monnet hailed the move as "the first expression of the Europe that is being born," and he became the ECSC's first president. Britain was invited to join, but declined.

The drive to unity reached a crescendo in March 1957, when France, West Germany, the three Benelux countries and Italy—soon to be known as the Six—signed the Treaties of Rome, setting up the EEC and the European Atomic Energy Community (Euratom). The EEC, or Common Market, was a customs union and free trade area that offered access to a

market of 180 million people. The EEC Treaty aimed to remove all internal customs barriers by 1970, and to establish the free movement of labor and investment between member countries. The purpose of Euratom was cooperation in the peaceful development of nuclear energy.

Inside the Six there were differences about how far union should go: should it stop at free trade, or should it move toward political federation? Paul-Henri Spaak, prime minister of Belgium, was tireless in his pursuit of closer Western European union. But General de Gaulle, who was returned to power as president of France in 1959, spoke of a Europe des Patries—a Europe of Nations—stretching from the Atlantic to the Urals.

In 1967 the three legs of the European tripod—the ECSC, the EEC and Euratom —were merged into a single body, the European Community (EC). It had a formidable array of institutions: a Commission to propose action; a Council of Ministers to take decisions based on those proposals; a European Parliament, sitting in Strasbourg, to discuss the proposals and EC budgets; and the European Court of Justice in Luxembourg, with authority to interpret the

ECONOMIC POWERHOUSE   The headquarters of the EEC in Brussels, center of administration and decision-making for a market that already numbered 180 million in 1957.

various European treaties and to resolve disputes between member states. Cases involving violations of the rights of individuals could be taken before the European Court of Human Rights in Strasbourg.

Britain, unwilling to give up political sovereignty, set up a rival customs union, the European Free Trade Association (EFTA), in 1959, with Austria, Norway, Denmark, Portugal, Sweden and Switzerland. They became known as the Outer Seven. But the ever-increasing prosperity of the Six was a compelling lure. In January 1963, under Harold Macmillan, Britain applied for EEC membership. De Gaulle, however, saw the British as reluctant Europeans, still too close to the Commonwealth and the U.S. He vetoed the application, announcing to a press conference: "The question is to know if Britain can at present place itself with the Continent and like it." A second British application, made under the premiership of Harold Wilson in May 1968, was blocked by a similar "Non" from de Gaulle.

However, following de Gaulle's resignation as president of France, the Six agreed at the end of 1969 to open membership talks with Britain, Denmark and Ireland.

MAN WITH A PLAN   France's Robert Schuman proposed the Coal and Steel Community, a key stage in Europe's drive to unity.

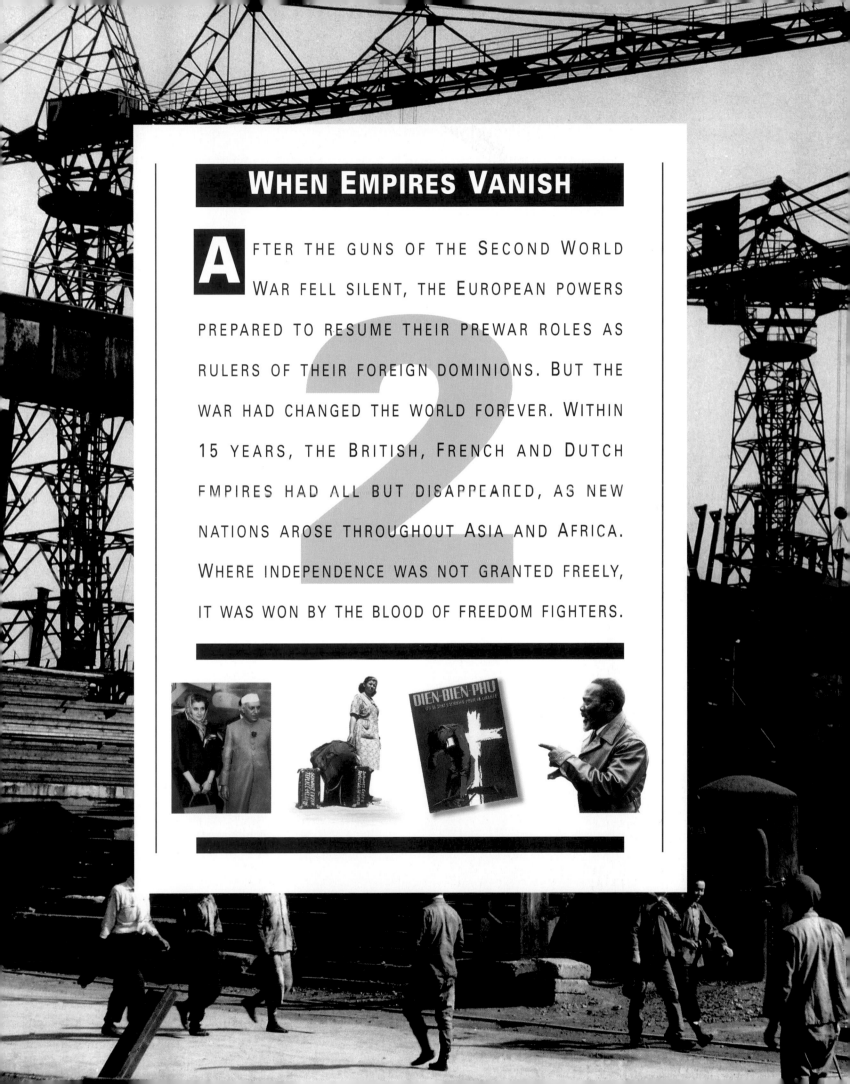

WHEN EMPIRES VANISH

AFTER THE GUNS OF THE SECOND WORLD WAR FELL SILENT, THE EUROPEAN POWERS PREPARED TO RESUME THEIR PREWAR ROLES AS RULERS OF THEIR FOREIGN DOMINIONS. BUT THE WAR HAD CHANGED THE WORLD FOREVER. WITHIN 15 YEARS, THE BRITISH, FRENCH AND DUTCH EMPIRES HAD ALL BUT DISAPPEARED, AS NEW NATIONS AROSE THROUGHOUT ASIA AND AFRICA. WHERE INDEPENDENCE WAS NOT GRANTED FREELY, IT WAS WON BY THE BLOOD OF FREEDOM FIGHTERS.

FREEDOM AT MIDNIGHT

INDIA AWOKE TO "LIFE AND FREEDOM" IN AUGUST 1947, BUT THERE WAS A HEAVY PRICE TO PAY FOR INDEPENDENCE—PARTITION

As the first stroke of midnight ushered in August 15, 1947, two new nations were born in Asia. India and Pakistan ended nearly two centuries of British domination and threw off the shackles of the Raj. "Long years ago we made a tryst with destiny," declared India's new prime minister, Jawaharlal Nehru. "At the stroke of the midnight hour, when the world sleeps, India will awake to life and freedom."

But the awakening was marked as much by struggle and blood as by rejoicing. For ancient fears and hatreds, largely suppressed under the British, burst to the surface in a frenzy of killing, arson and looting.

India's long march to freedom had been led by a saint who was also a political strategist of genius: Mohandas Karamchand Gandhi,

also known as Mahatma, "Great Soul," a name he was given by the Indian poet Rabindranath Tagore. Gandhi developed a strategy he called *satyagraha*, meaning "truth force," which demanded turning the other cheek to acts of violence and opposing unjust laws by passive resistance. It was a strategy that baffled and ultimately defeated the imperial power.

History held no comparable example of an empire being persuaded by nonviolent means to relinquish sovereignty over such a mass of humankind. But in 1947, India's

A DAY TO REMEMBER Jubilant citizens of Calcutta, once capital of British India, celebrate the end of the Raj and their first day of independence.

VICTIMS OF PARTITION Thousands of Hindus, fearful of being a minority in a Muslim land, flee from Pakistan to India after the partition map is drawn.

hour had come. No longer was it feasible for a nation of 400 million to be governed by 2,000 British civil servants, backed by a force of British regulars that never in peacetime numbered more than 60,000, and an Indian army led by 10,000 British officers.

This relatively small force could not have

1947 Independence and partition for India and Pakistan

1948 Gandhi assassinated

1949 UN imposes ceasefire line in Kashmir after first Indo-Pakistan War of 1947

held sway over such a multitude without the power of a myth, and the myth of British invincibility had been shattered by the fall of "impregnable" Singapore and by other wartime humiliations inflicted by the Japanese. There was a new attitude in London, too, with a Labor government in charge. The war had driven Britain close to the reefs of bankruptcy, and the prime minister, Clement Attlee, saw independence for India as both an economic necessity and a moral imperative.

In March 1946, Attlee sent Sir Stafford Cripps on a Cabinet mission to India to draw up a plan for handing over sovreignty, but the mission failed. Mohammed

LIVING SAINT Mahatma Gandhi, apostle of nonviolence, whose pleas for tolerance between Hindu and Muslim were not always heard.

1958 Ayub Khan takes power in Pakistan

1962 War between India and China

1965 Second Indo-Pakistan war over Kashmir

1966 Indira Gandhi elected India's prime minister

1969 Yahya Khan seizes power in Pakistan

Ali Jinnah, leader of India's 92 million Muslims, rejected Cripps's proposals, which he believed would see the Muslims swamped by India's 250 million Hindus. He called for a separate Muslim state— Pakistan, the "Land of the Pure"—and to show the strength of his support, he called a *hartal*, a business boycott and general strike, in Calcutta.

Riots and retaliation

The genie was out of the bottle. What began as a boycott turned into four days of riots that left between 4,000 and 5,000 dead. Hindu slaughtered Muslim and Muslim slew Hindu in Bombay, Bihar and Rawalpindi.

> ### DEATH IN THE PUNJAB
>
> A special correspondent for *The Times* gave a close-up view of the massacres in the Punjab, following the partition of India:
>
> "'A thousand times more horrible than anything we saw in the war' is the universal comment of experienced officers, both British and Indian, on the present slaughter in east Punjab. The Sikhs are on the warpath. They are clearing east Pakistan of Moslems, butchering hundreds daily, forcing thousands to flee westwards, burning Moslem villages and homesteads, even in their frenzy burning their own too . . .
>
> "The Sikhs attack scientifically. A first wave, armed with firearms, fires to bring the Moslems off their roofs. A second wave lobs grenades over the walls. In the ensuing confusion a third wave goes in with kirpans [sabres] and spears and the serious killing begins. A last wave consists of older men, often army pensioners with long white beards, who carry torches and specialise in arson."

Britain, represented by the viceroy, Lord Wavell, was clearly losing control. Attlee fired Wavell to make way for a far more glamorous figure. Britain's last viceroy was Lord Louis Mountbatten, Supreme Allied Commander, Southeast Asia, during the war, and cousin of King George VI.

Attlee had promised that Britain would leave India by June 1948, but at a press conference a year before that deadline, Mountbatten announced that the deadline was being brought for-

THE LAST VICEROY Resplendent in their viceregal regalia, Lord Louis Mountbatten and his wife, Edwina, bring glamour to the cover of a popular magazine.

ward, to August 15, 1947. That left just over ten weeks to complete the handover of power and the partition of India. Mounting violence had made it blindingly clear that the British Raj would be replaced by two nations, not one. Mountbatten gave the unenviable task of drawing up the frontiers of the new nations to a Boundary Commission, led by Sir Cyril Radcliffe.

The killings escalated to a new level of ferocity once people

BIRTH OF A NATION A dense throng gathers in Karachi to celebrate Mohammed Ali Jinnah's success in founding the separate Muslim nation of Pakistan.

knew where the boundary lines would fall. Some of the most horrifying scenes took place in the Punjab, homeland of many of India's 5.5 million Sikhs, but also home to millions of Hindus and Muslims. The new boundary line cut the Punjab in two. More than 3.5 million Hindu and Sikh refugees streamed across the border to seek safety in India, while more than 5 million Muslims fled to Pakistan. The migrations took place against a background of massacre, rape and looting. Bands of Sikhs, the *jathas*, armed with guns, grenades, sabers and spears, butchered fleeing Muslims, and Muslims retaliated equally savagely.

In one incident, typical of many, *jathas* attacked a trainload of Muslim refugees near Amritsar in a three-hour massacre. The Hindu guards on the train fired over the heads of the attackers, and the British officer in charge of the escort fought the *jathas* single-handed, with a machine gun, until he was killed. There was an even worse train incident at Gujrat station in the West Punjab, when Muslim Pathan tribesmen attacked a refugee train carrying 2,400 Hindus and

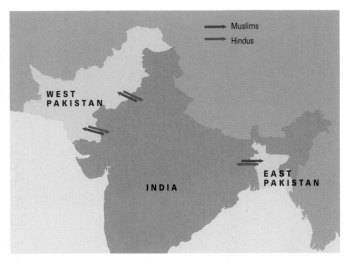

THE COST OF FREEDOM Independence brought partition between India and Pakistan, and the new boundaries left millions in peril on the wrong side of the line.

Sikhs, leaving more than 1,650 dead.

The Indian Independence Act not only separated Pakistan from India, but also split Pakistan: the nation was divided into two "wings"—West and East Pakistan, with 1,000 miles of Indian territory between them. Jinnah, awarded the title of Quaid-e-Aza, "Great Leader," became Pakistan's first president and governor-general.

Gandhi's sacrifice

In the nightmare that followed partition, an estimated 8 million refugees fled from Pakistan to India, and as many again from India to Pakistan. The number killed will never be known, but eyewitnesses reported that the canals were choked with bodies, and the trees laden with vultures. Estimates of the number of deaths vary from 200,000 up to 500,000. Jinnah issued a powerful appeal: "Are we now going to besmear this achievement, for which there is no parallel in the history of the world, by resorting to frenzy,

savagery and butchery?" But the most eloquent plea came not in the form of words. Gandhi brought peace to Calcutta by starting a fast unto death, vowing not to take nourishment until killings in the city stopped.

After shaming the rioters in Calcutta, Gandhi moved to Delhi, where, in January 1948, he began another fast. His object this time was not just to end the communal slaughter but also to force the Indian government to pay Pakistan 550 million rupees ($164 million) due from the splitting of assets of the two countries. He was 78 years old, frail and already weak from his Calcutta fast. After three days, with his health deteriorating rapidly, the government backed down and announced it would pay the debt.

It was to be the last victory of Gandhi's life. On January 30, 1948, as the Mahatma addressed a prayer meeting in New Delhi, he was shot dead by Nathuram Godse, a Hindu fanatic who had been incensed by the payment to Pakistan.

India was distraught. Nehru found the words to express the nation's emotions: "The light has gone out of our lives and there is darkness everywhere . . . and yet . . . a thousand years later that light will still be seen."

In death, as in life, Gandhi could move people's hearts. His assassination so stirred the conscience of both Hindus and Muslims that the widespread killings came to a halt. Some 35 million Muslims remained within the borders of India, and Nehru was to promise them: "We have never accepted, even when partition came to India, the two-nation theory—that is, that the Hindus are one nation and the Muslims are another."

The new India faced a host of problems: poverty, illiteracy, disease and a social structure dominated by the rigid caste system, with 6 million "Untouchables" at the bottom of the heap. Average life expectancy was just 32 years. Nehru set out to modernize the country, ignoring caste and making Untouchability illegal. Dams were built, irrigation plans launched, steelworks erected,

DEATH OF THE APOSTLE OF NONVIOLENCE

On January 30, 1948, a single act of violence brought an end to the life of the man who led India to freedom by preaching a doctrine of nonviolence. A Hindu fanatic, Nathuram Godse, thrust his way out of a crowd of Mahatma Gandhi's followers at a prayer meeting, bowed in reverence, and fired three bullets into the Mahatma at point-blank range. His spectacles dangling from one ear, Gandhi slumped to the ground, crying "Hey, Rama!" (Oh, God!). Godse, a 35-year-old journalist, was felled and smothered under a heap of bodies, amid cries of "Kill him!". He narrowly escaped lynching.

As the sounds of lament rose, Gandhi's niece Abha and great-niece Manu helped to carry him back to his room and tried to minister to him, but the 78-year-old pacifist was dead within 25 minutes. The crowd was chanting hymns by the time India's prime minister, Jawaharlal Nehru, arrived. He fell to his knees over the dead man and wept inconsolably.

Four months after the assassination, Godse went on trial, along with eight fellow conspirators. They had plotted to kill Gandhi because through all the violent days of partition he had tried to stop the massacres and bring peace to Hindus and Muslims. Only a few days before the tragedy, he had gone on a fast to force the Indian government to pay money it owed to Pakistan. Godse and another leading conspirator were sentenced to be hanged, five other conspirators were jailed for life, one was acquitted for lack of evidence, and one was given a free pardon for giving evidence against the rest.

LAID TO REST A niece places flower petals on Gandhi's brow, as he lies in state at Birla House, New Delhi, after his assassination by a Hindu fanatic in 1948.

TWO CULTURES MEET Indian women, carrying their burdens in a style that is more than 4,000 years old, walk past a symbol of the new India—a modern steel factory in Bihar.

and free primary education made available to all of India's children. But the march to prosperity was painfully slow because there were always more mouths to feed.

Conflict in Kashmir

By the time of independence, all but three of India's Princely States had declared their allegiance to either India or Pakistan. The exceptions were Hyderabad, Kashmir and Junagadh, a tiny state surrounded by Indian territory, whose Nawab, after some delay, decided to join Pakistan. Nehru promptly sent in the Indian army and the Nawab took a plane to Pakistan.

Hyderabad, a feudal state with 17 million people, presented a tougher problem. Its population was 80 percent Hindu, but the ruler, the Nizam, was a Muslim who tried to run his state as an independent country. It took Nehru until September 1948 to send in his troops and dash the Nizam's hopes.

Kashmir, a paradise of lakes and snow-capped peaks, was the reverse of Hyderabad: it had a Hindu maharajah, but a population that was 75 percent Muslim. On October 22,

1947, thousands of Pathan tribesmen swarmed across the border to claim Kashmir for Pakistan. They would have taken the capital, Srinagar, if they had not stopped to loot on the way. Indian troops were flown into Srinagar airport to repel the invaders.

Mountbatten, now governor-general of India, advised Nehru to call in the United Nations over the Kashmir dispute, and the

TEMPORARY TRUCE United Nations observers study the ceasefire line in the 1947 Indo-Pakistan dispute over Kashmir. War flared up again in 1965 and in 1990.

war was ended in 1949 by a UN-imposed ceasefire. Fighting flared again in August 1965, and again the UN imposed a ceasefire. Under the Tashkent Declaration of January 1966, sponsored by the Soviet Union, both sides agreed to stay behind the ceasefire line, and to settle future disputes peacefully.

Nehru's foreign policy was marked by suspicion of the U.S., although India's official stance was one of non-alignment. Nehru made friendly overtures to China, lobbying hard for Red China to have a seat in the United Nations and, four years after the Chinese invasion of Tibet, formally recognizing Tibet as Chinese territory. Both India and China attended a conference of unaligned Afro-Asian nations at Bandung in 1955, and used it as a platform to denounce colonialism.

But Nehru was mistaken if he thought he had found a friend in China's leader, Mao Zedong. For along the mist-covered ridges of the Karakorams and the Himalayas, India

RULING DYNASTY India's first prime minister, Jawaharlal Nehru, with his daughter, Indira Gandhi, who built on his policies when she became premier in 1966.

had a long, snaking border with Tibet. In March 1956, the Chinese started building a supply road in Tibet, part of it running through what India regarded as its territory in the inhospitable region of Aksai Chin.

Despite border skirmishes, Nehru and his defense minister, Krishna Menon, were convinced by their own rhetoric that China would not make war, and India was ill prepared to fight; factories that might have been making guns were turning out pressure cookers. The invasion came on October 20, 1962, when "human wave" attacks by 20,000 Chinese infantry swamped the Indian

THE LAST OF THE MAHARAJAHS

Even in the high noon of the Raj, less than two-thirds of India was directly ruled by Britain. The remainder fell into the category of Princely States, whose hereditary rulers owed allegiance to the King-Emperor and accepted advice on foreign affairs and defense but who otherwise, in theory at least, wielded total authority.

There were more than 500 Princely States, ranging in size from Hyderabad, one-third the size of Texas and with 17 million inhabitants, to tiny pockets of land less than a mile across. At one extreme, in the smaller, poorer states, the life of the ruler differed little from that of his subjects. At the other extreme, the rulers enjoyed a state of luxury and privilege rarely seen since the fall of the Roman Empire.

The Nizam of Hyderabad, listed in reference books of the time as the world's richest man, had his own private army, 10,000 strong, minted his own coinage, and printed his own stamps. He used the fabled 182.5 carat Jacob diamond as a paperweight, but for all his wealth he was notoriously stingy, wearing old suits and demanding a tribute of gold coins if he attended the wedding of one of his subjects.

The Maharajah of Gwalior served dinner to his guests on the world's most expensive model train set. Carriages running on solid silver rails conveyed course after course from the kitchens to the table. In Rampur, the Nawab had

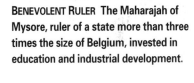

BENEVOLENT RULER The Maharajah of Mysore, ruler of a state more than three times the size of Belgium, invested in education and industrial development.

more than 90 hereditary cooks, each one specializing in a single ingredient. The Nawab of Junagadh kept his pet dogs in luxury apartments, with their own servants, and when they died had them laid to rest in a marble mausoleum. One of the favorite pastimes of the Maharajah of Patiala was collecting Rolls-Royces. He had a fleet of 27. Testimony to another of his pastimes was his harem of 350 concubines.

India's princes were descended from warriors, and their traditional sports bore witness to their lineage: polo, pig-sticking—pursuing wild boar on horseback, armed with a spear—and, most prestigious of all, tiger shooting. Other sports were picked up from British officers: tennis, squash, cricket and fox hunting, for which hounds were imported from England, although the quarry was often jackals rather than foxes. The ruler of Bhavnagar kept a pack of cheetahs to hunt black buck.

Some of the princes used their wealth and position to improve the lives of their subjects. The Nawab of Rampur built roads, canals and schools. Mysore had hydroelectric systems and a university. In Bhopal, women had equal status with men, and in Baroda, where education was free and universal, the ruler introduced reforms to improve the lives of the Untouchables.

Whether enlightened in their attitude or feudal, the Princely States, with their Maharajahs and Jamsabebs, their Nizams and Nawabs, their Badshas and their Begums, had no place in independent India and Pakistan. By August 15, 1947, with three exceptions, all the princes had surrendered their sovereignty and state assets in return for the right to keep their marbled palaces and private property, and to receive a

private pension based usually on 10 percent of annual revenues. Junagadh, Kashmir and Hyderabad were the last to concede. In the new India, demands grew for the total abolition of the princely order, and finally they were to lose their pensions. The mightiest of the princes had once been greeted with 21-gun salutes. In the future, they would have to work for a living, like any private citizen.

SPORTING RULER The Maharajah of Jaipur lived in prewar magnificence. His palace covered one-seventh of the area of his capital, Jaipur City.

WAR ON FAMINE   Prime Minister Indira Gandhi in Udaipur while touring areas stricken by drought and famine in 1966. She went on to secure aid and food from the U.S.

defenses. The Chinese, having made their point, declared a ceasefire and retired across the border. "Maybe we pinned too much faith in Chinese friendship," Nehru admitted.

Nehru died of a stroke on May 27, 1964, and his ashes were scattered, according to his wishes, "over the fields where the peasants of India toil, so that they might mingle with the dust and soil of India." Under his successor as prime minister, Lal Bahadur Shastri, India repelled a Pakistani incursion into the salty wasteland of the Rann of Kutch in 1965 and fought Pakistan over Kashmir. When Shastri died, in January 1966, Nehru's daughter Indira Gandhi became prime minister. She spoke out against America's policy in Vietnam, and inside India began a "green revolution," aimed at making the nation self-sufficient in food in three years.

The generals rule in Pakistan

With all its problems, India remained the world's largest democracy. In Pakistan, on the other hand, democracy had a precarious existence. The nation's difficulties included the separation of the country into two halves, a series of military rulers, and the festering sore of Kashmir.

Jinnah died of tuberculosis in September 1948, and the prime minister, Liaquat Ali Khan, was assassinated in October 1951. A Muslim sect, the Ahrars, tried to impose their puritanism on the country, and, following riots in Lahore, the government declared a state of emergency in September 1954. Two years later, Pakistan was declared an Islamic Republic, with General Iskander Mirza as its president. Mirza found it hard to govern through parliament, and in October 1958 he abolished political parties and proclaimed martial law. Within weeks he was ousted, in a coup led by General Ayub Khan.

SCHOOL WITHOUT WALLS   Pakistani children learn to recite the Koran by heart in their open-air school. For many, this is the main education they will receive.

A rising figure in West Pakistan was Zulfikar Ali Bhutto, who became Ayub's foreign minister but resigned in 1967 because he thought the government was not sufficiently aggressive over Kashmir. Bhutto founded the Pakistan People's Party (PPP), and was jailed in 1968 after denouncing Ayub as a dictator.

Ayub rooted out corruption, but his refusal to allow a greater degree of democracy led to strikes and riots, and in 1969 he was forced out of office by another general, Yahya Khan. The country was once again placed under martial law, but Yahya promised democratic elections in 1970.

Unlike India, Pakistan was firmly committed to the West in the Cold War. It joined the Southeast Asia Treaty Organization (SEATO) when it was set up in 1954 to resist communist advances in Asia, and qualified for massive military aid from America. The benefit of this aid, and the boost it gave to industry, was seen more in West Pakistan than in the East, where the Bengalis complained that they were treated as poor relations. The jute and rice that were among Pakistan's most important exports came from the East, but the money they earned was spent 1,000 miles away, in West Pakistan. Sheikh Mujibar Rahman and his Awami League led the Bengali protest, but the government's answer was to arrest Mujibar. Jinnah's dream of a Muslim nation united by religion and patriotism though separated by geography was fading fast.

NEW NATIONS FROM OLD

THE MYTH OF WESTERN INVINCIBILITY WAS SHATTERED BY JAPAN DURING THE WAR, AND NATIONALIST LEADERS LEARNED THE LESSON

Japan's dazzling series of victories in Southeast Asia, following the attack on Pearl Harbor, shattered forever the myth that the western nations were invincible. When Europeans returned to the region after Japan's surrender in 1945, it was to a world that had changed. Nationalist leaders who once would have been dealt with as agitators now had the backing to be taken seriously when they demanded independence.

The communists, who in many places had taken the lead in guerrilla fighting against the Japanese, were usually in the forefront of the new struggle. They simply turned their weapons against the colonial powers that had supplied the guns in the first place.

Freedom in the Philippines

The first step toward ending colonialism in the south Pacific was taken by the U.S. in 1946, in fulfilment of a promise made to the people of the Philippines before the war. The date chosen for independence was charged with significance: the Republic of the Philippines was born, like the U.S., on the Fourth of July. But the U.S. did not

TRAINED TO FIGHT Guerrilla war against the Japanese turned out to be good training both for the regular forces of the Philippines and for the "Huk" rebels.

entirely relinquish its influence. America was granted 99-year leases on 23 military and naval bases; U.S. nationals were given equal rights with Filipinos to exploit natural resources; and tariff-free trade was established between the two countries for eight years, with tariffs to be introduced gradually after that period and with Filipino exports to the U.S. limited by a quota system.

The wide gap between rich and poor in the Philippines led to a rebellion in the late 1940s by the Hukbalahaps or "Huks," originally a peasant party that rose up in protest against a sharecropping system under which landlords took 50 percent of the crops grown by their tenants. The Huks, who soon came to be dominated by the communists, at one stage threatened to capture the capital, Manila. But their power was broken in a jungle campaign led in person by the defense minister, Ramon Magsaysay. A charismatic man of the people, Magsaysay was elected president in 1953. He began a program of reforms in agriculture, and added to his

BORN ON THE FOURTH OF JULY Filipinos raise their flag over their embassy in Washington on July 4, 1946. The U.S. was fulfilling a wartime promise to grant independence.

popularity by winning better terms when he renegotiated the trade agreement with America. He also signed a mutual defense treaty with the U.S. and took the Philippines into the anti-communist SEATO alliance.

Magsaysay was killed in a plane crash in March 1957, and under his successors the Philippines faced three major problems: poor economic performance, a rising crime rate, and corruption in government. Hopes rose when Ferdinand Marcos won the 1964 election on a reformist program. Marcos was married to a former beauty queen, and he put himself forward as hero of the guerrilla struggle against the Japanese, though doubts about the claim were to surface later. In any case, Marcos began well. Launching a massive public works program, he built schools, dams and roads, and embarked on irrigation plans. He won praise inside the Philippines when he shortened the leases on U.S. bases from 99 years to 25.

HIGH HOPES When Ferdinand Marcos came to power in the Philippines, his beauty queen wife, Imelda, by his side, he started an optimistic program of massive public works.

But the economic problems remained—the peso had to be devalued in 1969. And the more the government spent on public works, the more opportunities there were for corruption. In January 1970, students clashed with police in Manila. It was an ominous sign for Marcos and his wife, Imelda.

Emergency in Malaya

In Malaya, a communist-staged insurrection actually delayed independence. Britain had neither the need nor the desire to continue ruling the Malay States after the war. Once the tin mines and rubber plantations were back in full production, a friendly Malaya could become a valuable dollar earner, and Britain was short on dollars. In February 1948, the British proposed setting up a Malayan Federation that would lead rapidly to full self-government.

The Malay States, nine of them ruled by hereditary Sultans, were a potentially explosive racial mixture in which native Malays feared being swamped by the Chinese, for they formed less than 50 percent of the population, compared with about 38 percent for people of Chinese descent.

The communists, almost exclusively Chinese, knew that a Malayan Federation would rule out any possibility of their setting up a People's Republic in Malaya, and they responded with a campaign of terror. The comfortable world of the white planters, downing a whisky and soda at the club after a round of golf, or taking tea with the memsahib, was shattered. In June 1948, the communists began to murder European plantation managers.

The Emergency, as it was termed by the British, was to last 12 years and to cost more than 11,000 lives—6,700 of them communist terrorists, nearly 2,500 civilians and over 1,800 soldiers and police. British and Commonwealth troops, along with 26,000 armed Malayan

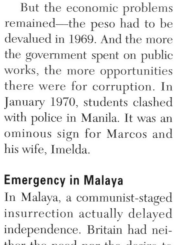

police, fought a savage war against the terrorists. They began to win it after more than half a million Chinese "squatters," who had provided food, shelter and recruits for the communists, were moved from their jungle clearings into protected villages. The British Colonial Secretary, Oliver Lyttleton, put it neatly: "You cannot expect to overcome the Emergency without the help of the civilian population; you cannot get the help of the civilian population without beginning to win the war."

The insurrection was defeated politically, too. General Sir Gerald Templer, in charge of British and Malayan forces, had the full backing of Malaya's leading politician, Tunku Abdul Rahman, the Cambridge-educated son of the Sultan of Kedah. Following an election victory in 1955, the Tunku became Chief Minister of the Malayan Federation. His campaign against the guerrillas was vigorous, and by 1958 the communist threat was reduced to the point where the British were ready to grant full independence.

The communists remained a threat, however, in Singapore, a tiny but flourishing

RIOT CONTROL A policeman rushes in to break up a fight between Chinese and Malays in downtown Singapore in July 1964—a period when racial tensions ran high.

Crown Colony and free port at the tip of the Malayan peninsula. Lee Kuan Yew, who became prime minister there in 1959, decided he would be better able to deal with that threat by linking with a country that had already shown it could defeat the communists. He and the Tunku joined forces to form the Federation of Malaysia, along with two former British States in Borneo, Sabah and Sarawak.

But Singapore was never comfortable as part of Malaysia—racial tensions between Malays and Chinese ran too high. There were serious race riots in the city in 1964, and Singapore left the federation the following year to pursue Lee's path to prosperity, based on free trade, private enterprise, social planning and an authoritarian lack of patience with those who broke the rules.

Cutting across the Equator south of Malaysia, in a great 3,000 mile arc, lies

VICTORY IN THE JUNGLE

The Malayan Emergency was a rare example of a communist rebellion in Southeast Asia being totally defeated by the returning colonial power. At the start, the insurgents seemed to have the cards stacked in their favor. They had learned their jungle craft in guerrilla warfare against the Japanese. They had hidden their weapons after the war, to be picked up when needed. And, since they were predominantly ethnic Chinese, they found food and shelter in the jungle, either provided willingly or extorted by fear, among the half million Chinese "squatters" who had moved into clearings to grow crops and raise a few pigs and hens.

Sir Hugh Gurney, the British High Commissioner in Malaya, made a start by clearing the squatters out of the jungle and resettling them in "new villages." Here, they were protected by high wire fences. The villages were supplied with water and electricity and were run by their own elected councils. Now the former squatters were safe from intimidation.

READY FOR ACTION A British soldier, fully equipped to survive for weeks in the jungle, searches for traces of communist rebels.

Gurney was killed in a road ambush in October 1951, and the dynamic Sir Gerald Templer became high commissioner and commander in chief. He took the bold decision to issue weapons to some 240,000 Malays and turn them into a Home Guard. He supported a drive by Malaya's Chief Minister, Tunku Abdul Rahman, to raise living standards and improve education. And he insisted that the communists were not fighting for liberation but against Malayan nationalism. The British, he made it plain, would grant full independence once the Emergency was under control.

Templer made sure that the men he sent into the jungle were properly trained. In the steamy tangle of the rain forests, they learned to rely on their senses of hearing and smell rather than vision, listening for the slightest sound that was out of place. The communists, never more than 7,000 strong, were beaten at their own game by Malays, Gurkhas, Fijians, Africans, Australians, New Zealanders, and some of the toughest units in the British army, including the SAS. Helicopters proved supremely useful in dropping men and supplies deep in the jungle.

Templer increased the prices on the heads of key guerrillas. Their leader, Cheng Ping, was worth $125,000 Malay ($45,000) dead and $300,000 Malay ($108,000) alive. He waged psychological warfare, dropping leaflets that called on the terrorists to join their comrades who had already surrendered, and sending "voice aircraft" to swoop low over the jungle, booming out the same message. Villages that gave

help to the guerrillas faced collective punishment, including curfews and fines. The Emergency was declared over on July 31, 1960, but it had effectively ended long before that. Its most important lesson was that an insurrection cannot succeed without the support of the local population. This lesson was not taken to heart by the French in Vietnam or by the Americans after them.

JUNGLE PEACE TALKS Two Malay Chinese terrorists emerge from the jungle in November 1955 to put out peace feelers from their leader, Cheng Ping.

Indonesia, a chain of 13,677 islands, of which just over 6,000 are inhabited. Prewar, most of these islands, including Sumatra and Java, formed the Dutch East Indies, and after the war the Dutch reclaimed their Pacific empire. The Japanese, however, had built up the standing of the nationalist leader Dr. Ahmed Sukarno, putting him at the head of a 120,000-strong army. Sukarno, who had been jailed and exiled by the Dutch before the war, took advantage of a breathing space between the Japanese surrender and the arrival of Allied troops to declare himself president of the independent Republic of Indonesia. He made his announcement on August 17, 1945, a date that became known as Merdeka (Freedom) Day.

The Indonesian nationalists rejected Dutch offers of partial independence, and in July 1947 open warfare broke out. It lasted for two years, and in military terms, victory went to the Netherlands. Their troops occupied the republican capital, Jogjakarta, and captured Sukarno and other nationalist leaders. But world opinion was turning against colonial wars. Under pressure from the United Nations and from public opinion at home, the Dutch released the captured rebels, called a conference in The Hague, and granted full independence.

"Guided democracy" in Indonesia

The Republic of Indonesia was officially announced on August 17, 1950, with Sukarno as president. His achievement was to give a national identity to a country that embraced some 300 racial groups, speaking 25 main languages and 250 dialects. But his regime was marked by rebellions at home, confrontations abroad and by ambitious plans that led to economic disaster.

Sukarno hosted the Bandung Conference of non-aligned nations in April 1955. "Wherever, whenever and however it appears," he declared, "colonialism is an evil thing, and one which must be eradicated from the earth." He had a tolerant attitude toward communism, and was awarded the Lenin Peace Prize by the Soviet Union. He also received 1.5 billion dollars' worth of Soviet military aid, in the form of warships, bombers and missiles.

Indonesia was desperately short of technicians and trained managers, but in 1957 Sukarno seized the property of Dutch citizens. This added another $1.5 billion to Indonesia's treasury, at the cost of a mass exodus of Europeans and Eurasians. Exports were paralyzed because the ships were idle. Rice prices soared.

AUSTRALIA, THE "LUCKY COUNTRY"

TWO RELATED THEMES EMERGE IN AUSTRALIA'S HISTORY SINCE 1945: A WEAKENING OF TIES WITH THE PAST AND AN OUTWARD-LOOKING OPTIMISM ABOUT THE FUTURE

When the war against Japan ended in victory, people danced in the streets in Sydney, and the bands played *Rule Britannia*. But most thoughtful Australians knew that this was looking to the past. In a vast land of barely 7.5 million people, with millions of Asians to the north, the slogan was now "Populate or perish," and the fastest way to build up the population was by attracting immigrants. Arthur Calwell, the ruling Labor Party's Minister of Immigration, targeted skilled workers and professionals from Great Britain—electrical and mechanical engineers, boilermakers, agricultural workers, architects, doctors, dentists, nurses and the like. Ex-servicemen and their families were given free passages to Australia, and other approved immigrants were asked to pay only £10 ($40) toward their fares.

Assisted passages brought in Europeans from the Continent, too —mainly from Italy, Holland, Greece, Germany and Yugoslavia. By 1968, more than 1 million Britons and 800,000 other Europeans had become new Australians. They arrived under an official "White Australia" policy that was increasingly questioned in the more tolerant postwar climate.

Australians shared the universal hope for a better life after the war. Prime Minister Ben Chifley introduced a welfare state, with unemployment and sickness benefits, widows' pensions and family allowances, and in 1946 set up the Australian National University at Canberra. Chifley put £3 million ($12 million) into launching Australia's car industry. The first all-Australian car, the Holden, rolled off the assembly lines in November 1948. His most ambitious project, the Snowy Mountains Hydroelectric Scheme, began in July 1949. It involved digging tunnels beneath Australia's highest peak, Mount Kosciuszko, and building dams to provide water for irrigation and cheap electricity for New South Wales, Victoria and Canberra.

NEW AUSTRALIANS   Many Europeans were eager to answer the call for immigrants, like these German women who arrived by ship in July 1959.

Chifley lost the 1949 election to a Liberal and Country Party coalition led by Robert Menzies. Staunchly Anglophile and fiercely anti-communist, Menzies aligned Australia with the U.S. in the Cold War, sending armed forces to Korea in 1950 and to Vietnam in 1962. Sir Robert retired in 1966, and his successor, Harold Holt, continued to support America in Vietnam. Holt disappeared while swimming in the sea on December 17, 1967, and his body was never found. His successor, John Gorton, in response to mounting public pressure, announced the first troop withdrawals in 1970, a process completed in 1972.

Australia is often called "the Lucky Country" after the title of a 1964 book by Donald Horne. Horne used the term ironically, to indicate that Australians were living on their luck, but the term has been generally understood to mean "a fortunate country," referring to Australia's pastoral wealth and prodigious mineral resources.

BACK TO THE SUN   Eight youngsters leave austerity-hit Britain in 1947, returning to Australia, where they had been wartime evacuees.

Under what Sukarno called "guided democracy," he dissolved the elected parliament in 1957 and banned the opposition Socialist and Masjumi (Muslim) parties. The Western pattern, he explained, was "not a true democracy in accordance with the ideals of the Indonesian people." Under his "guided economy," introduced in 1959, inflation increased 25-fold in five years.

Sukarno annexed Dutch New Guinea, which he renamed Irian Jaya (West Irian). He was stridently against the idea of a Federation of Malaysia because it blocked his plans for further expansion. *Ganjang Malaysia!* (Crush Malaysia!) was his slogan. He supported a rebellion in oil-rich Brunei in 1962, and though the rebellion was crushed by British troops, the Sultan of Brunei decided it would be wise to stay out of the federation.

The army did not share Sukarno's tolerance for the communists, and when he fell ill with kidney stones in August 1965, and there was speculation that he might die, the communists decided to strike first. Three generals were murdered in their beds, and another three dragged to Helim airfield, where they were tortured to death. The army's revenge was swift and bloody. Muslim mobs attacked the communists, most of whom were Chinese, and between 200,000 and 500,000 were massacred.

Sukarno, disgraced and placed under house arrest in his palace by General Suharto, died on July 20, 1970, knowing that his grandiose plans had ended in a bloodbath for his country, and that his successor, Suharto, was reversing most of his policies, including the confrontation with Malaysia.

Vietnam: the agony begins

It seemed only natural to the French in 1945 that, with Japan defeated, they should be restored as colonial rulers in Indochina. It was a region of mountains, jungles and fertile plains that embraced three separate countries—Laos, Cambodia and Vietnam—each with its own history and language.

The first Allied troops to arrive, in late September 1945, were British, under General Douglas Gracey, and they were assigned the task of disarming the Japanese in the south. With only 1,800 soldiers in his

PICKING UP WHERE THEY LEFT OFF French soldiers commanded by the war hero General Leclerc leave Marseilles in September 1945 to re-establish control of Indochina.

command, General Gracey found chaos everywhere. Nationalism was seething in Vietnam, and it had a born leader in Ho Chi Minh, who had declared independence before the British arrived. Bao Dai, emperor of Amman in central Vietnam, abdicated rather than argue with Ho's Vietminh guerrillas, but Ho still faced armed opposition from rival groups in Vietnam. Laos and

RAID BEHIND THE LINES In July 1953,
French paratroopers rain from the
sky in a surprise attack on Langson,
a Vietminh supply base only a few
miles from the Chinese border.

SCHOLAR AND FIGHTER
Ho Chi Minh, an admirer
of French culture, who
led Vietnam's fight
against France.

General Jacques Leclerc. In five months, Leclerc announced that victory was in sight, but it was a hollow claim. French forces might take the cities, but the countryside belonged to the Vietminh. Guerrilla units laid ambushes, blew up bridges, attacked isolated detachments, then vanished. Ho Chi Minh described the contest as one "between the grasshopper and the elephant."

With tragic inevitability, what had begun as a colonial war became drawn into the global struggle of the Cold War. Following the Chinese communist victory over Chiang Kai-shek and his Guomindang forces in 1949, supplies of modern weapons and artillery began to flow to the Vietminh from across their northern border. The Vietminh were led by General Vo Nguyen Giap, a former history teacher who had learned military theory by reading books; he mastered the practicalities by fighting the French.

Giap was always ready to learn from his mistakes, but was prepared to accept any level of casualties, provided they brought victory. His strategy was simple: "Is the enemy strong? One avoids him. Is the enemy weak? One attacks him." The aim was "to exhaust little by little, by small victories, the enemy forces, and at the same time to maintain and increase ours." Starting with bands of hit-and-run guerrillas, he built up a disciplined army that was capable of taking on the French in pitched battle.

Cambodia made their own declarations of independence. Gracey tried to establish order by declaring martial law and banning public meetings. Then he ordered Japanese troops to help to restore the French—an order that was swiftly countermanded by his chief, Lord Louis Mountbatten.

The French arrived back in force in October, and began their reconquest under

The U.S. had a long tradition of opposing colonialism, and initially there was little sympathy for the French attempt at reconquest. But in the context of the Cold War, France became a bastion of the free world against communism. The prevailing "domino theory" forecast that if Vietnam fell to communism, other nations in Southeast Asia would follow one by one, like dominoes in a row. America was to pump nearly 3 billion dollars' worth of aid into France's war.

With the end of the Korean War in July 1953, Chinese aid to the Vietminh was stepped up. Giap was now ready for the final battle—on ground of his own choosing. That was the village of Dien Bien Phu, a center for opium trading set among mountains near the northern border with Laos. In November 1953, on the orders of General Henri Navarre, French paratroopers dropped from the sky to capture the village. Navarre's idea was to use Dien Bien Phu as a base to strike at Giap's rear and prevent him from operating in Laos. Deep in almost impenetrable terrain, the French force would have to be supplied by air, but France held air supremacy.

THE LAST BATTLE   General Henri Navarre planned Dien Bien Phu as a strategic masterstroke, but it turned out to be a fatal mistake. Vietnamese paratroopers with the French army (right) land early in the campaign, and a French legionnaire (below) goes into action in the battle that lost the war for France.

DIEN-BIEN-PHU
...ILS SE SONT SACRIFIÉS POUR LA LIBERTÉ

PAUL COLIN

PAIX et LIBERTÉ

STRETCHER-BEARERS
French stretcher-bearers carry a wounded soldier to a field dressing station as Giap's men assault Dien Bien Phu.

TO THE FALLEN Both sides in Indochina believed their cause was just. "They sacrificed themselves for freedom," proclaims this French poster.

am completely dishonored."

Giap had a ring of trenches and tunnels built around the French garrison and relentlessly tightened the noose until the time came for the final assault, on May 7. The last French strongpoint fell in the early hours of the following morning, and 10,000 men, including de Castries, were taken prisoner. Only 73 escaped.

It was a crushing victory, but the Vietminh did not reap the benefits when they sat down at the conference table in Geneva. It did not suit either the U.S.S.R. or China to build up Ho's regime too far, and both were lukewarm in their support. Ho's delegate, Pham Van Dong, reluctantly agreed to a proposal to partition Vietnam along the 17th parallel, with the Hanoi-based communist regime in control in the north and a pro-Western regime, based in Saigon, in the south.

The partition was meant to be temporary, and it was agreed that general elections on the issue of reunification would be held in July 1956. Those elections never took place;

Dien Bien Phu turned out to be not a springboard but a death trap. Navarre's most serious mistake was to underestimate his enemy. As the French built up their forces, Giap secretly moved 50,000 battle-hardened Vietminh into the surrounding hills. Nearly 70,000 workers hauled howitzers, Soviet missile launchers, shells and rockets into the hills. They built makeshift roads, stripped down weapons into their parts, and carried loads on specially strengthened bicycles or on their backs. Hundreds of sampans and bamboo rafts brought supplies down the river. "We decided to take the enemy by the throat at Dien Bien Phu," wrote Giap.

His attack began on March 13, 1954, and for the next two months the French paratroops and Foreign Legionnaires, along with Algerians, Moroccans and African troops, were pounded day and night in their dugouts. The outpost's two airstrips were easy targets for Giap's guns, and the French artillery was out in the open. The French commander, Colonel de Castries, had been assured by his artillery officer, Colonel Piroth, that the French guns were more than a match for Giap's. When it became clear that Giap was winning, a humiliated Piroth pulled the pin out of a grenade with his teeth and blew himself up after announcing: "I

THE BESIEGERS AND THE TRAPPED AT DIEN BIEN PHU

For the Vietminh, Dien Bien Phu was a battle against the jungle as well as against the French. Colonel Bui Tin, a 27-year-old battalion commander, later told an American journalist, Howard R. Simpson:

"Our men died in many ways. They lost their way, they fell from high bridges, they suffered from appendicitis, and venomous snakebites . . . Tree falls during typhoons crushed them in their hammocks. Flash floods were very dangerous. There were fevers, malaria, even tiger attacks, and small jungle leeches attached themselves during the night, so that a man would awaken weakened and covered by his own blood."

Simpson also interviewed the French, and all the chaos of war comes through in this report by First Sergeant Bleyer, of the Foreign Legion:

"Heavy artillery fire smashed everything, and it had barely stopped when the Viets were in our wire. I went to get my orders, but the blockhouse of Lt. Carrière was under direct fire from bazookas and recoilless rifles. The lieutenant himself had been killed, and the controls of the defensive charges weren't working. I tried in vain to make contact with Lt. Jego. Then I found myself facing the Viets, who I welcomed with shots from my Colt. A grenade exploded between my legs."

America, wedded to the domino theory, threw its support behind the unpopular Saigon regime of Ngo Dinh Diem, who found excuses to block them. France had managed, at a cost, to extricate itself from the quicksands of Vietnam. America was about to be sucked in.

Japan's economic miracle

When the Second World War ended for Japan, there were few reasons for optimism about the country's future. Two-and-a-half million soldiers and civilians had been killed, 5 million homes were destroyed, and the country's industries were laid waste. Yet this defeated and starving nation, reeling from the shock of the atomic bombs that were dropped on Hiroshima and Nagasaki, was to become an economic superpower in less than a generation.

The recovery began during Japan's occupation by American troops, and was led by General Douglas MacArthur, Supreme Commander Allied Powers. His first task was to see that justice was done. Over 800 war criminals were executed, including wartime prime minister General Tojo, who had ordered the attack on Pearl Harbor. More than 200,000 officers, civil servants, politicians and teachers were fired from their jobs in a process described as "purging."

Emperor Hirohito offered to take the war guilt on himself, but MacArthur decided that putting him on trial could cause a national convulsion. Instead, the emperor had to

FIRST OF MANY In the 1950s, Japan began manufacturing television sets. At first they were expensive, selling for around $400. But as prices came down, exports went up.

FROM FOE TO FRIEND MacArthur made such an impact on the Japanese that a businessman had signs painted all over Tokyo supporting him in the Republican primaries of 1948.

renounce his supposed divinity. Schoolchildren were no longer required to bow to his portrait. Hirohito was allowed to keep his title, as a symbol of national unity, but he no longer held any political power.

MacArthur introduced democracy to Japan, presenting the country with a constitution in which women were allowed the vote, and the nation renounced war and the right to build up armed forces. MacArthur also gave Japanese trade unions the right to strike. And he pressed for a land reform law that gave tenant farmers 90 percent of the country's farmland.

A handful of major corporations, the *zaibatsu*, had served the military regime very well during the war, so the Americans decided to smash their power by breaking them into smaller units. Mitsui and Mitsubishi, for instance, became 300 separate companies. This policy was thrown into reverse when it became clear that it was interfer-

A SONG FOR JAPAN

Japanese workers identified very closely with the companies they worked for, and the company song was one of the ways in which the bond between worker and firm was expressed and strengthened. The company song at Matsushita Electric linked the company's success with the country's:

"For the building of a new Japan,
Let's put our strength and mind together,
Doing our best to promote production,
Sending our goods to the people of the world.
Endlessly and continuously,
Like water gushing out of a fountain,
Grow industry, grow! grow! grow!
Harmony and sincerity.
Matsushita Electric."

ing with Japan's capacity to recover.

The triumph of Mao Zedong's communist forces in China in 1949, and the outbreak of the Korean War in 1950, confirmed the Americans in their change of tack: Japan was now seen as a potential ally and bulwark against communism in the Pacific. A peace treaty and a U.S.-Japanese security treaty were signed on the same day in September 1951. America kept a number of bases in Japan after the occupation had officially ended.

The Korean War gave Japan's economy a much-needed boost, because the country became a supply base and workshop for America and its UN allies. But the war was far from the only reason for Japan's recovery.

Defense costs were low, even after a Special Defence Force of 180,000 men was set up—in defiance, said critics, of the constitution. In 1968, Japan spent only 0.8 percent of its budget on defense. The U.S. at that time was spending 13.4 percent of its budget on the Vietnam War alone.

The government, through its Ministry of International Trade and Industry (MITI), steered investment to selected industries—shipbuilding, iron and steel, cars and motorbikes, cameras, television sets, radios and electrical goods. It fostered a dynamic attitude to winning new markets in Western Europe, America and the Pacific, while protecting its own infant industries from foreign competition by raising high tariff barriers.

Most trade unions were based on factories and industrial plants, rather than on crafts and skills, and major policy decisions within a company were discussed beforehand with the unions. Management and shopfloor workers used the same cafeteria, teamwork was emphasized, and workers readily gave their loyalty to firms that provided them not just with a wage but with family holidays, medical care and sports facilities. The workforce was educated, too, with a firm emphasis on technical education.

Events in the rest of the world helped Japan to prosper—first the Korean War, and then the 1956 Suez crisis, which led to the

"SOLDIERS" IN THE SHIPYARD In the early days of the American occupation, Japanese workers turned up for work wearing old army uniforms. They applied army discipline to their work, too.

SUCCESS STORY Japan's postwar recovery and export performance astonished the world.

closing of the Suez Canal. Suddenly, the world needed oil tankers with a payload large enough to make the journey around Africa worthwhile. Japan was the first country to construct 300,000-ton supertankers, and by 1965, half of the world's new shipping was built in Japan.

In the 1960s, the country's output of steel increased more than fourfold, to 93 million tons a year; the production of TV sets went up nearly 8 times, to 13.8 million; and car production increased 18 times, to 3 million. In 1965, for the first time since the Second World War, Japan's exports were worth more than her imports, and the trend continued,

leading to massive Japanese trade surpluses and a strong yen.

For all its economic progress, however, the country faced stresses and problems. Burgeoning industries caused pollution. Cities were overcrowded and clogged with traffic. Close contacts between government and industry gave ample scope for corruption. The General Secretary of the Liberal Party was accused, in the early 1950s, of accepting bribes. Prime Minister Yoshida Shigeru refused to allow him to be arrested. Fears that Japan might be dragged into an American war in Asia led to clashes in the late 1950s between demonstrators and riot police, and in 1960 Prime Minister Kishi Nobusuke had to resign.

Despite these troubles, Japan grew steadily richer. Gross Domestic Product (GDP) is a measure of a country's wealth, and in the 20 years leading up to 1970, Japan's GDP increased a spectacular 18-fold. The country had gained in peace far more than it could ever have hoped to seize by war.

A NEW WIND IN AFRICA

BY 1960, A GREAT AWAKENING OF NATIONAL CONSCIOUSNESS
WAS EVIDENT THROUGHOUT THE COUNTRIES OF AFRICA

The winds that swept colonialism out of Africa after 1945 had to blow more fiercely in those colonies where Europeans had come as farmers and settlers than in those to which they had come as traders and missionaries. The Gold Coast in West Africa, humid and sticky, and in a part of the world once known as "the white man's grave," fell into the second category, and was the first British colony in Africa to be granted independence.

Ghana leads the way

The Gold Coast's march to freedom as Ghana set a general pattern that was to be followed by other British colonies, even down to the jailing of the man who eventually became prime minister. The British plan was to prepare the colony for self-government by delivering independence in stages, in the hope that what finally emerged would be close to Britain's parliamentary system.

First, traditional African leaders were appointed to the legislative council that advised the governor, then elected members were introduced. This process

was too slow for Kwame Nkrumah, leader of the Convention People's Party. He organized protests, boycotts and strikes against colonial rule, and was imprisoned for sedition. Nkrumah was allowed to fight the 1951 election from his cell, and was released when his party won an overwhelming victory. He became prime minister the following year, and in 1957 the Gold Coast, led by Nkrumah, became the first black African country to achieve full independence. Its name was changed to Ghana in 1960.

In its early years, Ghana prospered because world prices for cocoa were high, and Nkrumah secured aid from both the U.S. and the U.S.S.R. While holding up Ghana as a model to other emergent African nations, Nkrumah began to create a cult of

NOTHING CHANGES   A cartoonist's wry view of 300 years of African history. White colonists arrive in 1660; by 1960 they are leaving. But what is there, apart from the clothes they wear, to distinguish the new rulers from the old?

personality inside the country. He encouraged Ghanaians to call him "The Redeemer," built up his personal bodyguard to the size of a regiment, outlawed opposition parties, and jailed political opponents. In 1966, while Nkrumah was on a visit to Beijing, the army and police staged a coup that overthrew him.

Tribal rivalries in Nigeria

The early stages of independence in Nigeria owed much to the pattern set by Ghana, with the exception of the Regional Councils. These recognized the fact that the country was an artificial creation—the result of straight lines drawn on a map during the 19th-century "scramble" for Africa, with little regard for geographical boundaries and none for tribal homelands. Nigeria's 31 million people were made up of 250 ethnic groups, dominated by the Muslim Hausa and the Fulani in the north, the Yoruba in

1952 Nkrumah
becomes first black
African prime minister

1953 Jomo
Kenyatta jailed after
Mau Mau trial

Gowon's military regime, attempted to break away in May 1967 and to set up the state of Biafra. This led to a civil war, for Nigeria's oil fields were in Biafra. More than a million Ibo died of starvation or in the fight against Gowon's federal forces before their leader, Lieutenant Colonel Ojukwu, capitulated, in January 1970.

"Assimilation" in French West Africa

The French approach to colonial government was completely different from that of the British. The key word was "assimilation," and the thinking behind it was that French civilization was available to all.

The colonies were part of the French Empire, and Africans could become French citizens, provided they met the educational requirements. Black children used schoolbooks containing such phrases as "Our ancestors, the Gauls . . ." and those Africans qualified to vote sent their representatives to the National Assembly in Paris. The educated elite, however, was small in numbers.

Leaders such as Félix Houphouet-Boigny of the Ivory Coast and Léopold Senghor in Senegal began by campaigning not so much for independence as for equal rights and status for all Frenchmen, whether black or white. Senghor wrote poems in praise of Négritude (Africanness) but he wrote them in French.

When Charles de Gaulle returned to power in France in 1958, his biggest prob-

"REDEEMER" ON TOUR A warm welcome in Ghana for President Nkrumah. But his personality cult backfired when the economy failed, and the nation's "Redeemer" was ousted in a coup in 1966.

the southwest, and the Ibo in the southeast.

Nmandi Azikiwe ("Zik"), a leading Ibo, became governor general of independent Nigeria in 1960, and president in 1963. He was overthrown in 1966 by a coup in which Nigeria's prime minister, Sir Abubakar Tafawa Balewa, was killed. A counter coup by Hausa army officers the same year brought Lt. Col. Yakuba Gowon to power.

The Ibo, fearing for their future under

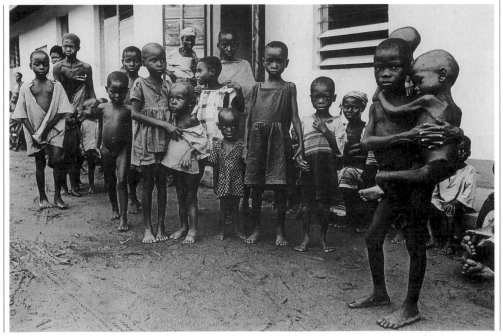

INNOCENT VICTIMS Ibo children in Biafra, facing the imminent prospect of starvation in July 1968, pay the price of a civil war fought over the control of oil reserves.

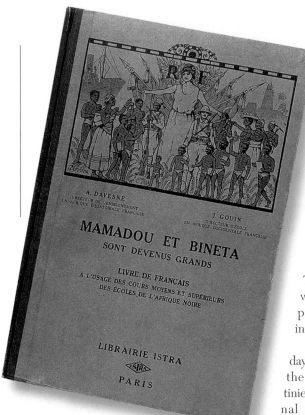

A GIFT FROM FRANCE
France's attitude to her African colonies is clearly shown in a schoolbook published in Paris. All of her "children" could enjoy the privilege of French culture.

lem in Africa was to end the war in Algeria, and he attempted to head off any trouble in France's 12 West African colonies with a dramatic offer: he created the French Community and told them they could either join it and continue to receive aid, or leave and have their aid cut off. Those who joined would be independent in all matters apart from currency, defense and foreign policy. Only Ahmed Sekou Touré of Guinea refused de Gaulle's offer, and French aid was promptly withdrawn. "We prefer poverty in liberty to wealth in slavery," he declared.

Two years later, while Guinea remained steeped in poverty, de Gaulle offered full independence without financial penalty to the other former colonies. They benefited, too, from France's insistence that they should be awarded associate membership of the European Economic Community.

Nightmare in the Congo

In the Congo, Belgium operated a paternalistic regime that delivered one of the highest standards of living in tropical Africa, with good medical care and primary education for large numbers of blacks in Roman Catholic mission schools. But the Belgians did nothing to prepare the country for self-government, with political parties banned until the 1950s. And what was happening in the rest of Africa could not be kept a secret.

Frustration, born of colonial restrictions and fueled by rising unemployment, broke to the surface in December 1959, with riots in the capital, Leopoldville (now Kinshasa). The Belgians' response astonished the world. They announced that they would pull out of the Congo and grant full independence by June 30, 1960.

It was a formula for anarchy. Within days of independence, the Congolese army, the 25,000-strong Force Publique, mutinied against its white officers and communal fighting erupted in the provinces

TIMETABLE OF FREEDOM

In 1945 there were only four independent nations in Africa—Ethiopia, Liberia, Egypt and the Union of South Africa. Independence was to come at a rate that matched the speed at which Africa had been colonized in the late 19th century. By 1970, 40 African countries had thrown off their colonial shackles, and only eight were still struggling to break free: Angola, Western Sahara, Mozambique, Guinea-Bissau, Zimbabwe, Djibouti, Namibia and Comoros.

between some of the country's 200 different tribes. As reports of the murder and rape of whites spread, the Belgian government flew in troops to protect its citizens, and families lined up for planes to get out of the country.

A mission-educated post office clerk,

THE CONGO ERUPTS   A mob on the rampage in 1960 in the newly independent Republic of the Congo. The country split into tribal factions. Here, members of one tribe are chasing members of another.

Patrice Lumumba, became prime minister of the Republic of the Congo, and Joseph Kasavubu, a leader of the Bakongo tribe who had once studied for the Catholic priesthood, became its president.

Vast deposits of copper-bearing ore made Katanga the richest province of the new republic, and when Moïse Tshombe, another mission-educated leader, declared it a separate state, Belgian mining interests gave him their backing. Lumumba appealed to the United Nations to end the secession, but although it sent a 3,000-strong peacekeeping force to the Congo, the UN stayed out of the Katanga dispute because it was regarded as an internal matter.

Lumumba turned to the Soviets for help against the breakaway province. They sent food, arms, 15 Ilyushin planes, and 300 technicians and military advisers. The U.S. now saw Lumumba as a Cold War enemy, and President Kasavubu dismissed him. Lumumba was handed over to the Katangans who shot him dead, in February 1961, allegedly while he was trying to escape.

Another notable death was that of Dag Hammarskjöld, Secretary General of the UN, who was killed in a plane crash in Northern Rhodesia on September 18, 1961, on his way to meet Tshombe. In that same month, the UN decided that it could, after all, act in Katanga and sent 20,000 soldiers, many of them Indian, to end the rebellion. Tshombe's army, led by Belgian officers, was defeated by the end of 1962, and he went into exile in Europe.

Kasavubu, faced with tribal opposition and ruling with the help of white mercenaries, called Tshombe back in 1964 and made him prime minister. The alliance lasted until October 1965, when Tshombe was dismissed and went into exile for a second time. Joseph Mobutu, a sergeant

CAPTURED AND CONDEMNED Patrice Lumumba, Soviet-leaning prime minister of the Congo, is arrested by Congolese troops. He was handed to rebel Katangans, who executed him.

during the days of Belgian rule, but now a colonel and army chief of staff, saw his chance to seize power in the confused situation following Tshombe's dismissal. He was backed by the U.S., which saw him as a barrier against Soviet influence in the Congo. He dismissed his white mercenaries once they had established him in power. Mobutu ran a brutal regime, holding the Congo together by fear.

The Mau Mau rebellion in Kenya

Kenya in 1945 was a classic example of a colonial country with a white settler population that was not prepared to yield its privileges without a struggle. In the decades before the war, white farmers had moved into the colony's most fertile region, the White Highlands, evicting Kikuyu tribesmen apart from a few illegal squatters or those allowed to stay on as laborers.

Protests by the Kikuyu, the largest of Kenya's 42 tribal groups, had changed nothing, even after their spokesman, Jomo Kenyatta, warned that the land problem "must inevitably result in a dangerous explosion." The settlers maintained that they had built the colony's prosperity, growing crops such as coffee beans, which needed long-term investment, whereas the Kikuyu, with their goats and their subsistence crops, would soon exhaust the land.

With the war over, fresh immigrants from Britain arrived to seek a new life in Kenya, increasing the pressure on both land and jobs at a time when many Kikuyu were unemployed. The explosion that Kenyatta had predicted could not be far away. It came in 1952 with the Mau Mau rebellion, a peasant revolt by the Kikuyu.

The Mau Mau began with arson attacks and cattle maiming, then moved on to murder. Recruiting members through ritual oaths, they brought terror to white settlers in lonely farmhouses and to Africans who remained loyal to the colonial regime.

Jomo Kenyatta was charged with being a Mau Mau leader and administering oaths. He denounced the accusation as "one of the most brilliantly calculated, fomented and perpetrated lies in the whole history of imperialistic intrigue." He was nevertheless found guilty and sentenced to seven years' hard labor.

Both sides proved capable of brutality. A

OPERATION ANVIL Police stand guard over some of the thousands of Kikuyu rounded up in the Nairobi area in "Operation Anvil," at the height of the Mau Mau rebellion.

British officer was cashiered and sentenced to five years' imprisonment for ordering his men to pierce the ear of a Mau Mau suspect with a bayonet, then lead him around by a wire threaded through the hole. At Hola Camp, 11 "hard core" Mau Mau were clubbed to death for refusing to carry out work that they said would have broken their oaths. An attempt was made to explain away the deaths by claiming they had drunk unsafe water in the heat of the sun. The incident caused an uproar in the House of Commons and the colonial secretary, Alan Lennox-Boyd, offered his resignation, but all that happened was that the camp commandant was retired early.

The security forces, 35,500 strong, included almost 28,000 Africans. Among their most effective fighters were the "pseu-

"MAY THIS OATH KILL ME"

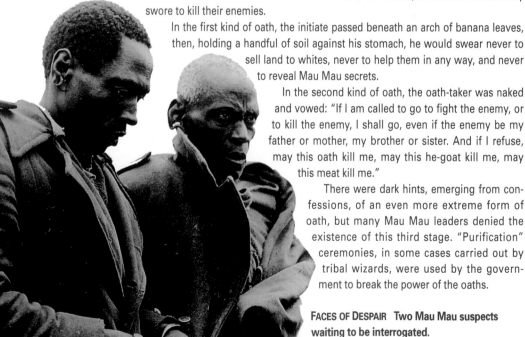

Confessions obtained from captured Mau Mau revealed their practice of ritual oath-taking, and confirmed white Kenyans in their belief that they were up against a barbaric enemy. There were at least two stages of oaths: the first was used to bind new members into brotherhood, and in the second they swore to kill their enemies.

In the first kind of oath, the initiate passed beneath an arch of banana leaves, then, holding a handful of soil against his stomach, he would swear never to sell land to whites, never to help them in any way, and never to reveal Mau Mau secrets.

In the second kind of oath, the oath-taker was naked and vowed: "If I am called to go to fight the enemy, or to kill the enemy, I shall go, even if the enemy be my father or mother, my brother or sister. And if I refuse, may this oath kill me, may this he-goat kill me, may this meat kill me."

There were dark hints, emerging from confessions, of an even more extreme form of oath, but many Mau Mau leaders denied the existence of this third stage. "Purification" ceremonies, in some cases carried out by tribal wizards, were used by the government to break the power of the oaths.

FACES OF DESPAIR Two Mau Mau suspects waiting to be interrogated.

do gangs" of former terrorists, who had gone through "purification" ceremonies to release them from their oaths. Led by young white Kenyans disguised as Mau Mau, the "pseudos" tracked down and ambushed their former comrades in dense forests in the Aberdare Mountains and on the slopes of Mount Kenya. The rebellion was finally broken with the capture of "Field Marshal" Dedan Kimathi, in October 1956. He was hanged the following February and became a hero in the eyes of the Kikuyu.

Official figures for the numbers killed in the rebellion were 1,877 civilians (of whom only 32 were European), 167 security forces (63 Europeans, 3 Asians, and 101 Africans) and 11,503 Mau Mau.

For Jomo Kenyatta, jail was followed by detention in exile until 1961. But the wind of change was blowing through Africa, and with the rebellion crushed, Britain had no stomach for holding on to a reluctant colony. Even though Kenya's governor, Sir Patrick Renison, had once described Kenyatta as "the African leader to darkness and death," talks were opened with him on Kenya's future. Independence was granted in 1963, and Kenyatta became prime minister when

FROM PRISON TO PREMIERSHIP Among the "credentials" that made him a popular leader in the new Kenya, Jomo Kenyatta spent seven years in a British jail.

JOMO KENYATTA, THE "BURNING SPEAR"

From the days when, as a boy, he ran away from home to enroll in a Church of Scotland mission school, Jomo Kenyatta combined an admiration for Britain with deep hostility to its policy in Kenya.

He became active between the wars in the Kikuyu "lost lands" movement, aimed at recovering land in the White Highlands, and because of his charisma and his command of English was an obvious choice to go to Britain to plead the Kikuyu case. The colonial secretary refused even to see him.

After two years in Moscow, Kenyatta returned to Britain, where he studied anthropology at the London School of Economics. His thesis, on the life and customs of the Kikuyu, was expanded into a book, *Facing Mount Kenya*. Freshly steeped in the traditions of his tribe, he took the name Jomo—"Burning Spear."

Returning to Africa in 1945, he became leader of the Kenya African Union, a position that made him a prominent target for arrest when the Mau Mau rebellion broke out in 1952. Kenyatta was charged with organizing the Mau Mau and administering oaths. He denied the charges and told the court: "We believe that the racial barrier is one of the most diabolical things we have in this colony." Despite a spirited defense, Kenyatta was found guilty and sentenced to seven years' hard labor.

Following his release from prison, Kenyatta was elected president of the Kenya African National Union (KANU) while still under a form of detention in exile. When Kenya won its independence in 1963, and Kenyatta became prime minister, he bore the whites no ill will. "We do not forget the assistance and guidance we have received through the years from people of British stock," he told them. "Our law, our system of government and many other aspects of our daily lives are founded on British principles and justice."

his party, the Kenya African National Union (KANU), won a sweeping victory.

Kenya enjoyed a measure of prosperity under his leadership. Realizing the value of Europeans to the country's economy, he moved black farmers into the White Highlands in stages, and used funds provided by Britain to pay compensation for land rather than seizing it. Although Kenya became a one-party state in 1964, with Kenyatta as president for life, he avoided tribal strife by appointing members of different tribes to positions in his government.

Rhodesia's breakaway bid

With sunny skies, an economy booming on the strength of Northern Rhodesia's copper, and a privileged life for whites, the two Rhodesias, Northern and Southern, were beckoning lands of opportunity to thousands in austerity-hit Britain after the war.

A British proposal to link them in a federation with Nyasaland held out still further promise: a thriving, white-dominated country in the middle of Africa, with the British government keeping a watchful eye on the interests of the blacks. The Central African Federation was set up in July 1953, but from the start it met opposition from the black majority, who suspected it was simply a means of maintaining whites in power.

Hastings Banda, a doctor, left his medical practice in London to lead the agitation in Nyasaland, while protests in Northern Rhodesia centered around Kenneth Kaunda, a former teacher and welfare officer. Both men were arrested, along with around 3,000 other blacks, following riots in 1959. The

OUT OF ORDER A white Rhodesian policeman reacts angrily to an African protestor who has threatened to harm his police dog.

federation's prime minister, Sir Roy Welensky, sent 3,000 troops into Nyasaland.

It was like trying to force the lid back onto a boiling pot; black consciousness was gathering momentum throughout Africa. The British prime minister, Harold Macmillan, made his "Wind of Change" speech in Cape Town in February 1960 and followed it up with a visit to Central Africa. Banda was released to meet him for talks, and Macmillan became convinced that the federation could no longer be held together.

Britain announced its break-up in March 1963—a decision that Welensky described as "treachery." Nyasaland became independent in July 1964, and was renamed Malawi, with Banda as its first president. In October 1964, Kaunda became president of independent Northern Rhodesia, renamed Zambia.

The whites in Southern Rhodesia, though outnumbered 15-1, felt that they had built the country, and were in no mood to hand it over. They found a leader in Ian Smith, a former RAF fighter pilot. As prime minister of Rhodesia, Smith rejected majority rule, which put him on a collision course with Britain's prime minister, Harold Wilson.

In November 1965, Rhodesia broke away from Britain with a Unilateral Declaration of Independence (UDI).

Harold Wilson refused to recognize its right to do so, but was in a quandary: he could not send British troops to fight against their "kith and kin" in the cause of black rule. Britain cut diplomatic and trading links

---

MACMILLAN AND THE WIND OF CHANGE

Harold Macmillan, prime minister of Great Britain, made his "Wind of Change" speech to members of the South African Parliament in January 1960. He told them:

"We have seen the awakening of national consciousness in peoples who have for centuries lived in dependence upon some other power. Fifteen years ago this movement spread through Asia. Many countries there, of different races and civilizations, pressed their claim to an independent life. Today the same thing is happening in Africa, and the most striking of all the impressions I have formed since I left London a month ago is the strength of this African national consciousness. The wind of change is blowing through the continent, and whether we like it or not, this growth of national consciousness is a political fact . . ."

with Rhodesia, and the UN followed up with economic sanctions. The two leaders met on board HMS *Tiger* in 1966 and HMS *Fearless* in 1968 for talks that turned out to be fruitless, because Ian Smith would not accept Wilson's formula of "No independence without majority rule." Despite the sanctions, vital supplies continued to reach Rhodesia through both South Africa and Mozambique. In fact, to some extent the sanctions actually helped the

---

FREE TO TALK Dr. Hastings Banda, freed from jail in Nyasaland (Malawi), arrives in London, smiling but suspicious of plans for his country's future.

WITH THE WIND . . . AND AGAINST IT Women in
Northern Rhodesia, soon to be Zambia, line up to
vote for nationalist leader Kenneth Kaunda as
prime minister. But Southern Rhodesia, led by
Ian Smith—far right, on board HMS *Fearless*
with Britain's premier, Harold Wilson—refused to
bend with the wind.

Rhodesian economy, forcing it to improvise
the manufacture of substitutes for goods that
it had previously imported.

South Africa on the edge of the abyss

Many white South Africans in the first few
decades after the Second World War could
not understand why "their" Africans should
be discontented. They had a higher standard
of living than blacks in the rest of the continent, and the country attracted migrant
workers in hundreds of thousands from
neighboring states. Nelson Mandela, a leading figure in the African protest movement,
called this line of argument "irrelevant," and
explained: "We are poor by comparison with
white people in our own country . . . The
lack of human dignity is the direct result of
the policy of white supremacy."

Racial discrimination, long a fact of life in South Africa's society, was elevated into a philosophy after the Nationalist Party won the general election of 1948, and Daniel Malan succeeded Jan Smuts as prime minister. A society known as the Broederbond (the Brotherhood) was the "think tank" that worked out the doctrine of Apartheid (Separate Development), a doctrine that the Nationalists set out with unashamed clarity in their election manifesto: "The policy of separation . . . is based on Christian principles of justice and reasonableness. Its aim is the maintenance and protection of the European population of the country as a

"HOMELANDS" FOR AFRICANS

Apartheid, the policy of racial separation, reached its logical conclusion in 1959 when, under Prime Minister Johannes Vorster, the South African government set up ten Bantustans as "homelands" for black Africans. The government allocated only 13 percent of the country's land area for the purpose, and the land chosen was generally plagued by drought. The Bantustans were the only territories where Africans were allowed to rightfully live.

pure white race [and] the maintenance and protection of the indigenous racial groups as separate communities within their own areas . . . Either we must follow the course of equality, which must eventually mean suicide for the white race, or we must take the course of separation."

The whites numbered 2.4 million at that time, compared with 7.8 million black Africans, 1 million "Coloreds" (people of mixed descent), and 300,000 Asians, whose forebears had been brought in as cheap laborers for the mines and railways. Nationalists were alarmed, because the nonwhite population was increasing at a rate approaching twice that of the whites.

Under Daniel Malan and his three successors, Johannes Strijdom (1954-8), Hendrik Verwoerd (1958-66) and Johannes Balthazar Vorster (1966-78), the Nationalist regime built up a crushing array of more than 300 apartheid laws. The Population Regis-

MAKING A BONFIRE OF APARTHEID Black South Africans burn their pass books in 1961, the year after Sharpeville, in protest at one of apartheid's most degrading laws.

tration Act allocated people to racial groups defined by the government. Somebody who had always thought of himself and his family as white could be reclassified as Colored— or, more rarely, a Colored person could be reclassified as white, and so win a passport to privilege.

The Group Areas Act meant that homes could be bulldozed or taken over, and their occupants left to build shanty towns, if people lived in the "wrong" area. Nonwhites had to carry passes proving they had a reason to be in a white area. The Suppression of Communism Act was all-embracing, for anybody protesting against the regime could be declared a communist, and become liable to severe penalties. The Mixed Marriages Act and the Immorality Act prohibited sexual relations across the color line.

Protests were organized by the African Nationalist Congress (ANC) as well as by liberal-minded whites. They tended to be nonviolent. In the Defiance Campaign of 1952, blacks deliberately broke the law and invited arrest, hoping to clog the country's jails; but only 8,500 were arrested. Chief Albert Luthuli, president of the ANC, won the Nobel peace prize in 1960 in recognition of his belief in passive resistance.

THE DEFIANT ONES With Nelson Mandela (right) urging nonviolent resistance, some black South Africans invite arrest by traveling in a "Whites Only" first class compartment in September 1952.

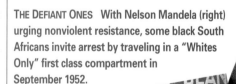

MASSACRE AT SHARPEVILLE Some of the dead, dying and wounded at Sharpeville—the tragedy convinced Nelson Mandela that peaceful protest would not work.

A protest against the Pass Laws, organized by the more militant Pan African Congress (PAC), ended in the tragedy of Sharpeville on March 21, 1960. As a crowd of African demonstrators advanced on the local police station, with jets swooping overhead, nerves snapped and the police opened fire. They left 69 dead and another 180 wounded. The ANC saw Sharpeville as a turning point. Nelson Mandela

argued that peaceful protest had failed, and it was time to turn to sabotage. He went underground and set up the ANC's military wing, *Umkhonto we Sizwe* (Spear of the Nation).

The government's attitude hardened too. In the 19th century, when Boer trekkers were attacked by hostile tribes, they drew their wagons into a defensive circle, the *laager*, and the battles they fought had become part of the national mythology. Reviled by world opinion and facing a UN-imposed economic boycott, the regime retreated behind its own laager after Sharpeville. It banned the ANC and the PAC, became a republic, and left the Commonwealth.

The boycott was an inconvenience rather than an effective sanction. Angola and Mozambique, under Portuguese rule, were prepared to break it, and so was Malawi, which depended heavily on trade links with South Africa. Oil, the only vital mineral South Africa lacked, could be obtained from Iran or synthesized from coal. When Britain refused to supply weapons, South Africa built up its own arms industry. The investment that was needed was affordable because South Africa was a treasurehouse of gold, coal, diamonds, copper, platinum, manganese and other valuable minerals.

More effective were voluntary boycotts by individuals in other countries, who simply refused to buy South African goods. In the late 1960s a new form of protest made the point to sports-obsessed white South Africans: the sports boycott. There were attempts to disrupt the 1968-9 Springboks' rugby tour of the British Isles, and an England cricket tour was canceled.

As the 1960s drew to a close, the outlook for nonwhites in South Africa was bleak.

Where people lived, the jobs they did, whom they were allowed to marry, the schools their children attended, even the park benches they were allowed to sit on—all depended on the color of their skin. Nelson Mandela, found guilty of treason in 1963, was serving a sentence of life imprisonment on Robben Island, off Cape Town. Alert and ready to crush dissent before it became serious was the sinisterly named Bureau of State Security—BOSS.

THE BOYCOTT BEGINS Students in London's Oxford Street appeal to shoppers not to buy South African goods, as part of a boycott launched by the British Labor Party.

VOICE OF THE VOTELESS

In 1962, the ANC leader Nelson Mandela was put on trial for inciting African workers to strike and for leaving South Africa without official travel documents. He told his judges:

"I am voteless because there is a Parliament in this country that is White-controlled. I am without land because the White minority has taken the lion's share of my country and forced me to occupy poverty-stricken reserves, over-populated and overstocked. We are ravaged by starvation and disease."

Mandela was sentenced to five years' imprisonment, but was brought from his cell the following year to face charges of treason, sabotage and violent conspiracy. This time he received a life sentence.

THE AGONY OF ALGERIA

A MILLION EUROPEANS IN ALGERIA FELT THEY HAD CREATED THE COUNTRY BUT MOST OF ITS 9 MILLION ARABS DISAGREED

France invaded Algeria to avenge an insult. In an argument over payment for Algerian wheat, the country's ruler, the Dey, struck the French consul across the face with his fly whisk. He refused to make a public apology, so the French government, in need of an easy victory to divert attention from problems in Paris, sent its troops to occupy Algiers.

That was in 1830, and over the next 17 years the French extended their conquest over the entire country, setting up the Foreign Legion, with its headquarters at Sidi bel Abbès, in the process. What had begun in near-farce was to end in tragedy.

When the French arrived, Algeria was a sparsely populated land, with 300,000 inhabitants. By the middle of the 20th century, it was struggling to support a population of 10 million, including 1 million European colonists, who had taken over the most fertile land along the coast. Unemployment was an inescapable part of daily life for many of Algeria's 9 million Muslims. But expectations were growing, especially among returning Arab servicemen who had fought alongside the Free French for liberation and against fascism during the war.

The first major outbreak of trouble came at a VE (Victory in Europe) Day parade in the town of Sétif on May 8, 1945. Shooting started when the local subprefect sent in gendarmes to seize a green-and-white Algerian flag and banners demanding independence. The enraged Algerians turned on Europeans, killing them in the streets. Sétif touched off anti-colonial riots around the country, and the French answered slaughter with slaughter. Bombers pounded rebellious villages from the air, and a cruiser shelled them from the coast. The French official figure for numbers killed in the riots and their aftermath was 103 Europeans and a little over 1,000 Arabs. But Cairo Radio claimed that 45,000 Muslims had died. General Duval, in charge of crushing the revolt, told Paris: "I have given you peace for 10 years."

His prediction was only one year off, but then, with neighboring Morocco and Tunisia moving rapidly toward independence, and France defeated in Indochina, the nationalist movement in Algeria could no longer be suppressed. Their Front de Libération Nationale (FLN), formed in October 1954, drew to its ranks men who had served at Dien Bien Phu and had seen the pride of France brought low by a peasant army.

"We must not lose"

To the French and to the European settlers, the *pieds noirs*, Algeria was an integral part of France—as much a province, say, as Brittany or Normandy. Jacques Soustelle, former head of the Free French Secret Service, who was appointed governor-general of Algeria, put the point unambiguously: "It is precisely because we have lost Indochina, Tunisia and Morocco that we must not, at any price, in any way, under any pretext, lose Algeria."

Toward the end of 1954, the FLN started an insurrection in the mountainous south of the country. In the cities, its weapon was terrorism, and its victims were both *pieds noirs* and *harkis*—"loyal" Arabs who cooperated with the French. General Jacques Massu, tough commander of the 10th Parachute Division, was sent to Algiers with full authority to crush the terrorists. His paratroopers broke them in the brutal Battle of Algiers—a battle in which both sides resorted to the use of torture.

Reports of the torture caused moral outrage in France and when, in February 1958,

DESERT SWOOP Rough, tough and ready for action, French paratroops storm off the chopper that has landed them near Timioune, deep in the Sahara, to tackle FLN rebels.

French planes attacked a Tunisian village thought to be harboring terrorists, France was criticized in the United Nations. Half a million French troops had not been able to defeat the FLN in the countryside, and it began to look as if the French government was losing its appetite for the struggle.

The *pieds noirs* staged a general strike in Algiers to put pressure on Paris, and in a move that deliberately harked back to the Reign of Terror in the French Revolution, set up a Committee of Public Safety under General Massu. This challenge brought down the Fourth Republic and led to the recall of General de Gaulle—the only man, thought the colonists and the army leaders, with the authority and stature to keep Algeria French.

They were mistaken in their calculations. A vast crowd cheered de Gaulle when he told

RIOT THAT TURNED AROUND Riot police hold anti-Gaullist *pieds noirs* demonstrators at bay in Algiers, in December 1960. When Muslims staged a backlash protest, the *pieds noirs* soon asked for police protection.

the *pieds noirs*: "*Je vous ai compris*" (I have understood you), but they were soon to learn what he meant. He sacked General Raoul Salan as commander in chief in Algeria for disloyalty in backing the colonists, and opened secret talks with FLN leaders.

De Gaulle proposed keeping Algeria within the French Union by granting Algerians full rights as French citizens, but too much blood had been spilled, and the moment for such concessions was past. His next proposal amounted to handing Algeria to the Algerians—provoking an attempted coup in Algiers by generals who could not

IN THE HANDS OF THE PARATROOPERS

Torture was made illegal in France by the revolutionaries of 1789, but during the Battle of Algiers, atrocities were committed both by the FLN rebels and by French paratroopers. Henri Alleg, editor of a communist journal in Algiers, was picked up by the paratroopers in the summer of 1957 and subjected to the electrical torture known as the *gégène* as part of his interrogation. He described the experience in *La Question*, a book that became a bestseller in France, and helped to bring an end to the condoning of torture:

"A flash of lightning exploded next to my ear and I felt my heart racing in my breast ... My jaws were soldered to the electrode by the current, and it was impossible for me to unlock my teeth, no matter what effort I made. My eyes, under their spasmed lids, were crossed with images of fire and geometric luminous patterns flashed in front of them."

1958 De Gaulle, back in power, visits Algeria

1961 General Salan's army rebellion crushed

1962 OAS leader General Salan captured; France agrees to Algerian independence

THE RISE AND FALL OF THE *PIEDS NOIRS*

The most likely origin of the term *pieds noirs* ("black feet") is that Algerians gave the name to French soldiers because of their highly polished black boots. It came to be applied to the colonists who arrived in the thousands, not just from France, but from Spain, Italy and Greece, in search of a better life than Europe could offer.

Many found what they were searching for in Algeria, and their descendants eventually numbered more than a million. For the richest of the *pieds noirs*, life could be sweet. Their fortunes were based on shipping, farming, wine production, banking or industry, and they could mix with others of their class at the yacht club or golf club, go skiing or gamble at the racetrack. For working-class colonists, the big attraction was the beach.

Few questioned the hedonistic values of this way of life, or acknowledged the extent to which it depended on the cheap labor of the Arabs around them. After all, they were inclined to reason, it was the colonists who had created the wealth of the country.

The slogan the *pieds noirs* repeated like a mantra once the Algerian rebellion started, was: "Algérie Française!" They gave it full throat at mass demonstrations or pumped out its rhythm on car horns. And they did not stop at slogans.

Led by Colonel Jean "Leathernose" Thomazo—so-called because he wore a leather strap to cover a war wound—they formed a militia to fight FLN terrorists. Their militant Front d'Algérie Française (FAF) fought a battle against 6,000 gendarmes during riots in Algiers in 1960.

Algeria was granted independence by the Evian Agreements of 1962, and the colonists abandoned the country that had abandoned them. Cars were left in the streets, and furniture piled up and burned, for emigrants were allowed to take out of the country only two suitcases per person. Only a handful remained behind to face life under Arab rule.

"LEATHERNOSE" Militia leader Colonel Jean Thomazo.

BROTHERS IN ARMS An OAS poster stresses links between the *pieds noirs* and *harkis*—Muslims who fought for France.

departure of the colonists left its economy in danger. The FLN leader Ahmed Ben Bella, who had spent the years since 1956 in a French jail, was released on independence and made prime minister in September 1962. He was toppled by a coup led by Colonel Houari Boumedienne in 1965.

face a second humiliation after Indochina. The coup failed because lower-ranking soldiers, many of them conscripts, stayed loyal to France and to de Gaulle.

Colonists and disloyal army leaders gambled once more. They set up the Organization de l'Armée Secrète (OAS), which carried out a terror campaign in Algiers and made a number of unsuccessful attempts to assassinate de Gaulle. In France, the OAS was smashed and its leaders jailed or executed.

In Algeria, the OAS had no power after the country had won its freedom at the Evian Conference in 1962. Independence was accompanied by an exodus of *pieds noirs*, but the Arabs were not slow in taking revenge on those *harkis* who were not able to get away. The new country's hopes of prosperity rested on the discovery of oil in the Sahara in the 1950s, but the war and the

VICTORY! Arabs in Algiers go on a celebration spree in July 1962, having won independence for their country after a savage war that lasted for 17 years.

MIDDLE EAST IN TURMOIL

FOR ARABS AND JEWS, PALESTINE WAS A PROMISED LAND: BRITAIN'S CONTRADICTORY PROMISES TO BOTH MADE CONFLICT INEVITABLE

TERROR IN THE STREETS Rescuers help the wounded after terrorist bombs exploded In Jerusalem in February 1948, just three months before the British mandate ended.

Jews all over the world end the feast of Passover with a solemn toast: "Next year in Jerusalem." It is a reminder that they have never lost their longing to return to the land from which their forefathers were driven after a failed revolt against the Roman Empire 2,000 years ago. For many, the toast was to become a reality in the 20th century.

Hopes of a return were boosted by the Balfour Declaration in 1917, issued by Great Britain in the heat of the First World War. The Declaration, by Britain's foreign secretary, pledged support for the creation of a Jewish national home in Palestine. Despite the proviso that nothing was to prejudice the civil and religious rights of non-Jews there, Arabs regarded the Declaration as a betrayal, for it contradicted a promise already made to them. They had been offered independence if they helped Britain to overthrow their Turkish overlords. The task of reconciling the two pledges would fall to a later generation.

It was against this background, and with the conscience of the civilized world seared by the deaths of 6 million Jews in Hitler's concentration camps, that Zionism, the Jewish movement for a return to the "Promised Land" of the Bible, became an unstoppable force after the Second World War. The problem facing the Zionists was that the land was already occupied. It was a problem shared by Britain, which controlled Palestine through a mandate handed down by the League of Nations, and had the thankless task of keeping the peace between Arabs and Jews.

Britain restricted Jewish immigration into Palestine after the war to 1,500 a month. But it proved impossible to enforce that quota. Boats laden with illegal immigrants began to slip across the Mediterranean from ports and harbors in Europe, running a gauntlet of Royal Navy patrols.

From America, President Truman urged the British government to allow the immediate entry of 100,000 Jews from refugee camps in Europe, but this would have provoked the Arabs. In Palestine the pressure on Britain intensified. Two underground groups, Irgun Zv'ei Leumi, led by Menachim Begin, and the Stern Gang, began a campaign of terror. On July 22, 1946, the Irgun blew up the King David Hotel in Jerusalem, with the loss of 91 lives, among them 41 Arabs and 38 Britons. In July 1947, they kidnapped and hanged two British sergeants.

Terrorism had its supporters among America's 5 million Jews. The screenwriter Ben Hecht wrote in the *New York Times*: "Every time you blow up a British arsenal or wreck a British jail . . . or let go with your guns and bombs at the British betrayers and invaders of your homeland, the Jews of America make a little holiday in their hearts."

Holding the Arabs and Jews apart required 100,000 British troops, and foreign

EXODUS IN HAMBURG A MARK OF CAIN FOR ENGLAND

BEVIN.WE WILL NOT LIVE YOUR REACTIONARY POLICIES!

PUTTING PRESSURE ON BRITAIN German Jews, survivors of the Holocaust, protest over Britain's action in turning back the Jewish immigrant ship *Exodus* from Palestine.

secretary Ernest Bevin decided to give up the mandate and pass the problem to the United Nations. The UN solution, announced at the end of November 1947, was to partition Palestine, with each side getting an incomplete jigsaw of territory that amounted to approximately half the country. Jerusalem, a holy city to both Jews and Muslims, was to become an international zone. The Arabs rejected partition totally, and the Zionist leader David Ben-Gurion would not give up Jerusalem. "Tens of thousands of our youth are prepared to lay down their lives for Jerusalem," he declared.

The birth of Israel

Open warfare broke out even before the British had left. On April 9, 1948, the Stern Gang and the Irgun joined forces to attack the Arab village of Deir Yassin, which they suspected of harboring Arab fighters. Moving through the village house by house, throwing grenades through the doors, they killed about 250 men, women and children. While the stories told by survivors

were horrifying enough, Arab propaganda spun them into tales of pregnant women raped and children deliberately murdered—setting off a panic.

Ben-Gurion proclaimed the birth of the State of Israel on the day the British left, May 14, 1948, and the next day the new nation was attacked by five Arab armies—from Egypt, Syria, Lebanon, Iraq and Transjordan. The invaders expected an early victory, for the Arabs numbered nearly 40 million, compared with only 600,000 Israelis. But the Haganah, the Jewish national army, had a training and mobilization plan that quickly built up its forces until they could effectively counter the invaders. After initial successes, the Arab armies were driven back or held on all fronts, except in Jerusalem, where Transjordan's Arab Legion, under a British commander, General John Glubb ("Glubb Pasha"), was their only effective fighting force.

During a month-long truce, arranged by the UN through Sweden's Count Fulke Bernadotte,

GOODBYE TO THE BRITISH David Ben-Gurion, father of the new nation of Israel, takes a farewell salute from the last British troops to leave the Holy Land (above). A newly arrived Jewish immigrant (right) waits at a reception center in Haifa.

1946 Irgun terror gang blow up King David Hotel

1948 Ben-Gurion proclaims State of Israel

1949 First Arab-Israeli war ends

1952 King Farouk toppled in Egypt

1954 Nasser seizes power in Egyptian coup

1956 Makarios deported in Cyprus; Nasser nationalizes Suez Canal

SIMON WIESENTHAL: JUSTICE, NOT REVENGE

After surviving Mathausen concentration camp, Simon Wiesenthal dedicated his life to tracking down war criminals. "I realized that I had a calling: to live on for the dead who were within me," he wrote in his memoirs. Early in 1947 he was given an office in a hut in Linz by the Austrian Government, and began tracing more than 1,000 war criminals. By entering on maps every piece of information he could find about Nazi escape routes, Wiesenthal revealed the existence of ODESSA, a secret organization that spirited former SS members to Spain, Italy, the Arab countries and South America.

His most spectacular triumph was to track down Adolf Eichmann, organizer of Hitler's so-called "Final Solution of the Jewish problem." Eichmann had escaped from Allied custody after 1945 and appeared to have vanished. His wife had him declared dead, and she remarried a German citizen, Ricardo Klement. Wiesenthal deduced that "Klement" was Eichmann, and passed a photograph of the SS man to Israeli agents. On May 23, 1960, David Ben-Gurion announced that Eichmann had been kidnapped in Argentina and brought to Israel for trial. He was found guilty and executed for his crimes. Franz Stangl, commandant at Treblinka death camp, was another prominent Nazi tracked down by Wiesenthal. Stangl, who was working at a car plant in São Paulo, Brazil, was betrayed by a former Gestapo man for $7,000, and arrested by the Brazilian police. Wiesenthal, fearing that Brazil might refuse to extradite Stangl, organized demonstrations by concentration-camp survivors outside Brazilian embassies, and persuaded Senator Robert Kennedy to make a special request to the Brazilian ambassador in Washington. Stangl was extradited to West Germany, tried, and sentenced to life imprisonment.

With a phenomenal memory, patience and a hunter's instinct, Wiesenthal was the embodiment of Nemesis, the Greek goddess of vengeance. But he entitled his memoirs *Justice Not Vengeance*. As he put it: "The realization that I had remained alive while so many others—better ones, cleverer ones, more decent ones—had died, at some moments almost seemed to me an offense against justice. I could restore the balance only by ensuring that the dead received justice."

NAZI HUNTER Simon Wiesenthal appeals for help in tracking down former Gestapo chief Walter Rauff, who fled to South America.

Israel regrouped its forces and bought arms from Czechoslovakia—the Soviet bloc thought at that stage that it might win a new ally. Then the fighting flared again, and when it looked as if Bernadotte might arrange a second truce that would have helped the Arabs, he was assassinated by the Stern Gang. A UN-imposed ceasefire, in January 1949, left Israel in control of three-quarters of Palestine, demonstrating the truth of Ben-Gurion's prediction at the start of the war: "Our strength will decide the size of the country."

The Israeli victory, known to the Arabs as "the Catastrophe," had far-reaching consequences. Some 600,000 Arabs fled in panic from Palestine, setting up makeshift camps on either side of the River Jordan and in the coastal Gaza strip. The land and property they had left behind were confiscated. This was the origin of the refugee problem that was to block the way to peace and cause bloodshed for decades to come.

In Egypt, a group of young army officers blamed the defeat of the Arab armies on the incompetence of their government, but public anger was also turned against the British, who maintained 70,000 troops in the country, to guard the Suez Canal. In this volatile

SUCCESSFUL, BUT SACKED Glubb Pasha (right) forged Jordan's Arab Legion into the Arabs' most formidable fighting force, but was still sacked by the youthful King Hussein.

political climate, the dissident officers staged a palace revolution. In July 1952, they toppled Farouk, Egypt's playboy king, from the throne of the pharaohs. As Farouk sailed off in his yacht to exile in Capri, the revolutionaries installed General Mohammed Neguib as president. But Neguib was only a figurehead. The driving force behind the coup had been Colonel Gamal Abdul Nasser, who took open control as president in 1954. Nasser's popularity was boosted by his success in persuading the British to agree to withdraw from the Canal Zone. The date set was March 1956.

Crisis over the Canal

Nasser's most ambitious plan was to increase Egypt's cultivable land by 25 percent and provide hydroelectric power for industry by building a high dam on the River Nile above Aswan. The $270 million needed for its construction would come from a loan, provided by the World Bank, America and Britain.

The two Western powers agreed to back the loan, largely to prevent Nasser from turning to the Soviet Union as an alternative

1964 Palestine Liberation
Organization founded

1967 Israel defeats
Arabs in Six-Day War

THE SHIP THAT HELPED TO BUILD A NATION

IN AN ECHO OF THE BIBLICAL EXODUS, A REFUGEE SHIP CLEARED THE WAY FOR JEWISH IMMIGRATION INTO PALESTINE AND THE CREATION OF THE STATE OF ISRAEL

The story of a single refugee ship has come to represent the Odyssey of the Jewish people after the Second World War. The ship, which was to become famous as the *Exodus*, was originally the *President Garfield*, and was rescued from a scrap heap in Baltimore, Maryland, by the Haganah, the Jewish militia. They patched it up and sent it across the Atlantic, manned by a crew of American volunteers. Their mission was to ferry illegal Jewish immigrants, survivors of the Holocaust, from Europe to the promised land of Palestine.

Britain, which ruled Palestine under an international mandate, was acutely conscious of its obligations to the Arabs, and would allow only 1,500 Jews a month to enter the country. The *President Garfield* slipped away from Sète harbor in the south of France on July 10, 1947, with 4,554 Jewish men, women and children aboard. Hope battled with fear in their hearts—the hope of a new life, the fear of being caught, for they knew that they were being shadowed by British Royal Navy destroyers.

When the refugee ship was about 25 miles from the coast of Palestine, up went its defiant new name: *Exodus 1947*, a reminder of the Bible's story of the flight of the Children of Israel from bondage in Egypt. The attack came while *Exodus* was still in international waters. Two destroyers moved in from either side and repeatedly rammed the refugee ship. "It looked like a matchbox that had been crushed by a nut-

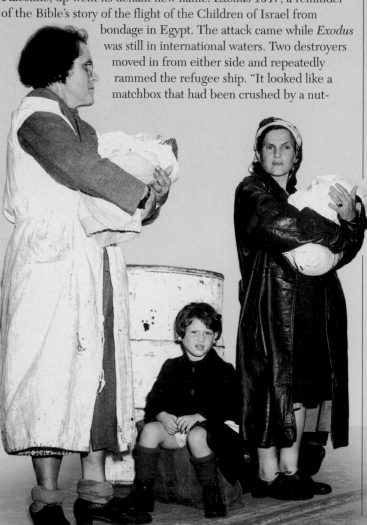

TEMPORARY SETBACK Showing the scars of its confrontation with two British destroyers, the *Exodus*, with its cargo of would-be immigrants to Palestine, is towed into Haifa under guard. Two weary Jewish mothers (left), defiance etched on their faces, wait to see what the future will bring.

cracker," said one of the passengers afterwards. Two passengers and one crewman were killed and 146 refugees injured in a short, sharp battle against boarders. But there could only be one outcome. *Exodus* was towed into Haifa harbor, a broken ship carrying a cargo of broken dreams.

Pictures were flashed around the world of passengers being taken off the ship, some of them injured, many in tears. The fate of the *Exodus* caused an international outcry, but the story was not over yet. Herded into three prison ships, the refugees were taken back to France, but the French authorities refused to accept any who did not disembark of their own free will. After more than three weeks of stalemate, the British, in a mood of frustration, sailed the refugees to Hamburg. British soldiers had to use force to drag Holocaust survivors aboard trains for their next destination. The *Exodus* refugees were to find themselves back behind barbed wire in Germany.

Worldwide outrage over the fate of the *Exodus* was an important factor in the decision taken by British foreign secretary Ernest Bevin to end Britain's mandate and to hand the problem of Palestine over to the United Nations. With Britain gone, the State of Israel was proclaimed on May 14, 1948. In the next few months, most of those who had taken part in the epic voyage of the *Exodus* found their way back to Israel and were prepared to start a new life in the new land.

NASSER'S MOMENT OF TRUTH
Colonel Gamal Abdul Nasser savors his Suez victory with Jordan's King Hussein at an Arab summit in January 1957.

lender. But Nasser's stream of anti-Western propaganda did not endear him to Western leaders. Anthony Eden, the British prime minister, blamed Nasser for the decline of British influence in Jordan, the country known as Transjordan until early 1950, when it took in 450,000 Palestinian refugees and annexed the West Bank of the River Jordan. Following anti-British riots, the young king, Hussein, asserted his inde-

pendence by dismissing Glubb Pasha from command of the Arab Legion.

For Israel, the ceasefire had not brought peace. Provoked by raids from Egyptian bases in Gaza, the Israelis hit back in force. Nasser's response was to apply to the U.S. for arms, so that he could improve Egypt's fighting capability. When this request was refused, he turned to the Eastern bloc, and soon MiG fighters, Ilyushin bombers, and Soviet

BLOCKED LIFELINE   Egyptian ships blocking the canal at Port Said, after the Anglo-French attack. Nasser sank 47 ships, successfully strangling the West's oil lifeline.

HUSSEIN, THE TIGHTROPE WALKER

Prince Hussein of Jordan had little choice but to grow up fast. On July 20, 1951, his grandfather, King Abdullah, was shot dead in a Jerusalem mosque, with the 15-year-old prince by his side. The assassin, who belonged to an extremist Palestinian group, was killed on the spot by the king's bodyguard.

Danger was to be Hussein's constant companion throughout the 1950s and 1960s, but he brought one of the shrewdest minds in the Middle East, as well as impressive physical courage, to the task of holding onto his life and his throne.

After the murder of King Abdullah, Hussein was sent to England to complete his education at Harrow, the school that boasted Winston Churchill among its alumni. There, and later at Sandhurst, he developed a fondness for British traditions and for driving fast cars. His father, Talal, occupied the throne for just over a year before abdicating on the grounds of mental unfitness, and Hussein, still not 17, became king of a desert land that had no oil and no shortage of problems.

The biggest problem was the presence of some 600,000 refugees, who had fled their homes in Palestine during the 1948 Arab-Israeli war, carrying little with them but dreams of vengeance and the hope that some day they would return. *Fedayeen* guerrillas among them would slip across the border to raid Israeli settlements, but retaliation was always severe. Hussein's tightrope act began. He saw it as his duty to rein back the *fedayeen*, but at the same time he had to convince fellow Arabs of his devotion to their cause.

One step toward this was to dismiss General John Glubb from his command of the Arab Legion. "Glubb Pasha" had forged the Legion into the most successful fighting force in the Arab world, but he and a number of its senior officers were British, and Hussein needed to demonstrate that he was not tied to Britain's apron strings.

The dismissal, in March 1957, was still not enough for President Nasser of Egypt. To him, the Jordanian monarchy was an anachronism, standing in the way of his vision of Arab progress. Some officers in the Jordanian army shared that view, and in March 1957, they mounted a coup. They had not taken into account the strength of the king's power base—the nomadic Bedouin tribes of the desert. These men were born fighters, and they had pledged their loyalty to a Hashemite king who could trace his ancestry back to the Prophet Muhammad. Hussein could have fled, but he stayed and defeated the plotters with the help of the Bedouin.

Hussein's bodyguards had to be especially alert after his cousin, King Faisal of Iraq, was killed in a nationalist coup, and their job was made no easier by the Arab tradition that gives ordinary people free access to their rulers. On one occasion, a plot to poison Hussein was exposed only when many dead cats were found in his palace grounds. The would-be killer, a cook in the royal palace, had been trying out his poison on local strays. On another occasion, two Syrian MiG fighters buzzed his plane and tried to force it down, but his pilot out-maneuvered them.

Hussein kept Jordan out of the 1956 Suez War, but the country was drawn into the Six-Day War in June 1967, because of defense pacts with Egypt and Syria. For Jordan, it was a disaster. Total defeat meant the loss of Old Jerusalem and the West Bank of the River Jordan, and the influx of another 200,000 refugees. The Palestine Liberation Organization stepped up its raids from bases in Jordan, bringing swift punishment from Israeli forces. So dangerous was the presence of the PLO that Hussein sent troops into the camps to clear out the terrorists. As the Sixties merged into the Seventies, he had lost none of his political skill, but his tightrope walking was becoming ever more difficult. His death from cancer, in February 1999, deprived the Middle East of one of its few statesmen trusted by all sides.

FROM SCHOOL DESK TO THRONE Prince Hussein as a Harrow schoolboy.

tanks began arriving from Czechoslovakia. Israel saw this arms build-up as a threat, for the weapons could have only one target. America saw it as a sign that Nasser was drawing too close to the Soviet bloc, and withdrew its loan offer.

It looked like a serious setback for Nasser. But he could not back down. On July 26, 1956, he played a dramatic card. He told a crowd in Alexandria that Egypt would seize the Suez Canal from its British and French owners and use its profits to pay for the Aswan Dam. Digging the canal had cost 120,000 Egyptian lives, he said. It was earning $105 million a year, but only $3 million was going to Egypt. The canal shareholders would be compensated, but its employees would be jailed if they left their posts.

The canal was a lifeline through which 60 million tons of oil from Saudi Arabia and the Gulf States reached Europe annually. For Anthony Eden, Nasser's seizure recalled Hitler's seizure of the Sudetenland in the 1930s. Appeasement of dictators had been a mistake then, and it would not be repeated. "Our quarrel is not with Egypt, still less with the Arab world," he told the nation in a broadcast. "It is with Colonel Nasser . . . he has shown that he is not a man who can be

trusted to keep an agreement."

Eden told American Secretary of State John Foster Dulles: "The only language Nasser understands is force," but the Americans did not agree with him. President Eisenhower warned the British prime minister: "I must tell you frankly that American public opinion flatly rejects the thought of using force."

Britain was not able to mount an immediate strike because its defense policy was based on the nuclear deterrent rather than on maintaining large conventional forces. Dulles, seeking a diplomatic settlement, proposed a Suez Canal Users' Association, which would collect canal fees and so deprive Nasser of revenue while making the use of force unnecessary. But Britain, France and Israel were each set on teaching Nasser a lesson: Britain because of all he had done against British interests in the Middle East; France because the French were fighting a vicious war in Algeria and believed Nasser was aiding and encouraging the rebels; Israel because the nation's very existence was threatened by Nasser's new weapons.

The three countries concocted a plan for Israel to attack Egypt in the Sinai desert, allowing Britain and France to step in later as "peacemakers." Nasser, it was hoped, would be humiliated and would be toppled by his own people.

Israel's attack came on October 29, 1956, and the next day Britain and France delivered their ultimatum: an immediate ceasefire, with both sides withdrawing to positions 10 miles away from the canal. The Israelis, who were still many miles from the canal, agreed. Nasser ignored the ultimatum, so British and French planes bombed Egypt's airfields, destroying Egyptian bombers on the ground, and an Anglo-French strike force landed at Port Said and Port Fuad in the Canal Zone.

Eden, who was a sick man throughout the Suez crisis, faced criticism at home, and had misjudged the strength of Eisenhower's opposition to the use of force. Eisenhower

AFTER THE BATTLE An Israeli tank and soldiers amid the debris of battle near El Arish in the Sinai Desert. Branded the aggressor by the UN, Israel later had to give up its gains.

COLLISION COURSE IN CYPRUS

On July 28, 1954, Henry Hopkinson, Britain's Minister of State for the Colonies, made a statement about Cyprus in the House of Commons that was to return to haunt him: "It has always been understood that there are certain territories in the Commonwealth which, owing to their particular circumstances, can never expect to be fully independent." On April 1, 1955, a group of Greek Cypriots gave their reply. The terrorist group EOKA, led by Colonel George Grivas, set off a series of bombs throughout the island. EOKA's aim was not independence but Enosis—union with Greece—and over the next four years, it was to wage a struggle that cost the lives of nearly 500 Cypriots and more than 140 Britons.

Enosis had been a dream of Greek Cypriots since the early years of the century, but there were two major obstacles in the way of attaining it. First, the Turkish Cypriots, amounting to 18 percent of the island's population, found the idea intolerable. They could rely on mainland Turkey for support, as the Greek Cypriots could rely on Greece. Secondly, Cyprus played a key role in Britain's Middle Eastern strategy, lying as it did only 250 miles from the Suez Canal. Britain, which had leased the island from Turkey in 1878, and made it a Crown Colony in 1925, was not prepared to leave.

While Grivas led the terror campaign from hideouts in the Troodos mountains, and Greek and Turkish Cypriots clashed, Enosis found a political champion in Archbishop Makarios. The British put a £10,000 ($30,000) price on the head of Grivas, and exiled Makarios to the Seychelles, accusing him of links with EOKA.

He had to be released in time to work on a ceasefire agreement under which Cyprus was to become independent in 1960, with a Greek Cypriot president and a Turkish Cypriot vice-president. Britain was to retain two military bases there.

THE PATH TO POWER Makarios in 1959, on his way to talks in London. By August 1960, he was president of a free Cyprus.

Elections were held in August 1960, and Makarios won decisively. He became president, with Dr. Fazil Kutchuk as vice-president. The two communities did not work well together, however, and it took only three years for civil war to break out. British troops and UN peacemakers helped to quell the fighting, though raids and reprisals continued. At one stage, the "homeland" countries of Greece and Turkey came to the brink of war. Neither Greek nor Turkish Cypriots had gotten what they really wanted in the 1960 settlement: the Greeks were still without Enosis, and the Turks, in their enclaves, did not have partition.

ENOSIS ABOVE ALL! EOKA leader George Grivas delivers a tirade against the deal that gave Cyprus independence rather than Enosis—union with Greece.

brought Britain to heel by instructing the U.S. Treasury to sell sterling, causing a run on the vulnerable pound. The British and French accepted a UN ceasefire, and a furious Eisenhower made it clear that they must withdraw their forces unconditionally.

The Suez adventure was Britain's last attempt, in the age of the superpowers, to behave like an imperial great power. If it was meant to protect the canal it was a failure, for Nasser blocked the waterway with sunken ships, and even after it was cleared and reopened, in April 1957, Israeli shipping was barred. In the outcome, it was not Nasser who was toppled, but Eden, for he had to resign as prime minister and was replaced by Harold Macmillan.

Britain and France, which had dominated the Middle East for over a century, saw their influence drain away at a rapid rate after the Suez debacle. By 1967 uprisings in southern Yemen had forced the British to withdraw from Aden. Both America and the Soviet Union tried to bring the region within their spheres of influence, but there were other powerful forces at work: Arab nationalism, militant Islam, and even dynastic rivalries.

The United States became alarmed when Syria, a former French mandate, began acquiring Soviet arms, and in January 1957 the U.S. proclaimed the Eisenhower Doctrine—a promise of economic and military aid to any Middle Eastern country that resisted the advance of communism. Iraq, Lebanon and Saudi Arabia took up the offer, but Syria encouraged a rebellion against the pro-Western regime of Camille Chamoun in Lebanon. The rising was crushed when, at Chamoun's request, 10,000 U.S. marines landed in Beirut, Lebanon's capital.

Iraq, traditionally a close ally of Britain, also tried to help Chamoun. But the army chiefs turned on their monarch rather than fight fellow Arabs. King Faisal and his prime minister, Nuri al-Said, were both killed, and Iraq was proclaimed a republic.

Nasser was more popular than ever among Arabs after Suez, but his dream of forging Arab unity did not take into account the real complexities of Arab politics. Syria came briefly into his orbit when, in February 1958, the two countries merged to form the United Arab Republic. The union ended in September 1961, when a group of army officers, concerned that Syria was being treated as a junior partner, evicted Nasser's envoy.

His voice, however, was still heard throughout the Arab world. In Yemen, a group of pro-Nasser officers rebelled against their ruler, the Imam Badr, and set up a republic. Badr escaped and rallied royalist forces among the desert tribes, so Nasser sent Egyptian troops to fight the royalists.

Israel, meanwhile, had been making the Negev desert bloom by diverting water from the River Jordan. Nasser's response was to call Arab summit meetings in Cairo and Alexandria, at which the Arabs agreed that in any future war with Israel they would place all their armies under the command of an Egyptian general. It was at the Alexandria summit, in September 1964, that the Palestine Liberation Organization

(PLO) was created to fight for a Palestinian homeland. Nasser hoped that this would help him to keep the *fedayeen*, the Palestinian guerrillas, under control. But Fatah, the largest guerrilla group, continued its raids on Israel. They were encouraged in this by the Syrians, who supplied training and equipment.

The Six-Day War

"We have resolved to drench this land with your blood," Syrian defense minister Hafiz Hasad told Israel in 1966. The following year, Israeli settlers started to move into the demilitarized zone between the two countries. Syrian artillery, lined up on the Golan heights overlooking the zone, opened fire on Israeli farmers on April 7, 1967. In response, Israeli jets screamed out of the sky to hit the Syrian positions with napalm bombs.

Nasser, who had a defense pact with Syria and had been building up his arms with Soviet help, saw this as an opportunity to consolidate his strength. He ordered UN peacekeeping forces out of Sinai and moved in Egyptian troops. He then signed a

ISRAEL ON THE ADVANCE Despite being surrounded by powerful Arab neighbors, Israel managed to extend its boundaries with every war it fought.

defense pact with Jordan and threatened Israel's oil supplies by closing the Straits of Tiran.

As Nasser was making warlike moves, Israel struck. On June 5, 1967, flying beneath enemy radar, Israeli planes attacked Egyptian and Syrian military airfields, destroying hundreds of enemy fighter jets on the ground. Secure against air attack, Israeli ground forces swept into Sinai, the Golan Heights, the Gaza strip, East Jerusalem and the West Bank of the Jordan.

In six days, Defense Minister Moshe Dayan had orchestrated a victory that vastly increased the size of Israel's territory, cost Egypt 20,000 men, and sent 100,000 Arab

(map legend)
— Borders in 1956
Israel's gains in 1949
Israel's territory in May 1948

LEBANON
SYRIA
WEST BANK
MEDITERRANEAN SEA
GAZA STRIP
JORDAN
ISRAEL
EGYPT
SINAI PENINSULA

SACRED SITE Soldiers pray at the Western Wall after the Six-Day War. The wall, the only remaining structure of the Second Temple in Jerusalem, was on land seized from Jordan by the Israeli army.

CALL TO A PEOPLE'S WAR

Following the crushing Arab defeat in the Six-Day War, the terrorist organization al-Fatah (Conquest or Death) fought back in the only way it knew. One of its leaflets distributed among Arab refugees on the West Bank exhorted:

"To the heroes of the Arab people in the occupied land! We call upon you in the names of the Arab heroes Omar and Saladin to rise against the foreign occupation and prohibit the Zionist occupiers from treading on our sacred Arab land. We must set up secret cells in every street, village and neighborhood . . . Roll down great stones from the mountain tops to block communications . . . If you happen to stand by an enemy's car, fill its gas tank with sand or sugar to put it out of action."

refugees streaming into Syria and more than 150,000 into Jordan. The total number of refugees had now swollen to well over 1 million. Yasser Arafat, leader of al-Fatah, became their spokesman and the leader of the PLO.

At the United Nations, the Soviet Union called on Israel to withdraw immediately from what became known as the Occupied

DESERT VICTORY Israeli soldiers with Egyptian prisoners taken during the Six-Day War in June 1967.

Territories, but with British and American support, this attempt was derailed. Instead, Israel accepted Resolution 242, under which it agreed to withdraw from all the land taken over during the Six-Day War on condition that its Arab neighbors officially recognized that Israel had the right to exist. But no Arab country was then willing to accept this condition, so Israel kept the Occupied Territories.

Nasser, worn out by defeat and bitterly disappointed by the failure of his attempts to bring unity to the Arab world, died of a heart attack on September 28, 1970. Millions of weeping Egyptians attended his funeral in Cairo.

TEARS FOR A HERO This woman is just one of the millions of Egyptians who wept for Nasser when he died in September 1970.

IN THE SUPERPOWER ERA

FEW COUNTRIES WERE ABLE TO REMAIN NEUTRAL IN THE GLOBAL STRUGGLE BETWEEN CAPITALISM AND COMMUNISM, WITH ITS FLASHPOINTS IN BERLIN, KOREA, CUBA AND VIETNAM. BUT IT WAS A CONTEST IN WHICH THE WEST HAD ONE HUGE ADVANTAGE OVER THE RIVAL POWERBLOC: THE WEST LEFT ROOM FOR THE ASPIRATIONS OF INDIVIDUALS, AND ALLOWED ITS PEOPLE TO REJECT UNPOPULAR GOVERNMENTS—A RIGHT THAT WAS DENIED UNDER COMMUNISM.

INSIDE THE U.S.

AMERICA REVELLED IN THE BOOM YEARS, THEN BASKED IN KENNEDY'S CAMELOT YEARS—UNTIL A FATEFUL DAY IN DALLAS

A square-jawed, straight-talking failed haberdasher turned politician from Missouri gave a press conference on April 13, 1945, as leader of the most powerful nation on Earth. Harry S Truman, who stepped up from the vice presidency on Franklin Delano Roosevelt's death to become the 33rd President of the U.S., told reporters: "Boys, if you ever pray, pray for me now . . . I've got the most terribly responsible job in the world."

Truman was a man who learned from his mistakes, and was not afraid of making decisions. A sign on his desk read: "The buck stops here," and he was to have plenty of chances to prove it. One of the first challenges the country faced was reabsorbing some 11 million servicemen and women into the economy. The task was made easier by the fact that demand had been suppressed throughout the war years, leaving the American people with billions of dollars in savings to spend. They were desperate for houses, cars and household goods, so when the dam burst, and factories returned to peacetime production, there was no shortage of jobs.

One result of the sudden rush of demand was inflation—food prices, for instance, rose by 25 percent in two years. Higher prices fueled the demand for higher wages. Car workers came out on strike at the end of 1945, and union boss John L. Lewis brought out 1.5 million miners. The year 1946 saw 5,000 strikes across the country, as workers flexed their industrial muscle.

Congress curbed the power of the unions through the Taft-Hartley Act of 1947. It was passed against Truman's veto, for in 1946 the Republicans had won control of both houses of Congress. The Act required unions to give at least 60 days' notice before striking, and outlawed the closed shop, under which workers could be forced to join a union.

When, against all predictions, Truman won the presidential election of 1948, he tried to repeal the Taft-Hartley Act, to improve civil rights, and to introduce other social reforms, in his "Fair Deal" program. But the Republican Congress was at loggerheads with the Demo-

cratic president. Little survived of the Fair Deal beyond an extension of social security benefits, public money for low-cost housing and an increase in the minimum wage.

The shadow of the Cold War fell heavily across America in the 1940s, and it became dangerous even to be suspected of having communist sympathies. The Loyalty Review Board, established by Truman in 1947, had the power to dismiss government employees who sympathized with totalitarian or subversive regimes, and over the next ten years it used that power in 2,700 cases.

"UnAmerican" Activities

It was in 1947, through its UnAmerican Activities Committee, that Congress turned its attention to rooting out communists in Hollywood. Among "friendly" witnesses called to the stand, Gary Cooper said he had turned down roles because the scripts were

THE GI BILL OF RIGHTS

Nearly 8 million of the 11 million Americans demobilized from the armed forces at the end of the war took advantage of the GI Bill of Rights. Passed by Congress in 1944, it offered them low interest loans to buy a house or farm or to start up in business. Veterans who wanted a college or university education were granted up to $500 a year for tuition fees and books, and were given a monthly living allowance of at least $75.

tinged with communism, and Walt Disney accused the Screen Cartoonists Guild of being communist-dominated. Other witnesses refused to answer questions about their politics—a stance in which they were supported by such stars as Gene Kelly, Humphrey Bogart, Danny Kaye and Judy Garland.

Ten screenwriters and directors, the "Hollywood Ten," were found guilty of contempt of Congress and were sentenced to jail terms ranging from six months to a year. After leaving prison, they spent years on Hollywood blacklists. Writers of the stature of Dalton Trumbo, who had once earned $200,000 a year for his scripts, and Ring Lardner, Jr., had to write under pseudonyms. Trumbo's script for *The Brave One* won an Oscar in 1957, but he could not attend the awards ceremony because he had written it as "Robert Rich," a man who did not exist.

"Red Scare" tension mounted when Alger Hiss, president of the prestigious Carnegie Endowment for International Peace, and

MAN OF DECISION Harry S Truman brought Missouri-style straight talking to the Presidency, and promised: "The buck stops here."

1945 Roosevelt dies; Truman becomes President

1950 McCarthy begins anti-communist witch hunt; Korean War begins

1953 Eisenhower becomes 34th president; Armistice ends Korean War

1954 Senate censures McCarthy

1955 Alabama bus boycott sets off civil rights protest

THE STARS MAKE A STAND Humphrey Bogart and Lauren Bacall (center) lead a star-studded protest outside the Capitol against the witch hunt in Hollywood by the UnAmerican Activities Committee. In the line-up are Richard Conte and Danny Kaye.

formerly a high-ranking official in the State Department, was accused of having been a communist in the 1930s. His accuser, the turncoat communist Whittaker Chambers, cut a sorry figure beside the elegant Hiss, an Ivy League product to the tips of his elegant shoes. The cloak-and-dagger aspects of the case mesmerized America. When Hiss sued for libel, Chambers invited federal agents to his Maryland farm where, in a hollowed-out pumpkin, they found microfilmed State Department documents that Chambers said had been handed to him by Hiss. Hiss denied the accusation. Because of the statute of limitations, Hiss could not be tried for espionage, so he was put on trial for perjury. In January 1950, he was found guilty and sentenced to five years in prison.

McCarthy's witch hunt

The Hiss trial, the Chinese communist victory over the forces of the American-backed Chiang Kai-shek, and then the news in September 1949 that the Soviets had caught up with the United States and exploded an atomic bomb, left the American public bewildered and dismayed. How could such things happen unless there had been treachery in high places? Paranoia was in the air, and celebrity of a sort was assured for whoever could focus and exploit it.

That role fell to Joseph McCarthy, the hard-drinking Republican Senator from Wisconsin. In February 1950, he told the Republican Women's Club of Wheeling, West Virginia, that the State Department was "infested" with communists, and went on: "I have in my hand a list of 205—a list of names known to the Secretary of State as being members of the Communist Party and who nevertheless are still working and shaping policy."

McCarthy clubs mushroomed in cities and small towns across the country, with the

THE PERSECUTORS Communist hunters Joe McCarthy (seated), Roy Cohn (left) and David Schine in a bullish mood. For their victims, McCarthyism was no laughing matter.

Senator leading the witch hunt from his position as chairman of the Senate's Investigations subcommittee. Nobody was safe from his accusations, not even former Secretary of State George Marshall, the architect of the plan to rebuild war-torn Europe. He was accused by McCarthy of "losing" China and of being "steeped in falsehood."

With his henchmen Roy Cohn and David Schine, McCarthy hunted for subversives in government offices. Nearly 500 State Department officials lost their jobs. Witnesses brought before his committee were under pressure to admit that they had been communists and to name fellow members of the party. Some "took the Fifth"— that is, relied on the Fifth Amendment to the U.S. Constitution, which says that

nobody can be compelled to be a witness against himself. It did not save them from being blacklisted or fired.

For four years, McCarthy seemed immune from attack, until Dwight D. Eisenhower, who won the presidential election of 1952, refused "to get into the gutter with that guy." In 1954 McCarthy went too far when he attacked the U.S. army. The hearings, televised over 36 days, showed him scowling, in need of a shave, browbeating witnesses and unable to back his accusations with solid evidence.

The Senate passed a motion of censure on him in December 1954, judging that his conduct "tended to bring the Senate into dishonor and disrepute." McCarthy, his

spell broken, died three years later of cirrhosis of the liver.

Eisenhower won the 1952 election partly on a promise that he would end the war America was fighting in Korea—a promise he fulfilled in July 1953. Eisenhower cultivated the public image of "Ike," the genial, easy-going president, who would rather spend time on the golf course than study policy documents in the Oval Office, but in fact, he was firmly in charge.

These were America's boom years, beginning with a "baby boom." Couples were marrying younger—the average age for a man to marry in 1957 was 22, and for his bride, 20. The population, just under 140 million in 1945, reached 180 million in 1960. In the same period, gross national product rose from $211.9 billion to $503.7 billion—a 37 percent increase, allowing for inflation.

The Eisenhower boom years

Diner's Club introduced the world's first credit card in 1950, giving further impetus to a consumer boom that saw nearly four in five American families owning at least one car by 1960. For winners in the race to prosperity, the treasured automobile was probably a chrome-plated gas guzzler with monstrous tail fins, garaged in a new suburban home complete with swimming pool, air conditioning, dream kitchen and landscaped garden.

Blue-collar workers, as well as the middle classes, benefited from the economic boom. Eisenhower's administration increased the

NO REDS WANTED Dwight D. Eisenhower ("Ike") and running mate Richard Nixon play on fears of communist infiltration of key government posts in a 1952 election poster.

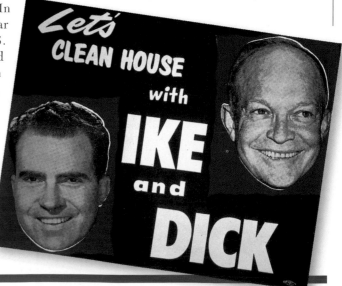

THE GANGSTERS WHO BUILT A CITY

Meyer Lansky, who came to America from Poland in 1911 as a boy of 13, graduated in crime in the Prohibition era of the Roaring Twenties and early Thirties. His partner in bootlegging, illegal gambling and murder was the ladies' man Benjamin "Bugsy" Siegel.

When Prohibition ended, Lansky built up gambling enterprises in Florida and Cuba and branched out into legitimate businesses, running hotels and golf courses. His most audacious project was to send his old bootlegging pal, Bugsy Siegel, to a quiet little town in the Nevada desert, a short plane hop from Los Angeles, to take advantage of Nevada's easy-going gambling laws.

With funds that Lansky had gathered from Eastern mobsters, Siegel built the Flamingo Hotel, laying the foundations from which Las Vegas, originally a Mormon settlement, grew into a vast casino, night club and entertainment complex. The city beckoned high-rolling gamblers not just from America but from all over the world.

The Flamingo cost $6 million to build—four times the estimate, and unfortunately for Siegel, Lansky worked out where the extra money had gone. On June 20, 1947, Bugsy Siegel was cut down by a hail of bullets at his Beverly Hills mansion. Lansky, whose personal fortune was estimated in 1970 at $300 million, was to die in bed, of lung cancer, in 1983.

FLAMINGO HOTEL The gambler's paradise created by mobster Bugsy Siegel.

BORN OF SUCCESS TO CHALLENGE THE FUTURE!
Presenting: New Push-Button Driving! New Trend-Setting Style! New Break-Away Power!
New '56 **DODGE**

STATUS SYMBOL With gleaming chrome and thrusting tailfins, American cars were icons of success in the booming mid-Fifties.

made the point forcefully in his "kitchen debate" with Soviet Premier Nikita Khrushchev at a Moscow trade fair in 1959. Standing in an American kitchen crammed with labor-saving wizardry, Nixon argued that it clearly demonstrated the superiority of the American way of life.

Nixon ran for president in 1960, but with his five o'clock shadow, and looking grey from the aftereffects of a chest cold, he presented an unattractive figure on television compared with the handsome, tanned, 43-year-old Democratic candidate, John Fitzgerald Kennedy. Even so, he lost by only 119,450 votes, in a total poll of 68,334,742.

"Ask not what your country can do for you," the new president said in his inaugural

ANYTHING YOU CAN DO Nikita Khrushchev sips a Pepsi in Moscow in 1959, before getting into an argument with Richard Nixon over the Soviet versus the American way of life.

minimum wage and improved social security coverage. The Highways Act of 1956 provided jobs for construction workers and gave drivers 41,000 miles of new expressways, coast to coast.

Recessions in 1953 and 1957 and the existence of pockets of poverty could not dent the confidence of millions of Americans that their standard of living was on an upward curve, and that life would be even better for their children. Vice-President Richard Nixon

MOVING TO SUBURBIA

Millions of upwardly mobile Americans turned their backs on the cities in the 1950s and 1960s, and moved out to what they hoped would be a healthier and safer life in the suburbs. In 1950 there were 35 million suburban dwellers; by 1970 the figure had reached 72 million.

The drift gathered pace soon after the war, when Bill Levitt and his architect brother Arthur came up with the answer to the country's housing shortage—instant homes. Bill, the builder and driving force, had developed a "Can do" approach to construction problems during the war, when he built airstrips for U.S. navy planes on islands in the Pacific. He broke down the process of building a house into 27 separate steps and applied Henry Ford's assembly-line principles. The difference was that in a Ford factory the assembly line brought the job to the workers, whereas on a Levitt site, groups of workers moved from one house plot to the next, each specializing in one of the 27 operations.

A Levitt home could be assembled in just over 15 minutes. The basic house contained a kitchen, a combination living/dining room, two bedrooms, a bathroom and an attic, and was offered at $7,990, at a time when the average family income was $2,500 a year. Veterans could buy one for $90 down, followed by payments of $58 a month. The first Levittown, built on what had been 6,000 acres of potato fields on Long Island, housed 82,000 people in 17,477 homes. Other Levittowns and other builders followed.

Suburbia had its critics. Writers and moviemakers joined the chorus of derision. Sloan Wilson's 1955 novel *The Man in the Gray Flannel Suit*, made into a movie starring Gregory Peck, told of a commuter lifestyle that was at once bland and stress-ridden. But those who lived in the suburbs were building up communities and changing the American way of life. Corner shops and downtown movie houses might be on the wane in the cities they had left behind, but suburban shopping malls were thriving, and by 1956, America had 3,000 drive-in movie theaters.

COMMUTER PARADISE A husband rising up the corporate ladder, a loving family and a home in the suburbs (above) were all part of the American dream. American suburbia, like the boom in drive-in movies (left), would not have been possible without the automobile.

address. "Ask what you can do for your country." The Peace Corps, founded in March 1961, gave thousands of idealistic youngsters the chance to spend two years of their lives overseas, helping underdeveloped countries.

Kennedy surrounded himself with high achievers from the academic and business worlds. For his National Security Adviser he chose McGeorge Bundy, Harvard's youngest Dean of Arts and Sciences; for his defense secretary, Robert McNamara, "whiz kid" president of the Ford Motor Company; for his secretary of state, Dean Rusk, a former

THE KENNEDY STYLE President Kennedy and his glamorous wife, Jackie, held court in the White House with wit and style, in what became known as the Camelot years.

Rhodes scholar at Oxford.

His glamorous wife, Jacqueline ("Jackie"), became a trendsetter in fashion and attracted poets, novelists, musicians and actors to the White House. Commentators began to liken the Kennedy "court" to King Arthur's fabled Camelot.

During his election campaign, Kennedy

MARCHING TO FREEDOM

AN INCIDENT ON A BUS IN ALABAMA BROUGHT MARTIN LUTHER KING, JR., TO THE FRONT OF THE CIVIL RIGHTS MOVEMENT AND GAVE AMERICA, AND THE WORLD, A BLACK HERO

After all the high hopes raised by victory in the Second World War, nearly 15 million underprivileged Americans found in 1945 that little had changed in the land of their birth. In the South, "Jim Crow" laws segregated blacks from whites in restaurants, buses, theaters, swimming pools, restrooms, and other public places, and kept black children out of white schools. Even in the North, a color bar blocked African Americans from a fair share in the nation's prosperity.

The National Association for the Advancement of Colored People (NAACP), founded in 1910, chipped away at the color bar for nearly half a century before notching up its first major victory. This came in May 1954, with a landmark decision by the Supreme Court, in the case of Brown v. Board of Education of Topeka. The NAACP brought the case to challenge the doctrine that it was within the U.S. Constitution to provide "separate but equal" facilities for minority groups. Chief Justice Earl Warren won the court around to his view that "in the field of public education, the doctrine of 'separate but equal' has no place. Separate educational facilities are inherently unequal." The court ruled that schools throughout the land should be desegregated.

By the mid-1950s, African Americans had what they needed most—a leader who was inspiring, articulate and fearless. Martin Luther King, Jr., a Baptist pastor in Montgomery, Alabama, was catapulted to prominence after a black woman, Rosa Parks, was arrested on December 1, 1955, for refusing to give up her seat on a bus to a white man. Parks, a seamstress in a local department store, asked the arresting officers, "Why do you push us around?" She was told, "The law is the law."

Martin Luther King, Jr., and other leaders of Montgomery's black community set out to change the law. They got Rosa Parks released on bail, and they organized a bus boycott. The bus company's profits nose-dived as blacks walked to work or joined car pools. Through all the 381 days of the boycott, and despite having his home bombed, King remained unshakable in his stance that the protest should be nonviolent. He quoted one 72-year-old woman as saying: "My feets is tired, but my soul is at rest." Victory came in November 1956, with a Supreme Court ruling that segregation on public buses was against the law.

A new weapon, the sit-in, was forged in February 1960, when four black students who had been refused service at a Woolworth's lunch counter in Greensboro, North Carolina, decided to stay put. Sit-ins spread all over the South, along with freedom rides, in which white sympathizers, many of them students, joined blacks in buses that took their protest to the heartlands of the South.

In August 1963, at a massive civil rights rally in Washington, King delivered what became his most famous speech:

THE WAY IT WAS Even after the Supreme Court ruled against segregation on public transportation, blacks in the South hardly dared believe they had won. Blacks on a bus in Dallas, Texas, continue in 1956 to sit at the back.

"I have a dream that one day this nation will rise up and deliver the true meaning of its creed: We hold these truths to be self-evident, that all men are created equal." President Lyndon B. Johnson did his best to make that dream come true, with his Civil Rights Acts of 1964 and 1968 and his Public Voting Act of 1965. Together, the Acts outlawed discrimination in such matters as jobs, housing and education, and gave African Americans the unfettered right to vote.

While King was promoting brotherhood and nonviolence, uprooted blacks in the cities were growing impatient. In the summer of 1965, black frustration boiled over in the urban ghetto of Watts, Los Angeles. In six days of looting and destruction, with rioters chanting "Burn, baby, burn!", 34 people died. The summer of 1967 saw riots and further loss of life in Newark, New Jersey and in Detroit. Martin Luther King, Jr., the man of nonviolence, was to die by an assassin's bullet. He was shot on April 4, 1968, as he stood on the balcony of a motel in Memphis, Tennessee. The murder, for which a white man, James Earl Ray, was sentenced to 99 years, triggered riots in more than 100 cities. Ray died in prison in April 1998.

MARTYR WITH A DREAM Martin Luther King, Jr., killed in the struggle for civil rights, proclaims: "I have a dream."

THE CANADIAN PATH TO PROSPERITY

Canada emerged from the Second World War as the fourth largest industrial power on Earth. But with a population of only 14 million, and with the war-damaged economies of Europe and Asia recovering, it was not a position the country could sustain for long. In any case, it had two major problems to tackle: working out its national identity and preserving national unity. History and kinship tied Canada to the United Kingdom and France—a bond confirmed during two world wars. However, geography ties Canada to the United States—they share the longest undefended border in the world. In the outcome, geography triumphed over history.

Links with Britain were weakened by a dramatic change in both the size and the nature of Canada's population. Immigration boosted the 14 million of 1945 to 20 million by 1970, and with immigrants coming

GATEWAY TO A CONTINENT The St. Lawrence Seaway opened in 1959, enabling oceangoing ships to reach the heart of the American continent.

in large numbers from Holland, Italy, Germany and other parts of Europe, the proportion of the British population fell from more than two-thirds to less than half. Canada remained a member of the Commonwealth, but was clearly determined to make its own decisions. In 1965, the nation symbolized its new attitude by dropping the Union Jack from its flag. In a world dominated by the superpowers, Canada recognized that it depended on America for defense.

The exploitation after 1947 of vast deposits of oil and natural gas in Alberta fueled an economic boom that culminated ten years later in the opening of the St. Lawrence Seaway—a long-cherished dream that gave oceangoing ships access to the Great Lakes, in the heart of the North American continent. But much of the investment in Canada's buoyant economy came from its southern neighbor. Well over half of the country's output, especially in mining, petroleum, pulp and paper mills, was owned by American parent companies. Many Canadians were worried, too, by the way that American culture was invading their lives, through television, movies, books and magazines. The tide of American influence was hard to stem. Equally irresistible, despite temporary setbacks, was the tide of Canadian prosperity. In January 1965, Canada became the second most affluent country in the world after the U.S., with an average income of $2,263 per capita and 347 cars for every 1,000 people.

This good fortune was not spread evenly across the country, however. Above all Quebec, homeland of the French Canadians, resented being among the have-not provinces. The Quebecois were proud of their French origin, language and traditions, and some began to talk of founding a separate state. The separatists cheered France's President Charles de Gaulle when he visited the Expo 67 world fair in Montreal, and proclaimed: "*Vive le Quebec libre! Vive le Canada Français!*"

Aware of the vital role played by language in holding a nation together, the Quebecois championed the use of French at the expense of English. Both became official languages, with equal status in all matters of government and in the courts after the flamboyant Liberal leader, Pierre Trudeau, won the general election of 1968. "We believe in a pluralist society, not merely as a political necessity, but as an enrichment," said Trudeau. This was not enough to appease the separatists. The Front de Libération du Quebec (FLQ) turned to terrorism, setting off a bomb in the Montreal Stock Exchange on February 13, 1969.

PAST AND PRESENT Young Quebecois recall an earlier struggle against Anglo-Saxon power.

PLATFORM SPELLBINDER President Kennedy in divided Berlin in 1963 challenging fence-sitters in the Cold War: "Let them come to Berlin." He had his audience spellbound with the claim: *"Ich bin ein Berliner."*

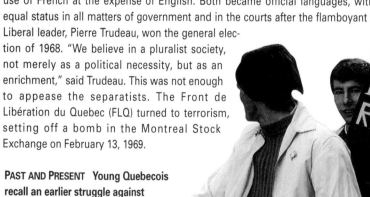

1837 RÉBELLION 1967 RÉVOLUTION

had promised to pioneer a "New Frontier" that would take America into uncharted areas of science and space, solve problems of peace and war, and end ignorance, prejudice and poverty. But in space, the Soviets were leading the way. On April 12, 1961, Yuri Gagarin became the first man in space, when he orbited the Earth in Vostok 1. Kennedy pledged that America would put a man on the Moon before the decade was out—an objective achieved, at a cost of $24 billion, on July 20, 1969, when Neil Armstrong stepped onto the Moon's

2:50 p.m. and charged with the president's murder. He was a former U.S. marine who had defected to Russia, married a Russian woman and tried, without success, to become a Soviet citizen.

Oswald denied killing the president, and if he had a motive, it went to the grave with him, for two days after his arrest, as he was being transferred to the county jail, a local strip-club owner, Jack Ruby, stepped forward with a .38 pistol. He thrust it into Oswald's stomach and fired point blank. Both events, the president's assassination and Lee Harvey Oswald's murder, were captured on camera, and people all over the world watched, hor-

continued on page 98

SHOTS RING ROUND THE WORLD The news of President Kennedy's assassination shook the entire world. A postcard from Dallas (bottom) shows the warehouse from which at least one shot was fired at the president.

surface from Apollo 11's moonlander, *Eagle*, with the words: "That's one small step for a man, one giant leap for mankind"—although the meaning of his sentence was spoiled somewhat when interference blotted out the "a."

Other items in Kennedy's New Frontier program did not fare so well. His small majority left him in a weak position when Congress stalled his plans for civil rights reforms, medical care for the elderly, and a $2.5 billion program of aid for schools.

The President assassinated

What Kennedy might have achieved had he lived will never be known. Around 12:30 p.m. on November 22, 1963, rifle shots rang out as the president's motorcade passed the Texas School Book Depository in downtown Dallas. Kennedy, who was visiting the city to strengthen his bid in the 1964 election,

slumped forward, his head shattered. John Connally, the Governor of Texas, who was in the car with him, was wounded in the back. Jacqueline Kennedy, spattered with blood, cradled her husband's head in her arms as the car sped to a hospital, but the president was dead on arrival.

Lee Harvey Oswald was arrested in a movie theater at

INSIDE LATIN AMERICA

FOR THE MILLIONS OF LATIN AMERICANS WHO WERE CAUGHT IN A THIRD-WORLD POVERTY TRAP, FIDEL CASTRO'S CUBA SEEMED TO OFFER THE WAY OUT—REVOLUTION

Poverty, inflation, and dictatorship have been the curses of Latin America. While people in other continents were enjoying an economic boom in the 1950s and 1960s, millions in South America were near starvation. In the early 1950s, when the average income per capita in the United States was around $3,000, in Latin America it was below $400—and that figure masked a chasm of difference between rich and poor.

In a continent rich in natural resources, many countries depended heavily on a single product—Bolivia on tin, Chile on copper, Cuba on sugar, Guatemala on bananas—and often the bulk of the profit from these resources went to foreign investors. America's United Fruit Company, for instance, was the biggest landowner in Guatemala. It also owned the country's main railroad.

A population explosion, brought about largely by improvements in medicine and public hygiene, left millions in the poverty trap. In 1945, the population of Latin America was around 130 million; seven years later, there were another 86 million mouths to feed, and the trend continued. Festering shanty towns grew up around the cities as peasants left the countryside in search of a living.

With the exception of Chile, there was no solid tradition of democracy; indeed, many countries had a tradition of military intervention in politics. Military regimes seized power in Argentina in 1955 and again in 1966, in Ecuador in 1961, in Brazil in 1964, and in Panama and Peru in 1968.

SLUM DWELLING Grinding poverty forced peasants off the land, only to face the filth and poverty of shanty towns such as this one near Buenos Aires.

One way of escaping from the poverty trap was to turn the economy around from an emphasis on exporting food and raw materials to industrialization. There could be a price to pay: inflation reached spectacular levels, with Uruguay setting a record of 9,000 percent during the period 1955-70. And rich landowners, who had benefited from the old system, did not always welcome moves to switch from agriculture to industry.

Another result of industrialization was the rise of an urban working class, a force whose potential was quickly appreciated by Colonel Juan Perón in Argentina. Perón ran for president in 1946 and won in a landslide. His fascist inclinations soon came to the fore: political opponents were jailed, and the press was muzzled. But his wife, Eva Duarte de Perón (Evita), had a genius for public relations and was loved by the masses. She helped him to turn the "shirtless ones" into a political force. Evita died in 1952, and Perón's touch without her was less sure. The economy suffered as sales of wheat and beef fell. Perón attacked the Church and was excommunicated, and finally he lost the confidence of the military. He was ousted in a coup in June 1955 and went into a long exile.

Ever since the Monroe Doctrine of 1823, which forbade European countries from setting up further colonies in the Americas, the United States had regarded Latin America as its special sphere of influence. In the Cold War era, this meant keeping communism out of America's "backyard"—either by aid or by intervention, the carrot or the stick.

An example of the stick came in Guatemala in 1954, when the left-wing President Jacobo Arbenz proposed reforms that included seizing uncultivated land from the United Fruit Company. This, coupled with the fact that Arbenz had accepted Soviet arms, smacked of communism to President Eisenhower. Arbenz was overthrown in a CIA-backed rebellion. John F. Kennedy's Alliance for Progress was an example of the carrot. He offered a total of $10 billion in aid to Latin American countries prepared to introduce land reform and social reforms.

Unremitting poverty for the masses and near-feudal privileges for the few led inevitably to protest movements. In 1961 in

Nicaragua—a nation run as a private profit-making enterprise by the Somaza family since 1937—the Sandinistas began what was to prove a long and blood-soaked struggle. In Uruguay, the Tupamaros demanded land reform and the end of foreign ownership of such key resources as banks and industries. The inspiration for those rebelling against the old order was Fidel Castro, leader of the rebellion that toppled the Cuban dictator Fulgencia Batista in January 1959.

Of all the Latin American revolutionaries, none appeared more glamorous than the Argentinian Che Guevara. His image, on posters and T-shirts, became an icon for a whole generation. Bearded and Christlike, his hair blowing in the wind, Che Guevara represented youth, idealism, the Sixties and revolution. In 1952, as a medical student in Buenos Aires, Ernesto Guevara joined in riots against the country's fascist-leaning president, Juan Perón. Believing that poverty and social injustice, common problems throughout Latin America, could be solved only by revolution on a continental scale, Guevara went in 1953 to Guatemala, where the reforming President Jacobo Arbenz was trying to create a new society.

Guevara —who had by now acquired his nickname from his habit of punctuating

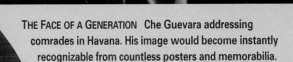

THE FACE OF A GENERATION Che Guevara addressing comrades in Havana. His image would become instantly recognizable from countless posters and memorabilia.

his speech with the Guarani Indian word *che* (a way of commanding attention)—went next to Mexico, where he became a close friend of two political refugees from Cuba, the brothers Fidel and Raul Castro. He joined their rebel invasion of the island in 1956, toughening himself up for guerrilla warfare by going for long endurance marches in the hills. He became a *commandante* in Castro's forces, and in January 1959, he and his 300 men entered Havana in triumph, after helping to overthrow the dictator Batista by derailing and capturing an armored train. Che became president of Cuba's national bank, then Minister for Industry. But his heart was not in administration, and he set out again to spread revolution.

After a time in the Congo, helping the cause of pro-Marxist Patrice Lumumba, he left Cuba for the last time in 1965 to spread the revolution in South America. Leading a guerrilla band in Bolivia, he was ambushed, wounded and captured by the Bolivian army in October 1967. His captors executed him. When the news of his friend's death was confirmed, Castro ordered three days of public mourning in Cuba.

VOICE OF THE SHIRTLESS From minor actress to most powerful woman in Argentina, Eva Perón never forgot the common people. That was her secret.

a sweeping Civil Rights Act passed in 1964. Where Roosevelt had his New Deal, Truman his Fair Deal and Kennedy his New Frontier, Johnson had a vision of the "Great Society" that he promised to build in America's cities, countryside, and classrooms. "The Great Society rests on abundance and liberty for all," he explained.

Turning the rhetoric into action, he won the agreement of Congress to reforms that included the Economic Opportunity Act (1964), which set aside more than $1 billion to fight poverty; the Housing and Urban Development Act (1965), under which $3 billion was invested in housing; improved Medicare for the elderly and Medicaid for the poor (both 1965); and the Education Act (1965), which allocated federal funds to the education of pupils from poor families.

America became bogged down in the Vietnam War under Johnson, and following a wave of protests against U.S. involvement, he declined to run for president in 1968. The Republican candidate, Richard Nixon, won the election that year, on a promise to "end the war and win the peace."

A WINNER AT LAST Richard Nixon beams out from a 1968 presidential election poster—a fight he won after the frustrating years that followed his defeat by John F. Kennedy in 1960.

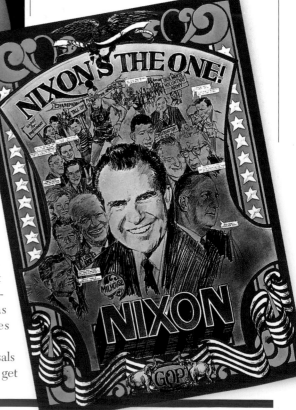

rified, as these dramatic incidents were relayed to their television screens.

Ruby said he had killed Oswald to avenge the president and to save Jacqueline Kennedy from the ordeal of attending a murder trial. But Dallas, and soon the entire nation, was awash with rumors of a conspiracy. The most persistent was that the Mafia, and even the CIA, had been behind the president's assassination, and that Ruby had silenced Oswald on their orders.

FBI chief J. Edgar Hoover said that Oswald had acted "in his own lunatic loneliness," and the same conclusion was reached, after listening to 522 witnesses and 26 volumes' worth of testimony, by a commission headed by Chief Justice Earl Warren. There remained many, however, who could not accept that a tragedy of such dimensions

THE TORCH PASSES ON On the very day of John F. Kennedy's assassination, Vice-President Lyndon B. Johnson, his wife Lady Bird Johnson at his side, is sworn in as America's 36th President.

could be brought about by one unstable individual, acting alone.

Lyndon Baines Johnson, the vice-president, was sworn in as president on the day of the assassination. LBJ understood the byways as well as the highways of politics. He had built up contacts during a stint as majority leader of the Senate, and was adroit at maneuvering his measures through Congress.

Where Kennedy's civil rights proposals had been blocked, Johnson was able to get

BEHIND THE CURTAIN

STALIN RULED WITH AN IRON FIST INSIDE AN IRON GLOVE, BUT AFTER HIS DEATH, CRACKS BEGAN TO APPEAR IN THE SOVIET FAÇADE

After the sacrifices made by the people of the Soviet Union during the Second World War, they might have hoped that their privations were over once it had come to an end. But Stalin had different priorities. The German invaders and Stalin's own "scorched earth" policy had, between them, left factories, communications, and farms in ruins. He intended to restore the Soviet economy through a five-year plan, concentrating on heavy industry.

Helped by crushing reparation payments from East Germany, the plan was a great success. By 1950, industrial output had soared to 40 percent above its prewar level. Less impressive was the performance in agriculture, with a crop failure in 1946 followed by a slow recovery.

Stalin, a ruthless social engineer, took his revenge on those ethnic groups that had shown a readiness to cooperate with the Germans. He uprooted millions of Crimean Tartars, Chechens, Ingush and Kalmucks, and resettled them in Siberia.

With the sinister Lavrenti Beria, head of the secret police, as his enforcer, Stalin stifled criticism before it was voiced. Anybody who opposed his view became an "enemy of the people." Nikolai Bulganin, who was to become premier of the U.S.S.R., once said, "It has happened sometimes that a man goes to Stalin on his invitation as a friend. And when he sits with Stalin he does not know where he will be sent next, home or to jail."

To millions of ordinary citizens, though, he was the "little father" who had saved the homeland in the war. Gigantic statues of the "sublime strategist of all times and all nations," as he was described in one official biography that he vetted himself, were erected in towns and cities all over the land. Stalingrad was just one of scores of places that bore his name. What Khrushchev was to call Stalin's "mania for greatness" was fed by adulation that reached its peak on his 70th birthday, December 21, 1949. The Soviet Academy of Sciences hailed "the greatest genius of mankind." A torrent of gifts and greetings flowed in from all over the world.

Stalin's other mania was suspicion. He even accused former Foreign Minister Vyacheslav Molotov, the man known as "M. Nyet" (Mr. No) in the West because of his inflexibility, of being an imperialist agent. Anti-semitism was never far from the surface with Stalin. When there was trouble at an aviation factory, he turned to Khrushchev and said, "The good workers at the factory should be given clubs so they can beat the hell out of those Jews at the end of the working day."

In his last year of life Stalin was preparing a bloody pogrom. In January 1952, he had

HAPPY BIRTHDAY TO YOU Many congratulations but few smiles were in evidence at Stalin's 70th birthday celebrations held in Moscow's Bolshoi Theater on December 21, 1949. Mao Zedong and other world leaders paid their respects alongside members of the Politburo.

nine Kremlin doctors, seven of them Jews, arrested and accused of killing Andrei Zhdanov, a high-ranking member of the ruling Politburo. He told his Minister of State Security: "If you do not obtain confessions from the doctors we will shorten you by a head."

Before the men arrested in the "doctors' plot" could be put on show trial, Stalin was dead. He had a brain hemorrhage on March 4, 1953, and died the following day. Perhaps understandably, in the light of events of the previous year, it had taken more than 12 hours for doctors to arrive at the dying leader's bedside.

Georgi Malenkov, the man named by Stalin as his successor, became prime minister and the far more powerful post of party secretary went to Nikita Khrushchev, a peasant's son. Naturally pugnacious, and with the backing of the Red Army, Khrushchev quickly emerged as the dominant force in the new leadership. He and Malenkov had Beria, the man they most feared, arrested and executed; then, at a secret session of the 20th Party Congress in 1956, Khrushchev took the dramatic step of publicly denouncing Stalin. The reign of terror was over, he announced, and it would be replaced by "Socialist legality."

The revolt of the satellites

An early sign that all was not as harmonious in Eastern Europe as Soviet propaganda claimed came a few months after Stalin died. Raising the lid of suppression, even slightly, carried with it the risk that hopes would be raised too. In East Germany, the grimness of life under the leadership of Kremlin-backed Walter Ulbricht contrasted sharply with the allure of West Germany, which was in the early stages of its "economic miracle."

In June 1953, thousands of workers in East Berlin put down their tools and marched through the streets shouting slogans against the regime. The protest spread to other towns and cities, and by the time it had been quelled by Soviet tanks and bayonets, 800 East German citizens were dead.

In Poland delegates who had attended the 20th Congress of the Communist Party spread the sensational news that Stalin and Stalinism had been denounced. Again, the lid had been raised. In June 1956, workers in Poznan took to the streets to protest against high productivity targets and low wages. They were joined by students, and the march turned into a riot. The response of the army and security police, who shot dead nearly 80 demonstrators, sent a shock wave through the country. Workers tore up their party cards and prepared to defend their factories as Soviet tanks rumbled toward Warsaw.

Khrushchev defused a perilous situation by restoring to power Wladyslaw Gomulka, who had been arrested under Stalin for advancing the view that there were more ways than one to socialism. Khrushchev knew that, although a Polish patriot, Gomulka as party secretary was also a loyal communist. He agreed that Poles imprisoned in the U.S.S.R. should be allowed to return home, and that Soviet officers should withdraw from the Polish army. For a few happy months, Poland enjoyed its new freedom. Cardinal Wyszynski, the Roman Catholic primate, was released from confinement, and censorship was abolished. But Poland's economy was stagnating, and Gomulka had no answer. As productivity and living standards fell, the Polish people found in the late 1960s that they were living once again under a regime that answered protests with rifle butts and police clubs.

In Soviet eyes, Hungary was an occupied country after the war, for it had been an ally of Germany, and its armies had fought alongside the Wehrmacht. Stalin's grip on the country was a brutal one, and even the hard-line communists he installed in power were not safe. In 1949 he had Laszlo Rajk, the foreign minister, hauled before a show trial and executed for "Titoism." Mátyás Rákosi, who became premier in 1952, was a Stalinist who imprisoned 200,000 of his own people and executed 2,000.

The ordeal of Hungary

Stalin's death swiftly brought changes. Imre Nagy replaced the hated Rákosi as prime minister, and in July 1953, announced his

TANKS IN THE CITY
Bewildered citizens of Budapest cluster around Soviet tanks, trying vainly to reason with their crews.

1948 Communists take control in Czechoslovakia

1952 Stalin arrests Kremlin doctors

1953 Stalin dies; Khrushchev becomes party secretary

1956 Khrushchev denounces Stalin; Hungarian rising against Soviet control

TOPPLING THE TYRANT A huge statue of the dictator Stalin is toppled by the citizens of Hungary's capital, Budapest. The uprising gave ordinary Hungarians, like the 15-year-old girl on the right, a chance to show extraordinary courage.

"New Course." Farmers would be allowed to leave the collective farms and sell their produce for profit. The powers of the secret police would be curtailed. To Rákosi this was political heresy; and Rákosi controlled the party machine. In April 1955, he overthrew Nagy and set about restoring a police state. So unpopular did this make him that,

in August 1956, he was forced to resign. He fled to Russia, carrying a list of 400 opponents whom he had planned to arrest.

News of the 20th Party Congress, and of the stirring events in Poland, started a ferment in Hungary that, on October 23, 1956, was to sweep Nagy back to the premiership. By then, the rebellion had already started. Thousands of students were voting to leave the party's youth organization, and were demanding a free press, free elections, and the withdrawal of Soviet forces. In Budapest, there were bloody clashes between demonstrators and armed security police, and a huge statue of the despot Stalin was toppled to the ground. Ominous troop movements showed that the Soviets had no intention of relinquishing control.

Nagy was a member of the government, but not yet prime minister, when a fateful decision was taken: with their own troops beginning to side with the demonstrators, the Hungarian Politburo called on the U.S.S.R. to help it to restore order.

From that moment the revolution became a matter of people versus tanks. Using captured weapons, the citizens of Budapest fought an unequal battle. It became dangerous to wear a leather coat, for that was the uniform of the hated secret police, who were being hanged from lampposts.

1970

1957
Sputnik 1
orbits Earth

1960 U.S.S.R.
withdraws advisers
in split with China

1961 Yuri
Gagarin is first
man in space

1962 Khrushchev
backs down in
Cuban missile crisis

1964 Khrushchev
ousted from
power in Kremlin

It was a battle that could have only one outcome. Radio Free Europe, broadcasting from Munich, borrowed Winston Churchill's words to announce that this was Hungary's "finest hour." But as Britain did in 1940, Hungary stood alone, and this time there was no happy ending. Soviet troops and tanks crushed the rebellion and installed Janos Kadar as head of a puppet government. Nagy sought refuge in the Yugoslav embassy, but when he left, on Kadar's promise of safe conduct, he was abducted by Soviet troops. On June 17, 1957, came the announcement that he had been charged with treason and executed, along with other leaders of the revolution.

Kadar proclaimed martial law, sent his militia to bring striking workers to heel, dissolved workers' councils and set up "peoples' courts" to try revolutionaries. Estimates of the number killed in the rising vary from 2,500 to more than 20,000. More than 20,000 Hungarians fled to safety and a new life in the West.

Western governments found that their protests had less moral force than was

intended, because Britain and France were engaged at the time in an act of aggression of their own—the invasion of Egypt during the Suez crisis. As one Western commentator put it, Khrushchev had "washed his hands in the Suez Canal." The Soviet line, expressed by their spokesman in the UN, was that they had saved the Hungarian people from "the specter of the fascist beast."

Khrushchev went even further when he made a visit to Hungary in April 1957, and warned: "You should not think that if a counter-revolution comes again you can depend on the Russians coming to your aid once more. You must help yourselves."

Inside the U.S.S.R., Malenkov and Molotov blamed Khrushchev and his 20th Congress speech for the Hungarian revolution, and

BATTLING PREMIER Nikita Khrushchev in forceful mood, haranguing a summit meeting after the U.S. sent a spy plane into Soviet airspace.

PAYMENT BY RESULTS Under the eye of Vladimir Lenin, a manager poses against charts showing targets and output for a collective farm near Moscow. Bonuses were paid for good results.

tried to have him unseated as party secretary. But Khrushchev had built up solid support within the party. He accused the pair, along with old-guard Bolshevik Lazar Kaganovich, of setting up an anti-party group, and it was they who were forced out. Malenkov was banished to manage a hydroelectric plant in Kazakhstan; Molotov was appointed ambassador to Outer Mongolia; and Kaganovich became a manager in a Siberian cement works. In Stalin's day they would have met a worse fate.

Triumph and failure for Nikita Khrushchev

Khrushchev followed up his attack on Stalin's memory with a program of de-Stalinization. He had the dictator's remains removed from their honored place in the mausoleum in Moscow and buried in a pit beneath a plaque that read simply: "J.V. Stalin." He rehabilitated millions of Chechens, Kalmucks and other ethnic groups who had been uprooted under Stalin, and allowed them to return to their homelands. He relaxed censorship, even permitting the publication in 1962 of Alexandr Solzhenitsyn's *One Day in the Life of Ivan Denisovich*, an uncompromising account of conditions inside the gulag.

One problem he seemed unable to solve was that of the poor Soviet performance in agriculture. While industrial output rose steadily, the collective farms were not reaching their production targets. Determined to catch up with the U.S. in food production, Khrushchev looked for quick results in the "virgin lands" scheme—a very ambitious project to grow crops on a grand scale in Siberia and Kazakhstan.

Many mistakes were made. Land that had been used by herdsmen for grazing turned out not to be suitable for crops, especially

COLLECTIVE PROPAGANDA An official photo of happy workers, bringing in the harvest on a collective farm in the Ukraine. Thanks to flawed agricultural policies by the state, the reality was often far different.

BIOLOGY, SOVIET STYLE

While agronomists in the rest of the world applied the classic laws of genetics, Trofim Denisovich Lysenko looked to Marxist-Leninist theory to find a way of growing bigger and better crops. Characteristics that were acquired, he believed, could impose themselves on those that were inherited.

He proved to his own satisfaction that he could give spring wheat the hardiness of winter wheat by moistening and refrigerating the seeds, thereby making them tough enough to stand the chills of winter on the steppes.

This kind of thinking appealed to Stalin, and Lysenko was made head of the Institute of Genetics in the Soviet Academy of Sciences. Biologists who spoke against his theories found that they were involved in something more dangerous than an academic debate. At least one opponent was found guilty of "bourgeois idealism" and died in a prison camp.

After the war, Lysenko proposed a grandiose plan to transform Russia's climate by planting "shelter belts" of trees across the steppes. Most of the saplings were killed by drought.

MISTAKEN MISSIONARY Lysenko, the geneticist who tried to apply political theory to crop raising.

Although the man and his theories were denounced after the death of Stalin, his influence lingered on. "We have much to learn from scientists like Lysenko," said Khrushchev as late as 1964. One of the Soviet leader's most damaging failures, an attempt to grow maize in the "virgin lands" of Siberia and Kazakhstan, owed much to Lysenko's theories.

In 1965, Lysenko was fired as head of the Institute of Genetics.

INSIDE THE GULAG

The full horror and extent of Stalin's prison camps was revealed to the world in 1974 when Alexandr Solzhenitsyn, their most famous inmate, authorized the publication of *The Gulag Archipelago*. Even so long after the events it describes, it had to be published outside the U.S.S.R.

"Gulag" is an acronym for the network of prison camps of the Stalin era, officially known as Corrective Labor Camps. It has been estimated that as many as 10 million people were sent to them. One reason why the camps needed to be so well filled was that they supplied slave labor for hacking canals out of the frozen earth and similar Herculean labors. Most of their inmates were political prisoners, some of them genuine opponents of the regime, but many were classified as "bourgeois wreckers" or "socially harmful elements" simply because they belonged to the wrong social group, or had merely been overheard complaining.

There were two waves of arrests during Stalin's purges before the war, and a third wave in 1944-6. This included many whose only crime had been contact with the West. These people were held to be dangerous because it was thought that comparisons between the West and the grimness of life in the U.S.S.R. might breed discontent. Suspicion fell even on those who had been taken as slave laborers to Germany, or on Soviet prisoners of war who had, on liberation, encountered the world outside their prison camps. Cossacks and Muslims who had fought with the Germans against the Red Army were obvious candidates for the gulag. Sentences could be anything from 10 to 25 years, and release was often followed by re-arrest. The "zeks" (gulag slang for a prisoner) were sent to the camps

LIVING HELL In a nightmare scene reminiscent of a Bosch painting, prisoners in one of Stalin's gulags build a canal in Soviet Central Asia.

with as many as 36 at a time crammed into railway cars intended to take 11 at most. Once there, they were liable to be robbed by the thieves and convicted criminals who held the privileges of "trusties."

Solzhenitsyn, himself a Red Army captain arrested for daring to criticize Stalin in a letter to a friend, describes life in the camps: ". . . the long waiting under the beating sun or autumn drizzle; the still longer body searches that involve undressing completely; their haircuts with unsanitary clippers; their foul-smelling toilets; their damp and moldy corridors; their perpetually crowded, nearly always dark, wet cells . . . the wet, almost liquid, bread; the gruel cooked from what seems to be silage."

JOURNEY'S END The final resting place in one of Stalin's prison camps for women and children.

during years of drought. The man appointed as Minister of Agriculture was under the influence of Trofim Lysenko, Stalin's favorite biologist, who applied Marxist theory rather than genetics or traditional common sense to crop-raising. In 1963 came the ultimate humiliation: the Soviet Union had to import grain from Canada, Australia, Romania and other countries whose agricultural methods were more productive.

Another area of concern for Khrushchev was the Soviet split with China. In the eyes of Mao Zedong, Khrushchev's denunciation of Stalin made him a revisionist—a man who was re-interpreting the true Marxist-Leninist faith. His pursuit of coexistence with the West was "a bourgeois pacifist notion." His visit to America in 1959 left Mao wracked with suspicions. The treaty banning nuclear tests in the atmosphere, which the Soviets signed in 1963, was "contemptible chicanery."

There were border differences, too. The Chinese claimed that tsarist Russia had stolen Vladivostok from them, and drew up a map showing their idea of the true boundary. "We took one look at it, and it was so outrageous that we threw it away in disgust," recalled Khrushchev. Trade and cultural contacts between the two countries fell away and in July 1960, the Soviets withdrew the 1,300 military and economic advisers who had been sent to help China when the two communist giants were on friendlier terms.

Mao regarded Khrushchev's backing off in the Cuban missile crisis of 1962 as a sign of weakness, and influential forces inside the Presidium, the successor to the Politburo, shared this view. Some spectacular propaganda successes had been scored under Khrushchev's leadership, especially in the Space Race with America. In October 1957, the Soviets launched Sputnik, the first man-made satellite to orbit the Earth. In April 1961 cosmonaut Yuri Gagarin became the first human being in space. But set against these successes were the Hungarian revolution, "adventurism" in Cuba, Khrushchev's problems in the virgin lands, the unresolved quarrel with China, and a natural ebullience that could lead to undignified behavior—as when, at a session of the United Nations in 1960, Khrushchev emphasized his point by taking off a shoe and banging it on his desk.

In October 1964, the 70-year-old party secretary was called back from a hunting and

fishing vacation to be told by the Presidium that he was being retired on health grounds. His successors, Alexei Kosygin, Leonid Brezhnev and Nikolai Podgorny, soon faced problems of their own.

The Prague spring

There had been signs of trouble in Czechoslovakia after Stalin's death, when a riot broke out at the Skoda car works in Pilsen. It was quickly suppressed by police and armed troops, and the country settled back into surly acceptance of the Stalinist regime of Antonin Novotny.

In the hope that he might reverse the government's unpopularity, Novotny made some concessions in 1963, lifting restrictions on the press and on cultural activities. The country's cultural life, never far below the surface, burst into flower. Czech films and theater made a global impact, and Czech writers dared to attack the regime. These criticisms, added to a poor economic perfor-

WINTER FOLLOWS SPRING Jubilant supporters flock around Alexander Dubcek during the "Prague Spring" of 1968. Their hopes were soon crushed by an invasion of Soviet troops (inset) backed by forces from four Warsaw Pact countries.

mance, led the party to lose confidence in Novotny. In January 1968, he was forced to resign, and the Slovak Alexander Dubcek was elected party secretary.

In what became known as "the Prague Spring," Dubcek embarked on a headlong program of reforms. Suddenly, people were free to travel without restrictions; the media could print news and views they thought important; people could even talk about leaving the Soviet bloc without fear of a knock on the door from the secret police.

Dubcek's policy of "Socialism with a human face" alarmed hard-liners in Moscow, and they decided on swift action. On August

21, 1968, a stunned world heard the news that Red Army tanks and soldiers were on the streets of Prague. They were supported by troops from Bulgaria and from three other Warsaw Pact countries whose own attempts at rebellion had been crushed earlier—East Germany, Poland and Hungary.

The Czech government made no call for a national uprising, and the Czech people had little, apart from sticks and their bare hands, with which to fight. People in Prague taunted the Soviet troops and climbed on tanks to argue with them. Some died when an ammunition truck exploded. But their most effective weapon was passive resistance. A 21-year-old student, Jan Palach, became a symbol of the national will to resist when, on January 16, 1969, he set fire to himself in Prague's Wenceslas Square. He died in a hospital, but before his death, copies of a note he had written appeared all over Prague: "Our group is composed of volunteers who are ready to burn themselves for our cause. I had the honor to draw the first lot . . ."

Dubcek, arrested and taken to Moscow, was forced to recant and rescind his key reforms. In April 1969, he was replaced as party secretary by the more reliable Gustav Husák, then steadily demoted. Following a brief period as ambassador to Turkey, he fell further into disgrace and eventually became a clerk in a woodyard.

The Prague Spring was over: Moscow had decreed it to be Winter.

AGAINST ALL ODDS Students stage a protest outside the National Museum, Prague, on November 21, 1968, the day the Soviet Union and forces from four satellites invaded Czechoslovakia, ending its bid for freedom.

KHRUSHCHEV LAYS TO REST A GHOST

It took almost three years after the death of Stalin for his rule to be put into something like its true perspective. In February 1956, with snow lying 4 feet deep outside the walls of the Kremlin, his former Politburo associate Nikita Khrushchev addressed a secret session of the 20th All-Union Congress on the subject of "The Personality Cult and its Consequences." Most of what he had to say was received in stunned silence, but it was a silence punctuated by occasional noises of indignation, by outbursts of prolonged applause, and at rare moments by laughter. When the speech ended, Khrushchev was given a tumultuous standing ovation. For he had dared to say what many had been thinking.

He contrasted Stalin's cult of personality and brutality with the modesty and compassion of Lenin, and revealed that as early as 1922 Lenin had serious doubts about Stalin's suitability to be the party's secretary general because of his "excessive rudeness." There was a commotion in the hall when Khrushchev read a letter in which Lenin threatened to break off relations unless Stalin apologized for rudeness to his wife.

Many party leaders and dedicated rank-and-file party workers had fallen victim to Stalin's despotism, said Khrushchev: "The formula 'enemy of the people' was specifically introduced for the purpose of annihilating such individuals." To loud murmurs of indignation, Khrushchev revealed that of 139 members of the Central Committee elected at the 17th All-Union Congress, 98 had been arrested and shot in Stalin's purges. Many thousands of honest and innocent communists had died as a result of "monstrous falsification" and as a result of "the practice of forcing accusations against oneself and others," charged Khrushchev.

He named old Bolsheviks, known to his audience, who had been tortured into making false confessions, then executed. He mocked Stalin's claims to be a military genius. And he bitterly mocked the man who had added to his own biography the words: "Although he performed his task of leader of the party with consummate skill and enjoyed the unreserved support of the entire Soviet people, Stalin never allowed his work to be marred by the slightest hint of vanity, conceit, or self-adulation."

For secret police chief Lavrenti Beria, Khrushchev had a special contempt: "In organizing the various dirty and shameful cases, a very base role was played by the rabid enemy of our party, an agent of a foreign intelligence service—Beria, who had stolen into Stalin's confidence."

COLD WAR CLASHES

THE KOREAN WAR AND THE CUBAN MISSILE CRISIS PUSHED THE SUPERPOWERS TO THE BRINK OF A NUCLEAR CONFRONTATION

Like two cautious heavyweights in the opening rounds of a championship fight, the superpowers tested each other in the 1950s and 1960s, jabbing, feinting, searching for areas of weakness. Their allies and client states were inevitably drawn in, as the giants struggled to establish a new balance of power. The "ring" for the contest was as vast as the globe itself, with flashpoints in places as far apart as Korea, Cuba and central Europe. Confrontation in the Nuclear Age carried with it a terrifying prospect, and a new strategy was put forward for reducing the risk: coexistence.

Hot war in Korea

The Cold War became a hot war on Sunday, June 25, 1950, when the rattle of artillery broke the predawn silence along the frontier between North and South Korea, and thousands of soldiers from the North, spearheaded by tanks, swarmed across the 38th parallel. The attack came as a surprise, though it should not have, as the two Koreas had been snapping and snarling at each other, like fighting dogs on leashes, almost from the day they had been separated at the end of the Second World War.

After the defeat of Japan, U.S. troops moved into the south of the Korean peninsula, and Soviet troops into the north—a division that was meant to be temporary but became rigid in the climate of the Cold War.

Both the occupying forces moved out by agreement in 1948-9, leaving the pro-Western Syngman Rhee as President of South Korea and the communist Kim Il Sung, a former guerrilla leader against the Japanese, in charge in the north. Both men claimed that theirs was the rightful government of the entire country.

Kim was in the better position to enforce his claim, since the U.S.S.R. kept him well supplied with tanks, planes and weapons. Rhee's position was not helped when, in January 1950, Secretary of State Dean Acheson stated publicly that America's "defensive perimeter" in Asia did not include Korea. Kim saw his opportunity and, with a nod of approval from Stalin, launched his attack on June 25.

He had made a bad misjudgment of the Americans. "Communism was acting in Korea just as Hitler, Mussolini, and Japan had acted

MOSCOW'S MAN Watched over by their Moscow-trained leader, Kim Il Sung, North Korea's army, navy and air force protect their land in a poster produced in 1951, at the height of the Korean War.

UNCLE SAM'S MAN Pro-Western Syngman Rhee, President of South Korea, was educated at Harvard and Princeton.

ten, fifteen, twenty years earlier," President Truman recalled in his memoirs. From his headquarters in Tokyo, General Douglas MacArthur immediately sent arms and ammunition to the panic-stricken South Koreans. On the day after the invasion, American fighter planes arrived in Korea, and the mighty U.S. Seventh Fleet headed toward the area, on Truman's orders.

The president moved swiftly on the diplomatic front, too. America put an emergency motion before the Security Council of the United Nations, which voted to repel the aggression. The Soviet Union could have vetoed this decision, but it was boycotting the Security Council at the time. MacArthur was given command of the UN forces, which were 90 percent American and South Korean, but drew from 16 nations, including Britain, Turkey, Australia, Canada, New Zealand and France.

Kim's army, with the impetus of its first onslaught, drove the South Koreans and the hastily assembled UN forces into the southeastern tip of the peninsula, around the port of Pusan. From there, General MacArthur carried off the boldest stroke of a spectacular

THE ANSWER TO AGGRESSION North Korea's attack on the South in June 1950 provoked a massive response from United Nations forces, led by the U.S. The battleship USS *Missouri* (above) blasts enemy concentrations along the North Korean coast, and an American machine-gun crew (below) covers a strategic bridge.

military career. On September 15, his troops made a seaborne landing at Inchon on the west coast, only 50 miles from the 38th parallel. "I realize that Inchon is a 5,000 to 1 gamble," he said, "but I am used to taking such odds. We shall land at Inchon, and I shall crush them!" The gamble worked. With their supply lines cut, the invaders fled north in disorder.

MacArthur pursued them across the frontier, pinning them against the Yalu River, on the border with communist China. A war that had begun to counter communist aggression had turned into a war to end communist rule in the north. MacArthur shrugged aside warnings from China to halt the advance. He believed the war would be over by Thanksgiving in late November, and told Truman that the Chinese could muster no more than 50,000 troops.

On November 25, 1950, more than 200,000 Chinese "volunteers," their 4th and 5th Red Armies, crossed the river. They attacked in "human waves," and the UN forces, bloodied and massively outnumbered, fell back behind the 38th parallel. MacArthur urged Truman to allow him to bomb supply depots inside China, to blockade the Chinese coast, and to add Chinese Nationalist troops from Taiwan to the UN forces. Truman vetoed all three requests.

At a press conference, however, Truman made an unguarded statement. Asked if the U.S. might use the atomic bomb in Korea, he said it was always under consideration, and that the military commander in the field was in charge of the use of weapons. The White House promptly issued a correction, pointing out that by law only the president could authorize the use of the atom bomb. But alarm bells had rung for America's allies. British Prime Minister Clement Attlee flew to Washington to argue restraint. Whether as a result of Attlee's visit or not, the Pentagon agreed that the bomb would not be used.

1948 Berlin blockade and start of airlift

1950 Korean War begins

1951 British diplomats Burgess and Maclean flee to U.S.S.R.

1953 Armistice ends Korean War; Rosenbergs executed

THE BRAINWASHING MYTH

During the Korean War, 21 American prisoners of war out of nearly 4,000, 315 South Koreans out of more than 8,000, and one Briton out of just under 1,000 defected to the communists. Some of the American defectors made broadcasts supporting the communist charge that the U.S. had resorted to germ warfare, filling bombs and shells with beetles, lice and ticks that carried typhus and bubonic plague. Commentators in the West began to hint darkly that the POWs had been "brainwashed"—subjected to a program of psychological pressure that expunged from their minds all their value systems and ethical beliefs, leaving the way open for new values and new beliefs to be implanted. Richard Condon's novel *The Manchurian Candidate*, later made into a movie, introduced the concept to a mass market.

But a U.S. Department of Defense study in 1956 concluded: "It is obvious that such a time-consuming conditioning process could not be employed against any sizable group such as a prisoner-of-war group because of the excessive time and personnel required." The communists certainly tried to win converts through group indoctrination in their POW camps, but so did the Americans. And the American program of movies and lectures was hugely more successful: when the war was over, nearly 76,000 North Korean POWs were repatriated, but approximately 25,000 said they would rather remain in the South.

MacArthur, more used to giving orders than taking them, appealed over Truman's head to the American public, describing the prohibition against bombing supply depots in China as "an enormous handicap, without precedent in military history." This was blatant insubordination, and the president, as commander in chief, had no choice but to fire him. MacArthur returned to America to a ticker-tape welcome, gave an address to Congress and then, following his own words, did as old soldiers do, and faded away.

Peace talks began in the summer of 1951, and after two years of tiring negotiations at Panmunjom, an armistice was signed in July 1953. Korea was back where it had started in 1950, divided roughly along the 38th parallel. The war had cost nearly 2 million lives, including 1,300,000 South Koreans, 500,000 North Koreans, 900,000 Chinese and some 54,000 Americans. It had reduced entire sectors of Korea's cities to ashes and laid waste to the country's industries. It left the South in the grip of the increasingly tyrannical Syngman Rhee and the North under the even harsher regime of the "Beloved Leader" and "Ever Victorious Captain," Kim Il Sung. On the other hand, it had strengthened the United Nations and demonstrated that America could and would stand up to communist aggression.

Crisis over Cuba

What worried newly elected President John F. Kennedy early in 1961 was not so much aggression as communist proximity. The island of Cuba, less than 100 miles from Florida, had been a haven for American businessmen and vacationers, and open house for gamblers and gangsters when it was run by the dictator Fulgencia Batista. He was toppled in January 1959 in a revolution led by Fidel Castro, a former law student. Once in power, Castro nationalized major industries and took land away from the landlords. When he seized oil refineries and other U.S. property, the U.S. retaliated by banning sugar imports from the island. Castro turned to the U.S.S.R. for loans, military aid and advisers, and in 1961 declared himself a Marxist.

Castro set up a police state, in which anybody suspected of working against the revolution might be jailed and, if unlucky, put before a firing squad. A stream of exiles began arriving in Florida, and a group among them spread the story that Castro was so hated that the island was ready to rise against him. The CIA, under its director Alan Dulles, was more than willing to believe this tale and put together what they thought was a secret plan to arm and train an invasion force of exiles. The plot, which began during Eisenhower's presidency, was inherited by Kennedy.

Kennedy's first major test in foreign policy turned out to be a disaster. The CIA's secret was so badly kept that the *New York Times* ran a front-page story: "U.S. HELPS TRAIN AN ANTI-CASTRO FORCE AT SECRET GUATEMALAN BASE." It was common gossip on the streets of Havana, the Cuban capital, that an invasion was coming, and Castro was put on full alert by a botched attempt, on April 15, 1961, to bomb his airfields out of action.

In the early hours of April 17, some 1,500 exiles were landed on Cuban soil at the Bay of Pigs. They were met, not by a joyous population eager to join them, but by tanks and 20,000 Cuban regulars. According to the plan, if things went wrong they were meant to escape into the mountains and from there carry out a guerrilla war. But the nearest mountains were 80 miles away. Incompetence dogged the invasion right to the end. Four B-26 bombers

PAYING THE PRICE FOR THE BAY OF PIGS
Despairing Cuban exiles under armed guard, after their failed attempt to topple Castro in the Bay of Pigs invasion. They had expected massive American aid.

| 1960 American U-2 spy plane shot down over U.S.S.R. | 1961 U.S.-backed Bay of Pigs invasion in Cuba; Berlin Wall goes up | 1962 Cuban missile crisis | 1963 President Kennedy announces in Berlin: "Ich bin ein Berliner" |

flown from Nicaragua arrived over Cuba to find no sign of their fighter escort, because nobody had taken into account the one hour time difference between Nicaragua and Cuba. Castro's jets shot down two of the unprotected bombers. After two days' fighting, the 1,100 survivors surrendered.

Kennedy accepted full blame for the invasion fiasco. The experience made him better equipped to deal with the next crisis in Cuba. This began with a challenge by the Soviet premier, Nikita Khrushchev. "We were sure that the Americans would never reconcile themselves to the existence of Castro's Cuba," he confided in his memoirs. "I had the idea of installing missiles in Cuba without letting the United States find out until it was too late to do anything about them . . ."

Aerial photographs taken by a U-2 spy plane revealed that launching sites were being installed for medium-range missiles that, armed with nuclear warheads, would be capable of destroying New York, Washington and other U.S. cities.

In an atmosphere tense with crisis, Kennedy went on television on October 22, 1961, to address the nation. "The purpose of these bases can be none other than to provide a nuclear strike capability against the Western Hemisphere," he said. The president ordered a "quarantine"—a naval blockade of Cuba to prevent any

A WORLD UNDER THREAT

The atomic bombs that fell on Hiroshima and Nagasaki in 1945 each had the power of 20,000 tons of TNT, and depended on nuclear fission—releasing enormous energy by splitting atoms of uranium. The hydrogen bomb first tested by the United States in November 1952 at Eniwetok Atoll in the Pacific works by fusing atoms of hydrogen into heavier atoms. Fusion liberates hundreds of times as much energy as fission, and the hydrogen bomb is so powerful that it uses an atomic bomb as its "trigger."

British and Canadian scientists played an important part in developing the first atomic bomb, so it came as a shock when, in August 1946, the U.S. passed the McMahon Act, prohibiting American scientists from sharing nuclear secrets with any other country. "No, Prime Minister, we've got to have this. We've got to have the bloody Union Jack on top of it," growled Foreign Secretary Ernest Bevin, persuading Clement Attlee to develop Britain's own atomic bomb. The first British bomb was exploded in the Monte Bello islands, off the northwest coast of Australia, in October 1952. In 1953 further British tests began at Woomera rocket range in central Australia.

The U.S.S.R. already had the secret of the atom bomb. The alarming news that it had broken the U.S. nuclear monopoly reached the West in September 1949. Other powers felt vulnerable until they, too, became members of the "nuclear club." France exploded an atomic bomb in 1960, and China in 1964. The Soviets tested a hydrogen bomb in 1953, Britain tested one on Christmas Island in 1957, and H-bomb tests were carried out by both France and China.

The arms race between East and West became a contest not just of nuclear know-how and building up stockpiles, but of finding the most effective long-range means of delivery. Fleets of V-bombers were replaced by Inter-Continental Ballistic Missiles (ICBMs) that could be fired from ground-based silos or from submarines. So terrifying was the destructive power placed in the hands of a few men that there were calls, particularly in Britain, for nuclear weapons to be banned.

more missiles from arriving. He put the armed forces, including America's entire fleet of B-52 nuclear bombers, on 24-hour alert and warned Khrushchev that a nuclear attack launched from Cuba against any nation in the Western Hemisphere would bring "a full retaliatory attack on the Soviet Union."

The world seemed poised on the brink of a third world war, and America steeled itself for the worst. Helicopters were put on standby to pick up leading politicians and officials and whisk them to underground nuclear shelters. In Cuba, Castro made impassioned speeches and the crowd roared back: "Cuba Si—Yankee No!" The tension almost reached the breaking

point as Soviet freighters, with a submarine escort, approached the quarantine line. Then came a report that the ships had stopped dead in the water. "We're eyeball to eyeball, and I think the other fellow just blinked," said Secretary of State Dean Rusk.

Khrushchev offered to withdraw rockets from Cuba if the U.S. would pledge not to invade the island and to remove its rockets from Turkey. Kennedy, combining firmness with diplomacy, accepted the first proposal and ignored the second, and Khrushchev accepted this offer of an escape route. After 13 days, the crisis was over, with the Soviets backing down.

Kennedy emerged with his prestige unassailable. He had shown he could keep his nerve in a game of Russian roulette for global stakes against the toughest of opponents. Khrushchev never recovered. Soviet hardliners accused him of "adventurism" and were soon to unseat him.

The Wall goes up
Kennedy had already shown signs of his nerve and increasing diplomatic skill in dealing with a crisis in the middle of Europe. In East Germany, the Iron Curtain consisted of an 850 mile-long strip of minefields and barbed wire entanglements, with one vital area left unguarded—Berlin. There, it was

EVIDENCE UNVEILED One of a number of photos released by the Pentagon, showing the build-up of missiles in Cuba before Kennedy called a halt.

BERLIN'S ORDEAL BEGINS Moments of danger and drama as barricades go up in Berlin. Left: Soviet and American tanks square off across a checkpoint. After 17 hours the Soviets backed away. Above: An East Berlin border guard leaps to freedom before barbed wire is replaced by a solid wall.

At one stage, Soviet and American tanks faced each other, gun barrel to gun barrel. Khrushchev knew there was an element of bluff on both sides. "We assumed that the West didn't want to start a war, and our assumption turned out to be correct," he recalled later. "Starting a war over Berlin would have been stupid."

As the barriers were going up, some East Berliners walked out through gaps in the wire, and others swam across a canal to freedom. Later escapers dug tunnels. One man was hoisted over the wall by a crane. Many died in the minefields or in the sights of Vopos' rifles. Khrushchev saw such tragedies in his own way: "There were illegal attempts to cross over to the West, resulting in some incidents along the border, some of them with unpleasant outcomes."

The Berlin Wall came to be a symbol of the Cold War. It separated workers from their jobs, parents from their children. When President Kennedy visited West Berlin in June 1963, he declared: "There are many people in the world who don't understand, or say they don't, what is the great issue between the free world and the communist world . . . Let them come to Berlin." To rapturous cheering he added: "All free men, wherever they live, are citizens of Berlin, and therefore, as a free man, I take pride in the words 'Ich bin ein Berliner.'"

possible to move from East to West simply by walking from one sector to another, or by catching the subway. Among the 3 million East German refugees who had fled to the West by 1961 were hundreds of thousands who used the Berlin escape route.

Khrushchev vowed to "remove this splinter from the heart of Europe," and in June 1961, at a summit meeting with Kennedy in Vienna, gave an ultimatum: no general peace treaty had been signed with Germany, but the U.S.S.R. was prepared to sign a separate treaty with Walter Ulbricht's East Germany—so removing any justification for Western garrisons to remain in Berlin.

In August 1961, passage between East and West Berlin was blocked by barricades and barbed wire. As the barriers went up, Ed Morrow, head of the U.S. Information Agency, noted that Khrushchev had "in the vernacular of our Western movies, told us to 'get out of town by noon tomorrow.'"

The wire was soon replaced by walls of brick and concrete, 13 feet high, overlooked by watchtowers, protected by minefields and more barbed wire, and patrolled by armed "Vopos" (*Volkspolizisten*, Ulbricht's security police) and fierce dogs.

The Western powers issued official protests and reinforced their Berlin garrisons.

A GALLERY OF TRAITORS

Greed, blackmail, revenge, bravado, misplaced idealism—the men and women who betrayed their country during the Cold War had many different motives.

Dr. Allan Nunn May was involved in nuclear research in Britain and Canada and claimed to have been motivated by the idea that scientific discoveries should be shared because they belong to the world. "I certainly did not do it for gain," he said when he was arrested in 1946. He was sentenced to ten years in prison.

John Vassall, secretary to Britain's naval attaché in Moscow, was a homosexual who was blackmailed with compromising photographs. "The Russians are not likely to take volunteers for this work," he wrote after his arrest. "They much prefer people under stress, because they can be controlled." He was sentenced to 18 years but released after ten.

Klaus Fuchs, a naturalized Briton who worked on the atomic bomb, was a communist who believed the world would be safer if the U.S.S.R. as well as the U.S. knew the secrets of the atomic bomb. Arrested in February 1950, a few months after the Soviets exploded their first atomic bomb, he confessed that he had been passing nuclear information to them. After release from prison in 1959, he went to East Germany.

Fuchs' arrest led to the arrests in 1950 of Julius and Ethel Rosenberg. An American couple who had been members of the Communist Party, they were accused of operating in and recruiting for a Soviet spy ring. After a month-long trial, they were both sentenced to death. The judge, Irving Kaufman, called their crime "worse than murder." After two years of appeals and public protests, the Rosenbergs were executed in 1953. They became the only Americans to be executed in peacetime for espionage.

In Great Britain, a famous band of spies was recruited at Cambridge in the 1930s. Diplomats Guy Burgess and Donald Maclean caused a sensation in 1951 when they disappeared. Both had served in the Washington Embassy, where Maclean had access to nuclear research findings. On the point of being arrested as spies, they were apparently tipped off by a mysterious "third man" and fled to Russia.

This "third man" was Harold "Kim" Philby, a Foreign Office colleague of the diplomats who had also been at Cambridge in the 1930s. He had become head of communist counter-espionage in British Intelligence and had served in Washington with the CIA. He fell under suspicion and was asked to resign in 1951. He vigorously denied the accusations until 1963, when he fled to Moscow. There he was made a KGB colonel in recognition of his services, which included betraying the names of many Western agents.

A fourth member of the Cambridge band of traitors, Sir Anthony Blunt, was investigated after Philby's defection and, in return for immunity from prosecution, admitted that he had worked for the KGB as a talent-spotter among the undergraduates. He was allowed at the time to keep his post as art adviser to the Queen, but was later dismissed and stripped of his title.

IN THE HANDS OF THE STATE A deputy marshal (center) leads Ethel and Julius Rosenberg into court. Evidence in the ensuing decades has indicated that, while Julius was indeed a Soviet spy, Ethel was most likely innocent.

TO RUSSIA WITH HASTE Guy Burgess (left) and Donald Maclean, who fled to the U.S.S.R. on a tip-off that they were under suspicion.

Relations between the capitalist and communist worlds were not marked exclusively by conflict. The very fact that each had the capacity to obliterate vast regions of the other by nuclear attack gave an urgency to the search for peace. Nikita Khrushchev began to talk of "peaceful coexistence" as early as 1955, at a summit conference with President Eisenhower in Geneva.

Khrushchev visited the United States in September 1959 with his wife, Nina Petrovna. During the visit, the Soviet leader agreed with Eisenhower on the need for the two men to hold another summit conference. It was scheduled for May 1960, in Paris. But it was never held.

On May 1 a high-altitude American U-2 spy plane was shot down over Sverdlovsk, 1,200 miles inside the Soviet borders. Its pilot, Francis Gary Powers, admitted that he had been on a spy mission, photographing Soviet military installations. Khrushchev accused the U.S. of piracy and angrily called off the summit. Powers was sentenced to ten years' imprisonment, but was later exchanged for a convicted Soviet spy, Colonel Rudolf Abel.

Despite all the setbacks, the search for coexistence continued. After their "eyeball to eyeball" confrontation in Cuba, when the U.S. forced the U.S.S.R. to dismantle missile bases, both countries realized how close they had come to the brink. One of the positive results that came out of the 1962 Cuba crisis was the establishment of a "hot line" between Moscow and Washington; another was a nuclear test-ban treaty.

The telephone link meant that in any future crisis the leaders of the superpowers could talk to each other and try to reach an understanding. The treaty, signed in 1963 by the U.S., the U.S.S.R. and Britain, and ultimately by 102 countries, banned nuclear tests in the atmosphere, in space and at sea. China and France refused to sign.

In 1968 came a Non-Proliferation Treaty, designed to prevent the spread of nuclear weapons to other nations. The following year, at Helsinki, President Johnson and the Soviet leader Leonid Brezhnev began Strategic Arms Limitation Talks (SALT) on reducing the number of weapons in their own nuclear armories. It was beginning to look as if Winston Churchill might have been right when he predicted that safety would be "the sturdy child of terror."

IN THE VIETNAM QUICKSANDS

AMERICA WAS SUCKED INTO WAR BY THE "DOMINO" THEORY: IF VIETNAM WENT COMMUNIST, THE REST OF SOUTHEAST ASIA WOULD FOLLOW

In April 1954, President Eisenhower spelled out the theory that was eventually to draw America into the Vietnam War: "You have a row of dominoes set up. You knock over the first one, and what will happen to the last one is a certainty—that it will go over very quickly."

According to the domino theory, the fate of Southeast Asia depended on the fate of Vietnam, a country soon to be divided along the 17th parallel by the Geneva Agreements that followed the French defeat at Dien Bien Phu. The northern half would be under communist control and the southern half under communist threat.

With the Korean war fresh in his mind, Eisenhower moved cautiously in Vietnam. He refused to send combat troops to prop up the anti-communist regime in the South, and limited U.S. help to sending supplies and around 1,000 military advisers. The regime Eisenhower backed was led by Ngo

UNCLE HO DEFIES UNCLE SAM A wartime poster of Ho Chi Minh. In reality a frail figure, he led North Vietnam with iron determination, calling for all-out sacrifice from the people.

Dinh Diem, appointed prime minister by the playboy emperor Bao Dai. While a student in an American seminary during the early 1950s, Diem had made a good impression on such influential fellow Catholics as the young John F. Kennedy. He was also, as it turned out, a tyrant, with no qualms when it came to jailing or executing his opponents.

Diem's authority was questioned from the start. His troops had to fight off a challenge from private armies controlled by his rivals. When Bao Dai, in Paris, made a feeble attempt to intervene, Diem abolished the monarchy in a rigged referendum and declared himself president. In the North, Ho Chi Minh pushed through a land reform which, though brutal against those accused of being landlords, at least gave land to the peasants. In the South, there were two million landless peasants in the Mekong Delta alone, and Diem held out no hope of reform.

Diem ran the country through cronies and through his immediate family, especially his brother, Nhu, and his sister-in-law,

DIVIDED LAND The era of French colonialism in Vietnam ended in 1954, when the country was divided along the 17th parallel into a communist North and a pro-Western South. America began by propping up the South, and ended by inheriting France's problems.

Mme. Nhu. She made the regime even more unpopular by abolishing divorce, making adultery and contraceptives illegal, closing nightclubs and banning beauty contests.

Diem's downfall

Free elections had been promised at Geneva as a first step toward reuniting the country, but Diem was afraid he would lose. He found excuses to avoid elections, and the U.S. accepted them. The communists in the South, the Vietcong, responded by murdering hundreds of government officials, and Ho Chi Minh, in the North, gave them his backing by announcing the formation of the National Liberation Front (NLF).

Faced with a mounting Vietcong threat, the U.S. steadily built up its presence. Eisenhower's 1,000 advisers grew to nearly 17,000 during the Kennedy presidency. In May 1962, the American advisers were joined in South Vietnam by a small Australian force of army instructors.

The line between adviser and combatant, which seemed sharp enough when explained to the U.S. public, became a hazy, easily crossed line in a world of bombings, ambushes and assassina-

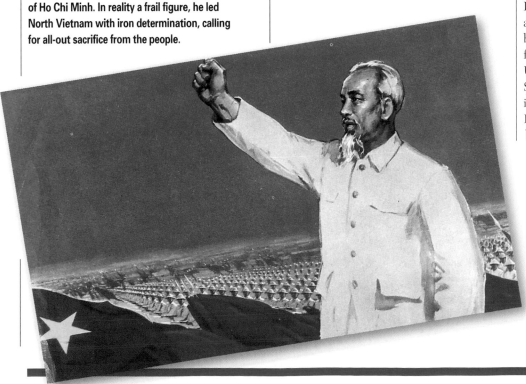

HIT-AND-RUN RAIDERS South Vietnamese infantry boarding U.S. "choppers" which will fly them to "zap" an area said to have been infiltrated by Vietcong guerrillas.

tions. As against the French, the communists used hit-and-run tactics, melting away into the countryside after a strike. Kennedy backed Diem's policy of "strategic hamlets"—clearing peasants from their villages and resettling them behind moats and stockades. In South Vietnam, peasants could not understand why they were being uprooted while their rice rotted in the paddy fields. Pham Van Dong, prime minister in the North, called the hamlets "camouflaged concentration camps."

Of all Diem's blunders, none was more

FUTURE UNCERTAIN Bandaged and barefooted, a U.S. airman who was shot down is marched at gunpoint through the streets of Hanoi.

catastrophic than his treatment of the Buddhists. Antagonism between Catholics and Buddhists was traditional in Vietnam, and it reached new heights when some 900,000 Catholics fled to the South after the country was divided. On May 8, 1963, government troops opened fire on a Buddhist demonstration in the old capital of Hué, killing eight people.

What Diem regarded as a private quarrel was thrust before the eyes of the entire world when a 66-year-old Buddhist monk, Thich Quang Doc, sat down in the lotus position in the middle of a busy Saigon crossroads, while fellow monks doused him with gas and set him on fire. An American photographer, Malcolm Browne, wired a picture of the horrific scene to newspapers and magazines around the world.

Diem was becoming an embarrassment to America. With the encouragement of the CIA, a group of his own generals ousted him on October 4, 1963. The coup revealed the limitations of America's position: it could influence events but not con-

COUNTING CORPSES

The American military in Vietnam relied heavily on the techniques of modern management, which lays great emphasis on measuring performance. In a war with no front line, results could not be assessed in terms of territory gained; instead, the U.S. army used "body count." The term sounded statistical and objective, but in fact body counts could be highly misleading, as they could be faked, bringing rewards in the form of bigger steaks or extra Rest and Recreation. Even General Westmoreland admitted that the counts were "somewhat overdone." Corporal Matt Martin recalls:

"The more regular you were, regular Marine, regular army, the higher the body count was. We had a colonel call, and he was all excited, and he said, 'What's the body count, what's the body count?' because we had called in a lot of heavy artillery, and we were really putting the job on this one village. So he wanted a real heavy body count. Well this second Louie we had with us—he'd come up through the ranks—and he yelled, 'Over 300.' So then the radio man said, 'You can't give them an even number. They're not going to go for an even number.' So he said, 'Well, okay, 311.' Three hundred eleven flat out deaths, sure kills. Well this officer loved it. He started yelling, 'Great, great, you did a great job.'"

trol them. For the plotters went too far, killing both Diem and Nhu.

Lyndon B. Johnson, sworn in as president after the assassination of President Kennedy, faced an early test in Vietnam. In August 1964, relying on reports (later questioned) that two American destroyers in the Gulf of

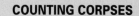

1954 Geneva Conference partitions Vietnam along 17th parallel   1955 Ngo Dinh Diem becomes South Vietnam's chief of state

Tonkin had been attacked by North Vietnamese torpedo boats, Johnson asked Congress for authority "to repel any armed attack against the forces of the United States." The Gulf of Tonkin Resolution, moved by Senator Fulbright, gave him men, weapons and supplies—and authorization to bomb the North. America was now engaged in a full-scale, if undeclared, war.

Pounding the North

Operation "Rolling Thunder" began on March 2, 1965, when 100 American aircraft hit an ammunition depot in North Vietnam. The strategic aim was to destroy communications and supply depots, and to smash Hanoi's will to continue fighting. In this it failed. In less than three years, 1.5 million tons of bombs fell on North Vietnam, yet North Vietnam's war production was protected from American bombs because it was located in China and the U.S.S.R.

Johnson insisted he had no wish to "supply American boys to do the job that Asian boys could do," but replacing Diem with a stable government that had the support of the people was proving impossible. Six prime ministers came and went as coup followed coup. A final coup, in June 1965, brought to power General Nguyen Van Thieu as chief of state and Air Vice Marshal Nguyen Cao Ky, a former pilot, as prime minister. Ky, a high-living gambler, woman-chaser and dandy, once told a journalist that the person he most admired was Hitler and added, "We need four or five Hitlers in Vietnam."

Despite Johnson's belief that the South Vietnamese should fight their own war, American boys were sent to help them in ever greater numbers. By the end of 1965 there were 184,000 U.S. troops in Vietnam, and by the middle of 1968 the number stood at 538,000. Australia, too, had been drawn into combat and had 8,000 troops on the ground by 1968. The Army of the Republic of Vietnam (ARVN, or "Arvins") was 750,000 strong, but contained enough reluctant recruits and enough corrupt officers to diminish its value as a fighting force. Desertion reached levels of one man in five. Ranged against these combined forces were 450,000 Vietcong and 70,000 North Vietnamese, supplied down the Ho Chi Minh Trail, a network of roads and tracks through neighboring Laos and Cambodia.

"HELL NO—WE WON'T GO!"

The anti-war protest movement in America had its roots both in the college campuses and in the civil rights campaign of the Sixties. Blacks, like poor and working-class whites, could not generally gain exemption from the draft by pleading it would interrupt a college education; and they were being killed in disproportionate numbers in the jungles of Vietnam. By mid-1965, blacks in Mississippi were urging blacks across the country to ignore the draft and refuse to fight in a "white man's war."

Martin Luther King, Jr., took up the cause in 1967 when he told a congregation at New York's Riverside Church: "Somehow this madness must cease. We must stop now . . . I speak for those whose land is being laid waste, whose homes are being destroyed, whose culture is being subverted." In the same year, another black hero, world heavyweight champion Muhammad Ali, was stripped of his title after rejecting the draft on religious grounds. "I ain't got nothing against them Vietcong," he proclaimed.

On the campuses, the protest movement found its most intense support in the prestigious colleges and universities. Students burned draft cards in public, with the defiant slogan: "Hell No—We Won't Go!" Burning or ignoring a draft card could mean up to four years in prison, and by the end of 1969, nearly 40,000 young men had been prosecuted and more than 3,000 jailed. Thousands escaped the draft by fleeing to Canada, Sweden, Mexico, and other countries.

The protest found support among a handful of politicians. Senator Fulbright, a "hawk" in 1964 when he introduced the Gulf of Tonkin Resolution, giving President Johnson authority to escalate the war, was calling it "unnecessary and immoral" by 1967. Senator Eugene McCarthy announced, in November 1967, that he would run on an anti-war platform in the Democratic primaries to choose a candidate for the next presidential election. McCarthy's campaign was to lead to a bloody confrontation at the 1968 Democratic convention in Chicago. Mayor Richard Daley turned loose a force of 12,000 police, backed by 5,000 National Guard, with 6,000 federal troops in reserve, on anti-war activists estimated at between 6,000 and 10,000. They were beaten with fists and clubs and assaulted with tear gas. The unequal battle lasted for five days, and in one single incident, 800 protesters were injured.

Opinion polls showed that what President Nixon was to call the "Silent Majority" supported government policy in Vietnam. But the minority against the war was sizable and growing. On "Moratorium Day," October 15, 1969, an estimated 2 million protesters took to the streets. In Washington, a crowd of 250,000 marched past the White House. Their voices were to sway a nation.

PENTAGON PROTEST An angry confrontation during an anti-war protest at the Pentagon in October 1967.

1960 Hanoi forms National Liberation Front—the Vietcong

1961 Kennedy sends Diem more advisers and steps up aid

1963 Diem overthrown and killed

1964 Tonkin Gulf incident; President Johnson given authority to hit back

1965 Sustained bombing of North Vietnam begins with Operation Rolling Thunder

1967 100,000 anti-war demonstrators at the Pentagon

1968 Vietcong launch Tet offensive

1969 U.S. begins secret bombing of Cambodia; Ho Chi Minh dies; My Lai massacre revealed

MASSACRE AT MY LAI

Originally, "search and destroy" missions by American troops in Vietnam meant tracking down Vietcong units in the jungle or in elephant grass—or forcing guerrillas out of hideouts in a honeycomb of underground tunnels. Since the Vietcong often moved among the peasants, where they were hard to identify, the term came to mean moving into a village with flamethrowers and automatic weapons. On March 16, 1968, a 30-man platoon from Charlie Company, 1st Battalion, 20th Infantry of the Americal Division, led by Lt. William Calley, went on such a mission to the hamlet of My Lai. The Company commander, Captain Ernest Medina, had been told that some 250 men of the Vietcong's 48th Battalion were in the area. He said in evidence later that he had also been told that My Lai's women and children would be away at a market when the attack came.

WHISTLE-BLOWER U.S. helicopter pilot Hugh Thompson, who helped reveal the story of the My Lai massacre, preparing to give evidence to an official inquiry.

Set down near the hamlet from helicopter gunships, Calley's platoon was edgy because just three weeks earlier some of their buddies from another platoon had wandered into a minefield and been blown to pieces. They moved in with weapons locked on automatic fire, lobbing grenades into hootches, or thatched huts, as they passed. One GI, who shot himself in the foot rather than take part, recalled: "People began coming out of their hootches and the guys shot them and burned the hootches—or burned the hootches and shot the people when they came out. Sometimes they would round up a bunch and shoot them together . . . Some of the guys seemed to be having a lot of fun. They were wisecracking and shouting, 'Chalk that one up for me!'"

Women and girls were raped. Some villagers were stabbed. Others were thrown down a well, with a grenade thrown in after them. Warrant officer Hugh C. Thompson saw the carnage from an observation helicopter, and put down in My Lai to try to stop it. He managed to save the lives of 16 children by threatening to open fire on Calley's men, and was later awarded the Distinguished Flying Cross.

Estimates of the number killed at My Lai range from around 100 to 700. It took more than a year before the facts were revealed to the American people. Calley was court-martialed, found guilty of murder and sentenced to life imprisonment. He served only three days in jail before being put under house arrest, pending appeals, and was later paroled by President Nixon.

General William Westmoreland, who became commander of the American forces in August 1964, attempted to defeat the guerrillas by superior military technology. Success in his war of attrition was measured by the "body count."

Flesh-burning napalm rained down on the Vietcong and on any peasants unlucky enough to be in the way. The defoliant Agent Orange stripped the jungle of its cover, and helicopters were used to land troops, evacuate wounded or as flying platforms from which to machine-gun the enemy. Whatever firepower they faced, however, the communist forces increased—leading to constant demands from Westmoreland for more men.

For America, this was a war fought by teenagers—the average age of draftees in Vietnam was 19. As is common in warfare, the very language was drafted into uniform. Killing human beings became "wasting gooks" or "zapping Charlie Cong." If civilian targets were hit by mistake, they counted as "collateral damage."

Out on patrol, the GIs fought bravely, but back at base, pilfering and corruption were rife. Drug-taking—marijuana, opium and heroin—took a hold among young men who were bored much of the time and close to death all of the time. Morale sank so low that unpopular officers were liable to be "fragged"—blown up with fragmentation grenades by their own troops. It was hard for both troops and peasants to reconcile Westmoreland's "Hearts and Minds" campaign with "Search and Destroy" missions. One sought to improve the quality of village life, while the other devastated villages that were suspected of concealing Vietcong.

By 1967, some U.S. leaders were beginning to realize they were in a war they could not win. On May 19, Defense Secretary Robert McNamara sent a memo to his president: "There may be a limit beyond which many Americans and much of the world will not permit the United States to go. The picture of the world's greatest superpower killing or seriously injuring 1,000 noncombatants a week, while trying to pound a tiny, backward nation into submission on an issue whose merits are hotly disputed is not a pretty one."

In January 1968, the Vietcong launched their Tet (New Year) offensive. They raided 39 provincial capitals, held the old capital of Hué for several weeks, and even fought their way into the U.S. embassy compound in Saigon. American troops threw them back, inflicting heavy casualties. A major who took part in the recapture of Ben Tré summed up America's dilemma in a war of high technology against guerrillas: "It became necessary to destroy the town to save it." General Westmoreland declared after Tet that the enemy was "on the ropes," then asked for another 206,000 U.S. troops to end the war. In propaganda terms, however, Tet was a Vietcong success: it showed they could still surprise the Americans.

SPIRIT OF THE VIETCONG "Better death than slavery" reads the message on this North Vietnamese poster, showing the people rising against U.S. forces.

越南必胜！美国必败！

RESCUE SERVICE A chopper rescues wounded marines from a hill near Khe Sanh—one of many tasks for U.S. helicopters in Vietnam.

Johnson had long decided that the war was "dirty, brutal and difficult." Now, it was costing more than $20 billion a year. American boys were being shipped home in body bags at a rate of more than 200 a week. Anti-war protesters were chanting, "Hey, Hey, LBJ! How many kids did you kill today?" There was no sign of a crack in Ho Chi Minh's endurance. On March 31, 1968, Johnson made a dramatic announcement: he would not run for re-election as president.

Richard Nixon, winner of the election in November 1968, was desperate to find a way out of the morass. He appointed as his adviser of national security a brilliant professor at Harvard, German-born Henry Kissinger, but the two men had an uneasy relationship. "I don't trust Henry, but I can use him," boasted Nixon. "The man is, of course, a disaster," was Kissinger's view: "That man is unfit to be president."

Both men were ego-driven and conspiratorial in style—so much so, in Nixon's case, that he proposed a massive nuclear bluff, his "madman" theory. He told his aide, H.R. Haldemann: "We'll just slip word to them that, 'for God's sakes, you know, Nixon is obsessed about communists. We can't restrain him when he's angry, and he has his hand on the nuclear button'—and Ho Chi Minh will be in Paris in two days, begging for peace."

Ho's conditions for peace were the same to Nixon as they had been to Johnson: an immediate and permanent end to bombing in the North, the complete withdrawal of American troops from Vietnam, and the presence of both North Vietnam and the Vietcong at any peace talks.

Nixon and Kissinger tried to "Vietnamize" the war by building up the fighting strength of the South, and to break Hanoi's resolve by stepping up the bombing. "I can't believe that a fourth rate power like North Vietnam doesn't have a breaking point," Kissinger told an aide. When no breaking point was found, he and Nixon ordered bombing sorties against North Vietnamese sanctuaries in neutral Cambodia. They tried to keep this bombing a secret from the American people.

By the end of 1968, the balance sheet of the war was not an impressive one. In the confident days of 1965, President Johnson had said, "We will not be defeated. We will not grow tired. We will not withdraw." But it was the North Vietnamese and the Vietcong, with what seemed an infinite capacity for absorbing punishment, who were living up to those brave words.

America had mistaken a nationalist revolution for a global communist conspiracy, and had lost more than 58,000 men dead, with another 153,000 wounded. Vietnam, both North and South, lay devastated.

RED DAWN IN THE EAST

THE LIVES OF MILLIONS OF PEOPLE WERE TRANSFORMED, RUINED OR ENDED BECAUSE OF ONE MAN'S VISION OF HUMAN HAPPINESS

An immense task faced Mao Zedong after his victory over Chiang Kai-shek's Guomindang forces in 1949: it was to revolutionize China's social and economic infrastructure in less than a generation. He knew the price that China had paid for economic and political weakness in the past 200 years: humiliating trade treaties and the loss of ports and territory to "foreign devils" from Britain, Russia, Germany and Japan. Famine was an even older enemy than imperialism, and China had the world's largest population to feed. From some 535 million in 1949, it would rise to 680 million in 1960, and 840 million in 1970—an average increase of nearly 40,000 a day. The fate of these millions was held in the hands of one of the most ruthless social visionaries of the 20th century, a man who enjoyed the excitement and drama of revolution.

After the chaos of war and civil war, China needed a strong central government. Mao called a conference of communist delegates at Beijing to organize elections for a National People's Congress. It met for the first time in 1954, and Mao was elected chairman, with Zhou Enlai as prime minister. But the Congress was no more than a front. Real power rested with the Communist Party and its governing Politburo, with Chairman Mao at the head.

Party membership grew steadily, reaching around 10 million by 1955. It carried privileges, even in a country committed to a classless society. There were 26 grades in the party, and the grade determined the standard of perks. Only Grades 13 and above could stay in a hotel room with a private bath, and traveling by plane was reserved to Grade 14 and above.

The country's rulers faced a host of problems. Inflation was rampant, industry primitive, agriculture barely at subsistence level, irrigation systems devastated, railways destroyed, canals blocked and dikes breached. The U.S.S.R. helped with loans, equipment and advisers. Under a Treaty of Friendship, signed in 1950, the Soviets gave credits that helped to build well over 100 industrial plants and projects, and sent technical advisers to show the Chinese how to run them.

Creating a new society

The new regime's social measures began to transform Chinese society. Education became open to all children and, in a land where concubinage, child marriage, female infanticide and foot-binding were well within living memory, women were given the vote. With emancipation came the right to own land and property, and equal rights with men to apply for divorce.

A major step in Mao's revolution was the Land Reform Law of 1950, which gave land to China's 300 million poor peasants. This meant taking it away from the landlords—a violent process in which an entire class was eliminated. At least 2 million landlords, supporters of Chiang Kai-shek and "rich" peasants—those owning more than about 30 acres—were denounced and killed.

SOMBER IN VICTORY Fresh from the defeat of Chiang Kai-shek's Nationalists, Mao Zedong proclaims the birth of the Chinese People's Republic.

1949 Mao Zedong proclaims People's Republic of China, after communist victory

1950 Chinese "volunteers" enter Korean War; China invades Tibet

1953 Armistice in Korea

1954 National People's Congress elects Mao chairman and Zhou Enlai prime minister

1957 "Hundred flowers" campaign

GENDER REVOLUTION   Women on a collective farm in Szechuan learn to use a new plough. The revolution put women on an equal footing with men, after centuries of oppression.

The nation was bullied into conformity. The "Three Antis" campaign of August 1951 was directed at corrupt officials. It denounced corruption, waste and inefficiency, and by the time it ended, a year later, 10 percent of the party membership had been expelled. The "Five Antis" campaign that followed was aimed at private profit. It attacked bribery, tax evasion, fraud, theft of State property and the betrayal of economic secrets.

Intellectuals, businessmen and professionals were brought into line by "Thought Reform," seen in the West as thought control. It involved being dragged before public meetings to offer self-criticism and confessions. In a break from Chinese tradition, children were forced to denounce their fathers. What Mao sought from his people was not just acquiescence but enthusiasm.

Just as China's emperors had needed their mandarins and scribes to run the country, so Mao needed his Communist Party cadres—

politically trained "shock troops"—to organize and energize the masses. At the same time, he needed experienced managers, bureaucrats and technicians. Mao's attempt to retain the loyalty of both groups helps to explain a series of what would otherwise appear to be a bewildering and irrational succession of lurches in policy.

Under a second Land Reform Law in 1952, communist cadres went out into the countryside to persuade peasants to combine in collectives of 100 to 300 families, pooling their labor, investing in new farm machinery and then sharing the profits. Families would still be allowed to keep a small private plot for growing vegetables and raising a few animals. Within two

GRASSROOTS REFORM   This propaganda woodcut shows a tangible benefit of the communist revolution—a new ox for the communal farm.

years, almost 200 million peasants belonged to such cooperative ventures. Even so, progress was not fast enough for Mao. "Some of our comrades are tottering along like a woman with bound feet," he complained. What he wanted for the revolution in the countryside was "More, faster, better and more economically."

Following the Soviet model, Mao embarked

1958 "Great Leap Forward," followed by famine

1960 Break with U.S.S.R.: Soviets withdraw advisers

1962 Border war with India

1964 China tests its first atomic bomb

1966 Cultural Revolution begins

1967 China explodes H-bomb

REPORTING TO THE CHAIRMAN
This idealized view of the new China shows workers submitting their production report to Mao Zedong.

in 1953 on a five-year plan to transform China's industry. Banks and other businesses were nationalized, and firms owned by foreigners were seized. Workers found they were expected to put in longer hours with no extra pay, but those who grumbled were shamed, along with persistent absentees, at self-criticism sessions.

While China had admittedly started from a low base, the results of the five-year plan were impressive: an industrial growth rate of more than 11 percent a year. Output doubled in the coal, oil and electricity industries. Steel production, which had been around 150,000 tons a year when Mao took over, was more than 5 million tons a year by 1957. By this time, however, the party cadres were coming under criticism from managers and technicians for their incompetence, while the cadres were accusing the professionals of a deficiency in revolutionary fervor. Mao's response was the "Hundred Flowers" campaign. Ordinary citizens were invited to point out faults in the regime. "Let a hundred flowers bloom and a hundred schools of thought contend," proclaimed Mao.

The campaign opened a Pandora's box. Some critics questioned whether socialism was the right basis for building the new China. Others called for the release of imprisoned intellectuals. Mao himself was accused of being "impetuous in making decisions without first making a careful study of the facts." It was even suggested that Chiang Kai-shek should be brought back. Mao abruptly ended the campaign and claimed that its deliberate aim had been to "entice snakes out of their lairs."

The Great Leap Forward

Following Nikita Khrushchev's denunciation of Stalin in 1956, relations between China and the U.S.S.R. became increasingly strained. Mao believed that Khrushchev had turned away from Marxist-Leninism, and that Soviet-style five-year plans no longer suited China. Impatient to push on with the revolution, he introduced in 1958 what was

MARCHING AS TO WAR Shouldering their farm implements like weapons, smiling women step out briskly for an afternoon of heavy work in the fields. In China, womanpower was as important as manpower.

to prove a shattering social experiment—the Great Leap Forward. Mao set a target of a 30 percent increase in industrial output, year after year, and pledged that China would surpass Britain in 15 years.

"WE SHALL CREATE A NEW HEAVEN AND EARTH FOR MAN," proclaimed one slogan. In practice, this meant the society of the anthill. Almost every aspect of daily life was brought under control, through elected communes. Half a billion peasants were regrouped from their 750,000 collective farms into 24,000 communes, each with its own schools, libraries and dormitories. Women were mobilized, so child care centers had to be set up in the communes. Private plots of land vanished, along with eating in private.

The Great Leap relied on China's greatest national asset, its manpower. Swarms of laborers, the "blue ants," equipped with little more than shovels and enthusiasm, were set to work digging canals, building roads, dams, reservoirs and irrigation systems. In industry, Mao decreed that the emphasis should switch from large-scale to small-scale production. He called for 600,000 "backyard furnaces" to produce iron and steel, farm machinery and spare parts. Patriotic music played through amplifiers as volunteers threw woks, bedsteads, railings, anything made of iron into their makeshift furnaces.

The Great Leap was a great disaster. The communist cadres sent out to direct the work of peasants proved to be incompetent. Many of the great earth-moving projects started by the "blue ants" were left half finished. Matters were not helped by droughts and floods that brought a run of bad harvests in 1959-61. Grain production in 1958 fell one-third below the forecast of 375 million tons, and by 1962 it was down to 175 million tons. Millions starved. Food rationing was re-introduced, and China had to import grain from Canada and Australia.

Industrial forecasts produced under pressure turned out to be unachievable. The "backyard" steel was of poor quality. Mao had to acknowledge failure. "I knew nothing about industrial planning," he confessed. "It is I who am to blame." He was quick, though, to point out that Marx and Lenin, in their time, had made mistakes. Mao resigned as Chairman of the People's Congress and was replaced by Liu Shao-chi, the party's expert on structure and organization.

CULTURAL GENOCIDE IN TIBET

To the Chinese, Tibet was a land of "three lacks and three abundances." The "lacks" were fuel, communications and people, and the "abundances" poverty, oppression and fear of the supernatural. They regarded Tibet as an integral, if backward, part of their motherland. But the Tibetans saw themselves as a separate nation with their own language and culture. Moreover, unlike the communist Chinese, Tibetans were intensely religious. Their mountainous country, inspiration for the legendary Shangri-la, was a Buddhist theocracy, ruled by a line of Dalai Lamas, each believed to be the reincarnation of his predecessors. It was a feudal land in which serfs could not even marry without permission from their lord.

In October 1950, Mao Zedong sent his People's Liberation Army across the border, to free Tibet from feudalism and to make its borders secure. Tibet's army could offer little more than token resistance. In any case, the Chinese were under orders: "You cannot take even one needle from the masses," and "You may not beat or scold people." The reality was to prove different. Ten years after the invasion, an International Commission of Jurists ruled that what was happening in Tibet amounted to cultural genocide.

The Chinese gave Tibet roads, telephones, banks, newspapers and hospitals. But they were wrenching an entire country out of the Middle Ages, against the wishes of many of its inhabitants. Landlords, aristocrats and other "enemies of the people" could be hauled before a *thamzing*, or public struggle session, to be humiliated, beaten, or even killed. In an attempt to break the hold of religion, Buddhist monks and nuns were forced to break their vows of celibacy in public. Some Tibetans formed guerrilla bands and fought back. When one such group took refuge in the monastery of Lithang, in western Tibet, Chinese planes bombed the monastery. The Dalai Lama's official protest was ignored.

In March 1959, alarmed by rumors that the Chinese planned to kidnap the Dalai Lama, citizens and pilgrims in Lhasa rose in revolt. They were defeated by tanks, machine guns and artillery, but the Dalai Lama escaped in the confusion, and made his way to safety and exile in India. There followed a systematic destruction of monasteries. The Chinese forced the peasants into collectives, and in place of the Dalai Lama they installed the Panchen Lama, the second highest spiritual authority in the land. For a time he proved docile, but in 1962 he sent a long protest note to Mao Zedong, and in 1964 he ended a public speech with the words: "Long live His Holiness, the Dalai Lama." This was enough to have him beaten, put on trial for planning a revolt, and sent to China.

In 1966, the Cultural Revolution spilled over from China into Tibet. Red Guards banned traditional songs and dances, destroyed shrines and religious monuments, and tore down prayer flags. Their manifesto declared: "We, a group of lawless revolutionary rebels, will wield the iron sweepers and swing the mighty cudgels to sweep the old world into a mess and bash people into complete confusion." It was a fairly accurate description of the Chinese impact on Tibet.

DIGNIFIED IN DEFEAT Tibetans lay down their arms after defeat in 1959—but the Dalai Lama escaped.

ALWAYS TIME FOR MAO In a scene repeated all over China, workers at the Anshan industrial plant give up their rest period to listen to the thoughts of Mao.

Liu was one of a group inside the Politburo who took a more pragmatic view than Mao of the way the revolution should develop. Prominent among them were two veterans of the Long March—Deng Xiaoping and Prime Minister Zhou Enlai who, despite policy disagreements, remained personally loyal to Mao. They argued that managers needed incentives to make the economy work efficiently, and that the peasants should be allowed private plots of land. To Mao, this looked like an argument for the introduction of capitalism and the profit motive.

The Cultural Revolution

As a preliminary to yet another devastating social experiment, Mao chastised his opponents in the Politburo as "capitalist roaders"—followers of the capitalist way. His plan was to create a state of constant revolution by drawing on the energy of the masses, especially the young. First, the "Great Helmsman" had to re-establish his prestige. He decided to prove that, although in his 73rd year, he was still vigorous enough to be the nation's leader. On July 16, 1966, followed by the bobbing heads of his entourage, he plunged into the Yangtse river and swam downstream for 9 miles. The swim took him 65 minutes. The photograph was shown all over the world and, more important for Mao, all over China.

The Great Proletarian Cultural Revolution, a colossal drama that was played out with the whole of China as its stage, began with an attack on a drama written for the theater. *Hai Rui Dismissed from Office* told the story of an official wrongly dismissed by a Chinese emperor—a tale uncomfortably close to the way Mao had dismissed his defense minister, Peng Dehui, for being too outspoken a critic of the Great Leap. A Mao-inspired article in the Shanghai journal *Literary Currents* attacked the play viciously, and the Cultural Revolution was underway.

With the backing of the army, through Defense Minister Lin Piao, Mao mobilized millions of teenage students to tear down the existing order. Formed into battalions of "Red Guards," they attacked the "Four Olds"—old culture, old customs, old habits, old ways of thinking. Waving their "little red books," which contained quotations from Chairman Mao and had been published by the army, these youthful Red Guards marched through towns, villages and cities, destroying temples, wrecking libraries, burning books and overturning authority. Even chess sets were smashed, because chess was bourgeois.

REBELS WITH A CAUSE Young Red Guards in Beijing pledging support to the Cultural Revolution. Mao harnessed their youthful energy to browbeat his enemies.

人 民 战 争 胜 利 万 岁
REN MIN ZHAN ZHENG SHENG LI WAN SUI

帝国主义者如此欺负我们，这是需要认真对付的。我们不但要有强大的正规军，我们还要大办民兵师。这样，在帝国主义__时候，就会使他们寸步难行。

TWO FACES OF THE CULTURAL REVOLUTION
Two propaganda posters show the joy of those supporting Mao's Cultural Revolution (right) and the reception awaiting its enemies (above).

Giant wall posters appeared in the cities, especially Beijing, criticizing "revisionist" members of the Politburo, and the slogans were reinforced in newspaper headlines. Mao made millions of Red Guards wild with enthusiasm when he appeared before them at mass rallies. Professors and teachers, journalists and high party officials were made to kneel before them, wearing dunces' caps.

Mao's third wife, the former film actress Jiang Qing, encouraged the staging of new plays and operas on revolutionary themes. "Our operatic stage is occupied by emperors, princes, generals, ministers, scholars and beauties, and on top of these ghosts and monsters," she said, making a case for operas that portrayed peasants and soldiers. She had a particular dislike for the Beijing ballet and took the opportunity to dispatch dancers to the countryside, to be "re-educated" by backbreaking work. Zhou held on to his position but could do nothing to save fellow members of his Cabinet. Liu was expelled from the party and banished to Hunan Province. Deng was sent for "re-education" to a tractor factory in Nanchang.

With an undeclared civil war raging between Red Guards and party cadres, Red Guards and workers, even between different factions of Red Guards, tens of thousands of people were being killed. China seemed to be on the verge of returning to the days of rival warlords. Then Mao decided the Cultural Revolution had gone far enough. "Too many people were arrested because I nodded my head," he

" THOUGHTS OF CHINA'S CHAIRMAN MAO

Galvanizing a nation the size of China called for simple messages that could be understood by the masses. The "little red books" of quotations from Chairman Mao, brandished by Red Guards on their marches, became a potent symbol, even for peasants who could not read. Mao's thoughts were based on his own experiences and struggles:

"Those to be trusted are not the experts, but the innocents, the amateurs, the lowly, anyone who has a heart bent to the public weal."

"Exploiting contradictions is the way to obtain and hold on to power."

"Nothing is gained if change comes by mere fiat from above, without the stirring up of the masses, whose own enthusiasm gives life to the change."

"Struggle purifies; it is not just a way of getting what you want, but the holy sacrament of politics."

"Political power grows out of the barrel of a gun."

"All reactionaries are paper tigers."

"We are advocates of the abolition of war. We do not want war, but war can only be abolished through war, and in order to get rid of the gun it is necessary to take up the gun." "

admitted. He turned to Lin Piao and the Red Army to end it. Over-enthusiastic Red Guards found themselves sent for "re-educa-

WAITING FOR MAO Their classrooms abandoned, Red Guards assemble in Beijing, hoping for the merest glimpse of their leader.

FOUNT OF WISDOM Mao's thoughts purveyed in his *Little Red Book* .

tion" among the peasants. Mao ordered that those who continued to oppose the army were to be annihilated.

China and the outside world

With so much frenzied activity inside China, Mao Zedong's concerns in foreign affairs were for the most part limited to absorbing territories that he regarded as parts of the "motherland" and to preserving China's borders from attack. The first concern led to the invasion of Tibet in 1950, to a "roof of the world" border war with India in Ladakh in 1962, and to border skirmishes with the Soviet Union in Kazakhstan in the late 1960s.

The second led to China's intervention in the Korean War in 1950, when United Nations troops under General MacArthur came perilously close to China's frontier on the Yalu river. Despite helping Ho Chi Minh with munitions, supplies and advisers, Mao took care not to become involved in the Vietnam War by sending combat troops. Any "hawks" in the Politburo favoring direct intervention were purged.

Chiang Kai-shek and his Nationalist forces found refuge on the island of Formosa (Taiwan) after their defeat in 1949, and their presence there was an irritant. Mao shelled Nationalists on the islands of Quemoy and Matsu, which lie close to the mainland, but made no serious attempt to invade Formosa.

China's explosion of an atomic bomb in October 1964, followed by its first hydrogen bomb less than three years later, gave some security to the man who had once told the Finnish ambassador that, even if American atomic bombs blew the Earth to pieces, this would "still be an insignificant matter as far as the universe as a whole is concerned."

CHANGING TIMES

PARADOXICALLY, AS STANDARDS OF LIVING IMPROVED IN THE WESTERN WORLD, SO THE YOUNG FOUND MORE TO REBEL AGAINST. THROUGH THEIR MUSIC, CLOTHES AND EXPERIMENTS WITH DRUGS, THE YOUNGER GENERATION THREW DOWN A CHALLENGE TO THE OLD. THE KALEIDOSCOPIC CHANGES IMPACTING ON SOCIETY INCLUDED SEXUAL PERMISSIVENESS, FEMINISM, AND THE SPREAD OF TELEVISION, WHICH BY THE END OF THE 1970S REACHED ALMOST EVERY HOME.

THE YOUTH EXPLOSION

THE FIRST RUMBLINGS OF REBELLION WERE HEARD IN THE FIFTIES, BUT IT WAS IN THE "SWINGING SIXTIES" THAT YOUTH ERUPTED WITH FORCE

Teenagers were a discovery of the 1950s, and they were first sighted in America. One consequence of the country's postwar prosperity was that, for the first time in history, large numbers of adolescents had surplus money to spend. And with money of their own went minds of their own. Where America led, Britain, France, Germany, the Netherlands, Australia and other Western countries followed. The teenager was now destined to become a worldwide cultural and commercial phenomenon.

By comparison with the European countries, America had come through the war unscathed, so the idea of putting money aside for a rainy day had little appeal to teenagers there. The Depression of the Thirties was something that had happened to their parents, not to them. There were fashionable clothes and pop records to buy, youth and life to enjoy.

Two of the earliest role models were film actors—Marlon Brando and James Dean. The heroes they portrayed were moody, mumbling, tormented, tough—and rebellious. In the 1954 film *The Wild One*, Brando played the leather-jacketed leader of a motorcycle gang who terrorized a small town. Asked what he was rebelling against, the Brando character spoke for an entire generation with his reply: "Whadda ya got?"

James Dean was a legend made to order for alienated youngsters. "Live fast, die young and have a good-looking corpse" was one of their slogans. Dean, who made only three films, died at 24, when he drove his custom-built Porsche Spider too fast on a California highway, and crashed. *Rebel Without a Cause*, released three days later,

ICONS FOR A NEW GENERATION James Dean in New York (left), with the hunched and vulnerable style that teenagers tried to copy. Marlon Brando (below) gives rebellion a more macho look.

1955 Mary Quant opens Bazaar boutique in King's Road, Chelsea; James Dean killed in car crash

1956 Elvis Presley's first No. 1 hit, "Heartbreak Hotel"

contained a strangely prophetic sequence in which the character played by Dean takes on a rival in a game of "chicken," both revving their cars toward the edge of a cliff to see who would be the first to swerve.

Some 2,000 fan letters a week were sent to the dead Dean—more than were received by any living star. And this was not just a tribute to the Hollywood publicity machine: it was because James Dean struck a chord with his audience.

The rock'n'roll era

Music was one channel through which America's teenagers could express their energy and demonstrate the gap between themselves and the older generation. The music they chose had a thumping, insistent, exciting rhythm, and was based on African-American music. Initially, rhythm and blues music—a fusion of gospel singing, blues and jazz—was banned by white radio stations as being too uninhibited. The ban merely incited white teenagers to tune in to black stations, to listen to R and B on juke boxes, and to buy the records. In 1951, disc jockey Alan Freed began playing the music with the powerful beat on his white radio station in Cleveland, Ohio. He called it rock'n'roll.

With black music spilling over into the white world, the search was on for a "great white hope" who could sing in the black style. Sam Phillips, studio head for Sun

ELVIS TAKES ROCK TO THE TOP Parents in the 1950s disapproved of his gyrating, but Elvis set the younger generation alight. Teenagers (above) were ready converts to rock'n'roll.

Records in Memphis, Tennessee, was quoted as saying: "If I could find a white man with the negro sound and the negro feel, I could make a million dollars." His wish was to come true.

A guitar-playing former truckdriver named Elvis Presley, who had been exposed to black gospel music since boyhood and had discovered R and B on black radio stations in Memphis, called in at Sun Records to make a record as a birthday present for his mother. Phillips liked what he heard and signed Elvis up. The record company RCA liked him too, and bought Elvis's contract. And America, in turn, liked what it heard. Within two years, Elvis Presley sold 28 million records.

His raunchy way of putting over such songs as "Heartbreak Hotel," "Hound Dog," and "Jailhouse Rock," with sneering lip-curl and gyrating pelvis, aroused teenagers

| 1963 First No. 1 hit for the Beatles, "From Me to You" | 1964 Berkeley Free Speech Movement in California | 1965 The miniskirt makes its impact on fashion | 1966 *Time* magazine publishes "Swinging London" issue | 1967 "Summer of Love" in San Francisco | 1968 Columbia University uprising | 1969 Woodstock defines a generation |

PUTTING ON THE STYLE Below: two British "Teddy Boys" of the Fifties. As the dress style developed, the jackets got longer and the drainpipe trousers got tighter. "Teds" rocked in the aisles when Bill Haley and his Comets (above) toured Britain in 1957.

and alarmed their parents. Southern churchmen described rock'n'roll as "the work of the devil." Television talk show host Ed Sullivan at first said that Presley was "unfit for a family audience," but then yielded to box office pressure and had him on the show. Elvis's likeable personality and his Southern politeness made such a good impression that he was invited back to do two more Ed Sullivan shows; but Sullivan made sure, on the third show, that the television cameras showed his guest only from the waist up—"Elvis the pelvis" was still considered far too controversial.

Like Elvis, other rock musicians, both white and black, made their impression on both sides of the Atlantic: Jerry Lee Lewis, Buddy Holly, Little Richard and Bill Haley and his Comets became household names, at least in houses where there were teenagers.

Rock'n'roll hysteria was not limited to the U.S. In Great Britain, in an era of National Service and church-based youth organizations such as the Boy Scouts and the Boys' Brigade, a spontaneous working-class youth movement called the Teddy Boys created its own culture and its own uniform. Teddy Boys wore long "Edwardian" jackets with velvet collars, "Slim Jim" bootlace ties, narrow trousers and crepe-soled shoes—and they were avid fans of rock'n'roll. They gave Bill Haley, who showed his country music origins in a kiss-curl on his forehead, a rapturous reception when he toured Britain in 1957. The previous year, Haley's film *Rock Around the Clock* had set off a series of minor riots when it arrived in Britain. Teddy Boys danced in the aisles and ripped up theater seats wherever it was shown.

Beatlemania

The United States had long dictated tastes in popular music, but four working-class boys from Liverpool were about to

before they signed a contract with George Martin of Parlophone, in May 1962. Then the careers of John Lennon, Paul McCartney, George Harrison and Ringo Starr skyrocketed. "Love Me Do" reached the Top Twenty; "From Me to You" was number one in the British charts in April 1963. "I Want to Hold Your Hand" topped both the British and U.S. charts. Lennon and McCartney turned out to have a genius for songwriting. They poured out hit after hit: "Please Please Me" . . . "She Loves You" . . . "All My Loving" . . . "Yesterday" . . . "Michèle" . . . Beatlemania swept Britain, America and the world.

JESUS AND JOHN LENNON

In March 1966, John Lennon gave an interview to Maureen Cleave of the London *Evening Standard* that was to scandalize America when it was picked up and published in a U.S. magazine around two months later. She wrote:

"'Christianity will go,' he said. 'It will vanish and shrink. I needn't argue about that. I'm right and I will be proved right. We're more popular than Jesus now. I don't know which will go first—rock 'n'roll or Christianity. Jesus was all right, but his disciples were thick and ordinary. It's them twisting it that ruins it for me.'"

Beatles sales slumped in America. The group's records were burned in public, and Lennon was forced to apologize.

WE LOVE YOU, YEAH, YEAH, YEAH! Girls in the throes of Beatlemania go wild at the sight of the "Fab Four," pictured (top) with their manager Brian Epstein, and (above) on an item of Beatles memorabilia—a tea tray.

challenge that domination. Liverpool, with a mixture of Irish, Welsh, English and blacks in its population, and the added advantage of being a seaport, was a cultural crossroads with a strong musical tradition.

Out of this tradition arose The Beatles, who spearheaded a whole new wave of musical energy. Playing in Liverpool's Cavern Club, and the rock clubs of Hamburg, they attracted fans by word of mouth. They were turned down by five major recording companies

THE TIMES SPEAKS UP FOR MICK JAGGER

It was a confrontation between the old England and the new in July 1967, when "flower child" Mick Jagger, lead singer of the Rolling Stones, stood in court before a bewigged judge, on a drug charge. With him in the dock were Rolling Stones guitarist Keith Richards and an art dealer, Robert Fraser. Sussex police had arrested all three in a raid on Richards' house.

Fraser pleaded guilty to possessing heroin and was jailed for six months. Richards was sentenced to 12

ROLLING INTO COURT Rolling Stones Keith Richards and Mick Jagger, on their way to face a drug charge.

months for allowing his house to be used, and Jagger to three months for possession of four pep pills that he had bought legally in Italy. The sentence brought a protest from an unexpected quarter. Under the headline "Who Breaks a Butterfly on a Wheel?," a *Times* editor argued:

"In the courts at large it is most uncommon for imprisonment to be imposed on first offenders where the drugs are not major drugs of addiction . . . It is surprising, therefore, that Judge Block should have decided to sentence Mr. Jagger to imprisonment, and particularly surprising as Mr. Jagger's is about as mild a drugs case as can ever have been brought before the courts . . . There are many who take a primitive view of the matter, what one might call a pre-legal view of the matter. They consider that Mr. Jagger has 'got what was coming to him.' They resent the anarchic quality of the Rolling Stones' performances, dislike their songs, dislike their influence on teenagers and broadly suspect them of decadence . . .

"Has Mr. Jagger received the same treatment he would have received if he had not been a famous figure, with all the criticism and resentment his celebrity has aroused? If a promising undergraduate had come back from a summer visit to Italy with four pep pills in his pocket, would it have been thought right to ruin his career by sending him to prison for three months? Would it also have been thought necessary to display him handcuffed to the public?"

Neither Rolling Stone served the jail sentence. The conviction against Keith Richards was quashed on appeal, and Mick Jagger was given a conditional discharge.

songs. It was commonly believed that The Beatles' song "Lucy in the Sky with Diamonds," which was packed with psychedelic imagery, deliberately echoed the initials of LSD.

The search for enlightenment

In their eagerness to break with traditional ways of thought, the hippies sought enlightenment in the wisdom of the East—in Zen Buddhism, in Hindu mantras, in the I Ching, a Chinese technique for predicting the future. The Beatles went to India to sit at the feet of the Maharishi Mahesh Yogi, exponent of transcendental meditation (TM), which claimed to be a direct route to a deeper level of consciousness. Some followers of TM believed it could bring about physical as well as psychological changes, and that it could enable them to levitate their bodies or walk through walls.

Ronald Reagan, the newly elected governor of California, drew on his movie-actor background to describe a hippie as someone who "dresses like Tarzan, has hair like Jane and smells like Cheetah." The hippies ignored such put-downs from the older generation and held a "Summer of Love" in San Francisco in 1967. "Make Love, Not War"

The Beatles opened the gates for a flood of British musical talent, including the Rolling Stones, the arrogantly strutting "bad boys" of rock, and The Who, a group whose performances at times reached such a pitch of frenzy that they smashed their guitars and electronic equipment on stage.

Dylan sings his protest

America, where rock'n'roll had started, was also the home in the late 1950s and the 1960s of the protest song. In 1959, civil rights activists were keeping up their spirits by singing Pete Seeger's "We Shall Overcome," based on an old gospel song.

Strumming his guitar, picking out links on his harmonica and singing such songs as "Blowin' in the Wind" and "The Times They Are A-Changin'" in his nasal, rasping yet compelling voice, Bob Dylan gave expression to the sense of injustice felt by the young at problems created by their parents. Dylan was also capable of writing dreamy, lyrical

songs, as in his "Mr. Tambourine Man" of 1965, which caught the mood of a movement in America—hippiedom. Spreading out from the Haight-Ashbury district of San Francisco, the long-haired, bead-wearing hippies believed in gentleness, flower power and the search for fulfilment. Some found it in drugs. Among their gurus was Professor Timothy Leary, who was dismissed from Harvard University for advising the young to "turn on, tune in, drop out."

Leary's preferred drug for turning-on was the hallucinogenic LSD (lysergic acid diethylamide), widely known as "acid," but marijuana, or "pot," was more widespread. Both drugs were openly referred to in pop

THE VOICE OF PROTEST Tousle-haired folk-singer and guitar player Bob Dylan, who gave teenage rebellion a social and political focus.

down. With food shortages, rain, overcrowding and often indiscriminate drug use, the situation could easily have turned into a riot.

It didn't. Organizations and neighbors donated food. Members of The Hog Farm commune acted as security, a job that expanded to include organizing water stations, free kitchens and medical tents.

Woodstock became a defining moment for the counterculture of the late Sixties—but it also marked the time when that culture started to decline.

Later that year at Altamont, near San Francisco, some 300,000 turned out for a Rolling Stones concert. But the atmosphere was one of violence, not peace and love, and culminated in a black teenager being beaten and stabbed to death by Hell's Angels who had been brought in as security. The dream had turned sour.

LA LOVE-IN Flower children capture the spirit of 1967 at a Los Angeles "love-in," watched by bemused elders and members of their own generation.

was the slogan with which they opposed America's war in Vietnam, and in November 1969, they gathered in the thousands at the Washington memorial and sang John Lennon's "Give Peace a Chance."

Free rock concerts attracted vast numbers of young people as the Sixties came to a close. In August 1969, nearly half a million gathered at Woodstock, in New York state, for what would become the world's most famous festival of music and hippie culture.

Organized by four men in their twenties—John Roberts, Joel Rosenman, Artie Kornfeld, and Michael Lang—Woodstock was originally conceived as a festival for 50,000. Inexperienced and facing local opposition, the organizers managed to rent out 600 acres of Max Yasgur's dairy farm in Bethel, New York, and sign on some of the era's biggest names in music—including Jefferson Airplane, Janis Joplin, Arlo Guthrie, the Grateful Dead, and Jimi Hendrix. With the slogan "Three Days of Peace and Music," the organizers advertised through both mainstream and under-

PEACE, MUSIC, AND CROWDS Above, a couple catches some sleep as Woodstock concert-goers stumble home after three long days. Left, Michael Lang, one of the concert's youthful organizers, on Max Yasgur's farm.

ground channels, with a turnout far beyond what they anticipated.

Nearly half a million people flooded Yasgur's farm. Traffic jams were 20 miles long; food supplies were quickly used up; the fence around the concert (and with it any attempt at selling tickets) was taken

ENGLAND SWINGS

The tremors of a culture shift in Britain, with its epicenter in the capital, were detected a year before *Time* magazine published its issue on "Swinging London." In April 1965, the American journalist John Crosby wrote in the *Weekend Telegraph*:

"The nightlife is just a symptom, the outer and visible froth, of an inner, far deeper, turbulence that boiled up around—if we must date it—1958, though some say as late as 1960. In that period, youth captured this ancient island and took command in a country where youth before had always been kept firmly in its place. Suddenly, the young own the town . . . The most astonishing change for me is the muscular virility of England's writers and dramatists and actors and artists—this from an island we'd mostly thought of in terms of Noel Coward and drawing room comedy. Now it's all anger, sweat and the working classes."

Global style

Across the world, fashions were changing. In Great Britain, the revolution began in 1955, when Mary Quant decided to offer young women something different from what their mothers were wearing, and opened her boutique, Bazaar, in what was then a run-down part of Chelsea. It wasn't until the Sixties that her simple, boldly designed clothes made their real impact on world fashions. In 1965 she helped make the miniskirt famous, and the following year she wore one at Buckingham Palace. Even Paris succumbed to her spell. After displaying her dresses at a fashion show there in 1967, she sold 30,000. "Good taste is death. Vulgarity is life," she said in an interview that year. "Fashion doesn't really influence the climate of opinion. It reflects what is already in the air. It reflects what people are reading and thinking and listening to, and architecture, painting, attitudes to success and to society."

"Swinging London" was a trend commented on by *Time* magazine, in its April 15, 1966 issue: "In a decade dominated by youth, London has burst into bloom. It swings; it is the scene." Britain had its own "Summer of Love" in August 1967, when a Festival of the Flower Children at Woburn Abbey in Bedfordshire attracted thousands of teenagers to dance and listen to music.

Students in revolt

Rebellion and protest were in the air throughout the Sixties. Students rebelled against the Vietnam War, discrimination and increasingly bureaucratic universities.

One of the first student uprisings was the Berkeley Free Speech Movement in 1964. Protesting a rule limiting campus political advocacy, students held a sit-in at an administrative building at the University of California Berkeley campus. The police were called, and the school formed committees to address the issue. The rule was eventually overturned, and Berkeley students—as well as students across the country—became aware of their newfound power.

In 1968, students at Columbia University in New York staged a rally to protest the uni-

versity's involvement in the Vietnam War. The rally turned into a week-long takeover of the school. Students stormed buildings, shutting down the college for a week. The uprising ended in the arrest of 720 students in what was then the largest police action on a college campus. This was to be the first of many such takeovers.

Students were active off-campus as well. In 1966 two Oakland, California, college stu-

POLICE ACTION The National Guard surrounds a group illegally demonstrating in Berkeley in 1969. After 1964, Berkeley became a crucible for activism and radical politics.

dents founded the Black Panthers, a paramilitary organization whose initial goal was to combat police brutality in the Oakland ghetto. Armed with legally carried weapons, tape recorders, cameras and a copy of the penal code, they policed the police, following cruisers throughout the city. The Black Panthers eventually became a nationwide movement, taking a confrontational and often controversial stand for the rights of African Americans in the United States.

Despite the explosions of youthful energy, the experiments with drugs and the challenges to authority, most people held fast to traditional values while enjoying their increasing prosperity. The success stories of the Sixties could almost have come from a Victorian primer on how to get ahead in life, for they depended on talent, self-belief and a readiness to take risks. This applied as much to celebrity artists such as Andy Warhol as it did to entrepreneurs like Britain's Mary Quant, or to the pop stars who set the tone for the entire decade.

PEACE Students occupying an office at Columbia University greet a professor during the 1968 uprising.

A NEW DEAL FOR WOMEN

WITH GREATER FINANCIAL INDEPENDENCE, WOMEN BEGAN TO QUESTION TRADITIONAL ROLES AND TO DEMAND EQUALITY

One of the many lessons society learned from the Second World War was that a woman could do a man's job. In America, for instance, Rosie the Riveter became a national symbol. But even as shipyards, factories and other traditional male preserves were being breached, women were paid less than men for doing the same work and only very rarely rose to the executive ranks.

It was a French intellectual who sounded the rallying call for women. In 1949, Simone de Beauvoir, a professor at the Sorbonne and lifelong companion of the Existentialist philosopher Jean-Paul Sartre, published *Le Deuxième Sexe* (translated into English as *The Second Sex* in 1953). She argued that women, half the human race, were denied equality and their true importance in society, not because of any biological weakness but because of their upbringing and of the expectations placed on them by a male-dominated society. "One is not born a woman; one becomes one," she wrote. "In the past, all history has been made by men."

Women at work

De Beauvoir's call was taken up on the other side of the Atlantic, in an increasingly affluent America, where women's struggle for equal status was based on their increasing importance in the workforce. The number of women workers in America had dipped briefly after the war, as millions of veterans moved back into the jobs they had left behind. But it soon became clear that many families needed two incomes if they were to afford a dream home and give their children the best possible chance in life.

By 1962, the man was no longer the sole breadwinner in many U.S. homes. Some 24 million women were at work, but they were earning only 60 percent of a man's wage and 75 percent of them were in low-status factory, office or cleaning jobs. Less than 7 percent of America's doctors, and fewer than 4 percent of its lawyers, were women. Whether working or not, many women felt something important was missing from their lives. Advertisers saw them as the key to success in the consumer society—potential buyers of washing machines, vacuum cleaners, refrigerators, furniture and cosmetics. Magazines told them that getting married and raising a family was life's most fulfilling role. "The two big steps that women must take are to help their husbands decide

THE PIONEER Simone de Beauvoir, who spoke out trenchantly for women's rights in 1949. "All history has been made by men," she wrote in *The Second Sex*.

where they are going and use their pretty heads to help them get there," wrote Mrs. Dale Carnegie. Television sitcoms, based on comic misunderstandings within happy families, reinforced the message.

Betty Friedan, who had tasted the excitement of being a political activist in New York's Greenwich Village before getting married, did not agree. In 1963, she caused a stir with *The Feminine Mystique*. The book was based on a survey of her class of 1942 at Smith College, the long-established women's college in Massachusetts. Before being published, her work had been turned down by several of the magazines whose values it questioned. Friedan argued that "the

SPEAKING OUT FOR WOMEN

Simone de Beauvoir, the novelist and companion of the French Existentialist philosopher Jean-Paul Sartre, became a pioneer of the women's movement when she published *Le Deuxième Sexe* in 1949. In it, she declared:

"Woman has always been man's dependent, if not his slave; the two sexes have never shared the world in equality. And even today woman is heavily handicapped, though her situation is beginning to change. Almost nowhere is her legal status the same as man's, and frequently it is much to her disadvantage . . . In the economic sphere men and women can almost be said to make up two castes; other things being equal, the former hold the better jobs, get higher wages, and have more opportunities for success than their new competitors. In industry and politics men have a great many more positions and they monopolize the most important posts . . . it is a world that still belongs to men."

problem that has no name" left suburban women who devoted themselves to husbands, children and homes dissatisfied but afraid to ask even themselves, "Is this all?"

President Kennedy, alert to new movements in society, prohibited federal agencies from discriminating against women when hiring staff or deciding on promotions, and set up a Presidential Commission on the Status of Women. Its report, issued in October 1963, found that women, as well as being poorly paid, were being consistently passed over for promotion and for management training. In Congress, only two out of 100 Senators and 11 out of 435 Representatives were women.

In its origins, the women's struggle for

GLAMOUR MAKES A COMEBACK

For women who had lived through the drab years of wartime austerity, the New Look that Christian Dior launched in February 1947 was a taste of feminine luxury. It soon became, for those who could afford it, a necessity. Dior set out to release women from what he described as "a poverty-stricken, parsimonious era, obsessed with ration books and clothing coupons."

His ultra-feminine dresses banished the square-shouldered military look. They were tiny in the waist, full in hips and bust, and their hemlines fell well below the calf. They used up yards of material, at a time when many women in Europe were struggling to feed their families, and for this they came under official disapproval. Harold Wilson, President of the Board of Trade in Britain, criticized the New Look as irresponsible, frivolous and wasteful. Working-class women in Paris attacked Dior's elegant models in the street. Even in affluent America, a group of women tried to mount a rear-guard action with hemlines that were higher, and so less extravagant.

THE NEW LOOK   After years of austerity, Christian Dior's New Look brought back femininity and elegance.

But fashion writers and fashionable women in Paris, London and New York adored the New Look. It brought back glamour. It restored Paris to its pre-eminence in world fashion. And it represented the hope of better times to come.

equality was closely linked with the black struggle for civil rights. White women were schooled in political protest when they joined freedom rides in the deep South and risked the taunts and blows of white reactionaries. Even so, they sometimes encountered prejudice among those they were trying to help. Stokely Carmichael, a black civil rights leader, asserted: "The place of women in the movement is prone."

The birth of "Women's Lib"

Feminism benefited in a direct way from the civil rights movement. Lyndon B. Johnson's 1964 Civil Rights Bill proposed a ban against discrimination on the grounds of race, color, religion or national origin. Representative Howard W. Smith, a southern Democrat from Virginia, extended the list to include discrimination on the grounds of a person's sex, expecting that it would cause the entire Bill to be rejected. To his surprise, the Bill was passed in its entirety.

An Equal Employment Opportunities Commission was set up under the act to enforce its provisions.

To turn support into effective action, the National Organization for Women (NOW) was founded in 1966, with Betty Friedan as its first president. Its aim was "to bring women into full participation in the mainstream of American society now, exercising all the privileges and responsibilities thereof in truly equal partnership with men."

Students played a key role in America's feminist movement. In the late Sixties, women in a group called Students for a Democratic Society began to talk of "Women's Liberation" and introduced the concept of "male chauvinism." A convention at Ann Arbor, Michigan, resolved: "We demand that

STILL ASKING FOR MORE   Betty Friedan, whose question "Is this all?" stirred housewives in the Sixties, takes the platform at a Women's Lib meeting in the Seventies.

our brothers recognize that they must deal with their own problems of male chauvinism in their personal, social and political relationships." The movement was international by the end of the decade, which saw the publication of Germaine Greer's *The Female Eunuch*.

Signs of the times

At the same time as women, on both sides of the Atlantic, were asserting their right to social equality, the availability in the Sixties of an effective oral contraceptive, the Pill, made possible a new era of sexual equality. It meant, more than ever, that pregnancy could be a matter of choice, rather than a penalty for carelessness.

A more open attitude toward discussing sex was pioneered by Alfred Kinsey, a professor of zoology from Bloomington, Indiana, who in 1948 published *Sexual Behavior in the Human Male*, based on thousands of interviews and questionnaires. *Sexual Behavior in the Human Female* followed in 1953. Although his methodology has since been questioned, the reports highlighted a gap between the conventions of sexual conduct and what people actually did.

1947 Christian Dior introduces the New Look | 1948 Kinsey Report on male sexual behavior | 1949 *Le Deuxième Sexe (The Second Sex)* by Simone de Beauvoir published in France | 1953 Kinsey Report on female sexual behavior | 1957 Wolfenden Report proposes homosexual law reforms in U.K.

One husband in two and one wife in four, according to Kinsey, had experienced sexual relations outside marriage. Homosexuality was more common than had been supposed, with some 10 percent of men admitting to sexual experiences with other men and 4 percent claiming to be exclusively homosexual. Both reports became bestsellers.

Legal reforms

As women began to speak up for their economic, political, and reproductive rights, the courts began to reflect these changes in the law. The U.S. and Great Britain passed laws and made court decisions that allowed for more open speech, helped assimilate women into the work force, and gave women more legal equality.

In 1957 the Supreme Court, while reinforcing the fact that obscene language was not protected by the First Amendment, lim-

THE RIGHT TO READ Paperback copies of *Lady Chatterley's Lover*, priced 3s 6d ($.60), sell briskly in Leicester Square, London (below), on the day Penguin Books announced a victory over censorship (right).

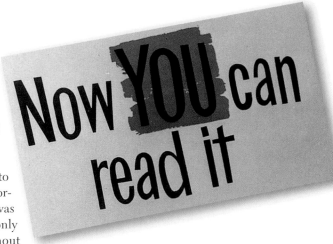

ited the definition of obscenity to works that were socially unimportant. In 1966 this definition was further narrowed to include only works that were "utterly without redeeming social value."

In Great Britain, the 1960 Chatterly Trial marked a watershed in obscenity rulings. When Penguin Books attempted to publish an uncensored version of *Lady Chatterly's Lover*, which had been banned since 1920, it was charged under the Obscene Publications Act. During the trial, the prosecuting counsel revealed the chasm

between the old Britain and the new when he invited jury members to ask themselves: "Is it a book that you would even wish your wife or your servants to read?" The jury gave its answer after a three-hour deliberation: it found Penguin Books not guilty.

Although the U.S. Civil Rights Act of 1964 forbade workplace discrimination on the basis of sex, it remained up to the Equal

1960 U.K. jury rules that *Lady Chatterley's Lover* is not obscene; contraceptive pill on sale in U.S.

1963 Profumo, U.K. war minister, resigns in scandal

1964 U.S. Civil Rights Bill outlaws discrimination on grounds of gender, as well as race

1965 Capital punishment abolished in U.K.

1969 Gay rights riots in New York after police raid on Stonewall bar

THE SEARCH FOR THE PILL

The American scientist Russell E. Marker, searching for an oral contraceptive in the early 1940s, knew that for centuries Mexican women had avoided pregnancy by eating the roots of a particular kind of yam. Working in a friend's laboratory, he isolated the chemical diosgenin from the yam, and discovered that it could easily be processed into the female hormone progesterone. An over-abundance of this hormone can suppress ovulation, the monthly release of an egg. Two of his colleagues synthesized cortisone and the male hormone testosterone from the same yam.

Marker set up a company to exploit his discovery, but then lost interest in biochemistry and spent the rest of his life manufacturing copies of silver antiques. Research work on the contraceptive pill in America was taken up by, among others, Gregory Pincus and John Rock. They set out to find a means of contraception that was "harmless, entirely reliable, simple, practical, universally applicable and aesthetically satisfactory to both husband and wife."

Clinical trials carried out in Puerto Rico in 1955 demonstrated that estrogens were also needed to make the Pill an effective method of contraception. The early Pill could have unfortunate side effects, including migraine, thrombosis and diabetes, but once a way was found of controlling the dosage of estrogens, these problems largely disappeared. The Pill became widely available in America in the early Sixties, and in Britain a few years later. The Pill was as much a result as a cause of the New Age of sexual freedom. Family planning clinics in Britain did not, in the early years of its availability, issue it to unmarried women, and as late as 1970, fewer than one married couple in five was using it as a means of contraception.

THE PILL A month's supply of the popular contraceptive.

the movement for women's rights, a gay rights movement began to emerge in the Sixties. In the previous decade, a few gay and lesbian organizations had formed in the United States, most notably the Mattachine Society in 1951 and the Daughters of Bilitis in 1955.

With protest so much part of the climate in the Sixties, it was inevitable that members of the gay subculture should start making protests of their own and demanding their own equal rights. They banded together in places where they were most likely to find tolerance—colleges, universities and cities such as New York and San Francisco. Ironically, it was an act of intolerance that gave their cause its greatest boost.

In June 1969, New York police raided a gay bar, the Stonewall Inn, in Greenwich village. Such raids were not uncommon, but this time the patrons and a sympathetic crowd fought back. The bar was set on fire, with police inside, and though they were rescued, the battle spilled over onto the streets. The Gay Liberation Front was set up in New York within weeks of the riot, with Stonewall as its rallying call.

Employment Opportunities Commission (EEOC) and the courts to determine which actions were actually discriminatory. In 1968, the EEOC ruled to eliminate sex segregation in newspaper help-wanted ads. The following year, *Weeks v. Southern Bell*, the first court case to apply the Civil Rights Act to sex discrimination, forbade employers from barring women from jobs that required lifting more than 30 pounds.

Beyond the workplace, women were gaining general legal rights. In 1968, U.S. courts started overturning state laws that required longer prison sentences for women than for men convicted of the same crimes. Great Britain's Divorce Reform Act of 1969 introduced the concept of "irretrievable breakdown," in which a married couple could achieve a divorce simply because one or both of them felt they needed one.

In both countries, laws concerning contraception and abortion began to give women some measure of control over their reproductive lives. In *Griswold v. Connecticut*, the Supreme Court ruled that married couples' right to privacy ensured them legal access to contraception. Some states began introducing abortion reform laws, which made abortion legal in situations where the physical or mental health of the mother was clearly threatened. In Great Britain, the Abortion Act of 1967 stated that a medical abortion could be carried out legally under similar circumstances. In that same year, abortion became available through the National Health Service. *Roe v. Wade*, which legalized abortion in the U.S., would follow in another 6 years.

Gay liberation

Rather more cautiously than

A MESSAGE FOR THE NATION With America enmeshed in the Vietnam War, the youth counterculture used eye-catching posters to put across its message.

Make love not War

DREAMS AND DIVERSIONS

TELEVISION BROUGHT ENTERTAINMENT AND THE OUTSIDE WORLD INTO THE HOME AT THE FLICK OF A SWITCH, AND BECAME BIG BUSINESS

A world that had grown comfortable with books, magazines, newspapers, the theater and radio as its main sources of information and entertainment was given a wake-up call in the late 1940s by a small, flickering screen that beamed its message from a corner of the living room.

Before then, television had been the preserve of the rich—fewer than 1.1 million sets had been sold in America and only 70,000 in Britain by 1949. It was in the United States, where TV had massive potential as an advertising medium, that the infant industry benefited from improvements in technology to begin its almost vertical takeoff. By 1970, there were TV sets in well over 90 million American homes; and in Britain, with nearly 16 million sets, there were few households that did not own at least one television.

The medium might be new, but those who performed on it were, for the most part, well established. They had learned their trade on radio, and sometimes on stage in front of an audience. America's first major TV star was Milton Berle, who had won a Charlie Chaplin lookalike contest at the age of six, and honed his skills in vaudeville. On TV, he hosted a comic variety show, the *Texaco Star Theater*, which had started its run on radio. By 1951, people were buying TV sets just to watch him, and he was earning $200,000 a year. Ed Sullivan, host of *The Toast of the Town*, was a former sports reporter and Broadway columnist who was to give Elvis Presley and The Beatles their first national coverage on U.S. TV.

TV BREAK   All eyes are on the television at a drugstore in 1954. Restaurants and other stores often attracted customers by installing a set on the premises.

THE WORLD LOVES LUCY   An instant success on home ground in America, the sitcom *I Love Lucy* was a long-lasting hit in many countries, and made household names of its stars Lucille Ball and Desi Arnaz.

Jack Paar, on *Tonight*, pioneered the talk show, dominated by conversation rather than by variety acts. He was succeeded in 1962 by the up-and-coming Johnny Carson, whose chirpy professionalism was to make him a television legend.

Television ate up scripts and ideas at a much faster rate than theater and vaudeville, where performers polished their timing by delivering the same act in city after city. This meant that the success of a TV show depended on the writers almost as much as on the performers. Sid Caesar and Imogen Coca gave Mel Brooks, Neil Simon and Woody Allen an early showcase for their writing talents on *Show of Shows*. Another showbusiness veteran, Jackie Gleason, made America laugh at the comic situations built into the scripts of *The Honeymooners*, in which he played a Brooklyn bus driver with a yearning for the good life.

American television was funded almost exclusively by money earned from advertising, so the networks kept a watchful eye on audience ratings. The show that toppled Milton Berle from the top of the table was the situation comedy, or sitcom, *I Love Lucy*, starring film actress and radio comedienne Lucille Ball and her Cuban

band-leader husband Desi Arnaz. It began on the CBS network in October 1951, and presented a version of the everyday mishaps and misunderstandings of married life. The approach was so successful that within six months *I Love Lucy* was being watched in more than 10 million American homes.

The man with too many right answers

U.S. network revenues were $7.28 million in 1949, but had climbed to $460 million by 1960. Sponsors put their advertising budgets behind the shows with the top audience ratings, and by the late 1950s that meant game shows. *The $64,000 Question*, on the CBS network, pushed *I Love Lucy* off its perch at the top of the ratings.

NBC's rival game show, *Twenty-One*, was at the center of television's first major scandal. Since viewers found the drama of winners and losers so compelling, it seemed like a good idea to build up tension by coaching a contestant in the questions and then, when he seemed to be on a winning run, arrange for him to lose to a more glamorous figure. The man chosen as the first big "loser," Herbert Stempel, was deliberately made to look unappealing in comparison with

A Cheat's Reward Quizmaster Jack Barry (right) congratulates Charles Van Doren on winning what was then a record amount on a game show. Van Doren later admitted cheating.

AGAINST THE TIDE: THE BEAT GENERATION

While most Americans were doing their best to acquire a share of the affluence that followed the Second World War, one group was rejecting the career ladder, spurning respectability, turning its back on the American dream, and seeking a different kind of fulfillment. The Beat generation, whose central figure was the writer Jack Kerouac, sought heightened awareness through sex, drugs, jazz and Zen Buddhism.

"The only people for me are the mad ones," wrote Kerouac in *On the Road*, his saga of crossing America by hitchhiking and in stolen cars. "Mad to live, mad to talk, mad to be saved, desirous of everything at the same time." Kerouac and his fellow Beats alienated conventional people with their riotous lifestyles. They borrowed slang from bebop and from black culture. Money was "bread," somebody they admired "hip," the rest of society "square."

Another prominent Beat writer, William Burroughs, a narcotics addict and author of *The Naked Lunch*, accidentally killed a girlfriend when, as a party trick, he tried to shoot a glass off her head with a .38 automatic, William-Tell-style. The "Beats"—a word that implies both "exhausted" and "beatific"—became "Beatniks" in April 1958. Herb Caen, a San Francisco columnist, coined the term six months after the U.S.S.R. put the first Sputnik into space.

Kerouac died in October the following year, from the effects of a poor diet, too many drugs and heavy drinking. By then, the Beatniks had run their course. Their protest had been against a lifestyle; the rising generation was occupied with other matters, such as the color bar and the Vietnam War.

Cult Hero Jack Kerouac, whose novel *On the Road* expressed the restlessness of the Beat generation.

The Experimenter In his books, as in life, William Burroughs pursued new experiences.

the eventual "winner," Charles Van Doren, bearer of an illustrious name in America's academic world.

But Van Doren was also coached, not only in the questions, but also in how to mop his brow and stumble convincingly for the right answer. Stempel made a fuss after he lost. New York's District Attorney began investigations. Congress held special hearings. And Van Doren, who had won $129,000, had to confess: "I was deeply involved in a deception." The networks cancelled all big-money game shows.

Lunch boxes and coonskip caps

Television revolutionized how people viewed entertainment. In addition, through advertising and through the shows themselves, it transformed Americans' consumer habits. The medium could reach millions of people at once; as people saw the same shows and the same advertisements, they often then bought the same products. This was very

1945

1946 BBC restarts TV transmissions after wartime shutdown

1951 TV sitcom *I Love Lucy* begins in U.S.

1953 Coronation of Queen Elizabeth II boosts U.K. TV sales

1954 Army-McCarthy hearings televised in U.S.

1955 Independent television starts in the U.K.

GROUP ENTERTAINMENT
Above: Television drew family and friends together in the Fifties. Below: Children in "Hoppy" hats and shirts watch an episode of Hopalong Cassidy. Left: Children wearing Davy Crockett "frontier" clothing appear on TV.

noticeable—and often blatantly capitalized upon—in children's television. Productions featuring cowboys, super heroes and cartoon characters fascinated millions of children and often had them clamoring for toys and clothing from their favorite shows.

In 1949, Hopalong Cassidy and his horse Topper broadcast their first national television show. That year, a personal appearance by William Boyd, the actor who played Cassidy, could draw up to 300,000 fans at once. Children's demands for black "Hoppy" hats, shirts, guns and other merchandise reportedly created a national shortage of black dye.

On December 15, 1954, Disney aired the first of a three-part series starring Fess Parker as "Davy Crockett, King of the Wild

Frontier." It was watched by 40 million viewers, most of them between the ages of 5 and 15. By February, Davy Crockett was a nationwide craze. Children clamored for coonskin caps, frontier outfits, Davy Crockett lunch boxes and bikes, and whatever else merchandisers could think to sell. "The Ballad of Davy Crockett," released on nearly 20 different labels, sold over 7 million copies in less than 6 months. By the time the fad faded in November 1955, merchandisers had sold over $100 million worth of paraphernalia.

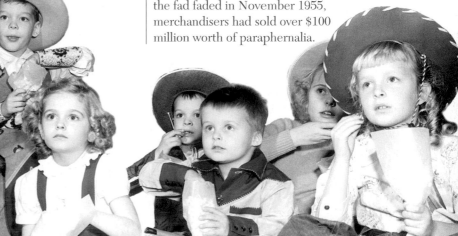

1957 Beatnik Jack Kerouac publishes *On the Road*

1959 "$64,000 Question" scandal shocks America

1963 Assassination and funeral of President Kennedy on worldwide TV

1967 BBC2 is first in Europe with color TV

1968 French TV strike against government interference

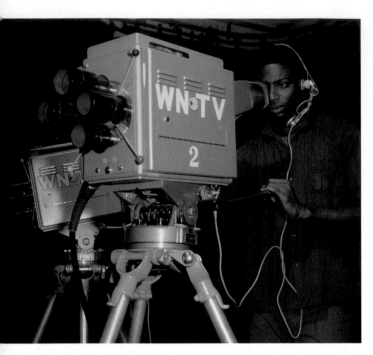

TV TAKES OFF A cameraman in action in Nigeria. As TV spread, it took on an important educational role in the developing world.

Television conquers the world

In the long run, television was to reach every country in the world, but in the short term, some countries had their reasons for resisting its introduction. In Tanzania, the stumbling block was finance. President Nyerere needed money for his program of radical social reforms, and was not prepared to see investment "wasted" on television. Well into the 1980s, mainland Tanzania remained without a TV station, although programs could be picked up from Zanzibar. South Africa was another latecomer, largely because the government feared TV might stir discontent among the black population. Cabinet minister Albert Hertzog was blunt about it: "The effects of the wrong programs on children, the less developed and other races can be destructive." Television finally arrived there in 1976. Sri Lanka's minister of broadcasting was introduced to TV in America in 1966, and did not like what he saw. It was, he said, "the deadliest instrument to create a non-thinking generation of people, gun-happy and brought up on mayhem and mur-

A SERVICE FOR THE PUBLIC Few homes in Haiti could afford a TV set, so early broadcasts were from public kiosks— sometimes to a public that found them less than absorbing.

der." Sri Lanka held out until the early 1970s. Latin America, by contrast, was an eager market for the new entertainment. The Arab countries tended to be latecomers, partly because those in authority needed reassuring that television did not offend religious laws.

Just as Hollywood movies appealed to audiences all over the world, so U.S. television programs brought American values and the American way of life to millions outside America. Especially popular were game

WHEN TELEVISION ARRIVED

Television took its time to spread around the world, arriving relatively late in many countries:

1950: Brazil, Cuba	1961: Zambia
1951: Argentina, Mexico	1962: Pakistan, Indonesia
1952: Venezuela	1963: Malaysia, Kenya,
1953: Japan	Singapore, Ghana
1954: Morocco	1965: Saudi Arabia
1956: Algeria, Australia	1968: Jordan, Turkey
1958: China, Chile	1976: South Africa
1959: India, Nigeria	1985: Cameroon
1960: Egypt, New Zealand	1986: Chad

shows, sitcoms and Westerns. *The Price is Right* became *Der Preis ist Heiss* in Germany, *El Precio Justo* in Spain and *Kac Para* in Turkey. *Beat the Clock*, which began in the U.S. in 1952, and *The $64,000 Question* (1955) were licensed and reformatted for other countries. Westerns, their popularity well established by the movies, found a ready audience. *Cheyenne*, *Bonanza* and *Maverick* were dubbed into a score of languages. So were comedy shows, detective series and sitcoms. *The Honeymooners*, *Dragnet* and *77 Sunset Strip* reached audiences around the world. Sergeant Bilko and Lucille Ball became as instantly recognizable in Nairobi and Nagasaki as on Nantucket. *I Love Lucy* reached Japan in 1957 at a time when the audience was relatively small, but a royal event sent people rushing to buy sets: 2 million were sold in 1959 to people wanting to watch the wedding of Crown Prince Akahito.

PATERNALISTIC PROGRAMMING In France (above) television had to struggle to break away from state supervision. In the U.S.S.R. (left), it was a tool of Marxist-Leninism.

As well as providing entertainment, television had enormous potential as a means of persuasion. The more authoritarian the government, the more the new medium was seen as a political weapon. In the U.S.S.R., the head of Gosteleradio, the State Broadcasting Committee, was a Politburo appointee, and his mandate was to use television to "mold a Marxist-Leninist outlook." As late as 1964, there were only 14 million sets in the entire Soviet Union, and apart from sports, what was offered was very serious—current social issues, ballet and other cultural activities, or epics on the history of the Communist Party or the works of Lenin. Television in the rest of the Iron Curtain countries followed much the same pattern, though in some areas it was possible to pick up Western programs. Throughout the Fifties and Sixties, it was a punishable offense in East Germany to watch West German TV.

In China, television was seen from the start as an arm of government. Broadcasting began in the Beijing area, in May 1958, but few could afford sets, and the programs concentrated on government announcements, news and education. It was not until the Cultural Revolution of 1966 that television began to take off, with patriotic operas and plays designed to enthuse the masses. Even then, TV had a rival in the wall posters that were pasted up in Beijing and other cities, and the drama in the streets outdid any drama on TV screens.

Television in the democracies

In Great Britain, the BBC held a television monopoly until commercial TV began broadcasting in 1955. Drawing its money from a license fee payable by all viewers, the BBC's mission was to inform as well as to entertain. It regarded television as the junior partner of radio, or the

A SELLER'S MARKET Latin America rushed to join the television boom. London dockers load a transmitter that will help to start a TV station in Venezuela.

NEW FORMS OF EXPRESSION

In the mid 1940s a bold new movement in art, Abstract Expressionism, started in New York. It was to become the first American school of painting to gain international prominence. Led by artists such as Jackson Pollock, Mark Rothko, and Willem de Kooning, the Abstract Expressionists did not share a style so much as an outlook. They valued individuality and spontaneity, and—during a time when the world was struggling with the aftermath of the war and the rise of a society under the shadow of the atomic bomb—often tackled weighty themes.

One of the most famous of the Abstract Expressionists was Jackson Pollock. He is best known for his action paintings, in which he would put a canvas on the floor or a wall and approach it from all sides, dripping or splashing paint—often thickened into a paste with bits of ground glass or other materials—and then shape the paint with sticks and knives. By relying on spontaneity and full body involvement, he hoped to bypass the intellect and create a direct expression of the subconscious. Although often subject to popular ridicule—Time magazine once referred to him as "Jack the Dripper"—Pollock became recognized as the most important figure in one of the most important movements in American painting.

DOCUMENTS II **Pollock's action paintings took a new approach to art. Films of Pollock painting a canvas were often as interesting and revealing as the paintings themselves.**

In the 1960s, artists began to react against the intensity of Abstract Expressionism. They developed Pop art, a minimalist style of painting that reflected a culture increasingly steeped in commercialism and materialism. Instead of tackling subjects with moral or psychological depths, they celebrated the ordinary. Andy Warhol, the most famous of the Pop artists, said, "The Pop artist did images that anybody walking down Broadway could recognize in a split second...all the great modern things that the Abstract Expressionists tried so hard not to notice at all."

Warhol produced images of common items and celebrities, including his famous Campbell's Soup cans and portraits of Marilyn Monroe and Jacqueline Kennedy. His silk-screened images looked mass-produced, and to an extent they were. At his studio, "The Factory," Warhol made over 2,000 pictures between 1962 and 1964.

A cult figure in pop culture, Warhol did not limit himself to painting. He made movies such as the 6-hour *Sleep* and the 8-hour *Empire*, wrote a book of phone calls recorded in his studio, and produced records for The Velvet Underground. In 1968 he was shot (but not killed) by Valerie Solanas, the only member of S.C.U.M. (Society for Cutting Up Men), whose book—*The S.C.U.M. Manifesto*—he had bought to make into a movie.

CULT HERO   Andy Warhol was as much a celebrity as the people he painted.

wireless. The standards set for the wireless were epitomized in rules issued in January 1948 to writers of the popular serial *Dick Barton, Special Agent*. There was to be no sex, swearing or lying by the hero, and if he had occasion to use violence, it should be restricted to "clean socks on the jaws."

Television in West Germany inherited a legacy of checks and balances from 1945. Britain, France and the U.S., fully aware of the way that state-controlled radio had spread the contagion of Nazi ideas, divided broadcasting in their zones into a number of networks run by the states that made up Germany. Each network had editorial freedom, but was responsible to a Broadcasting Council appointed from political parties, the unions, churches and other influential groups in society. This system resulted in programs that were worthy, balanced, sometimes excellent, but rarely lively.

France had 1 million sets in 1960, compared with more than 10 million in the U.K. One reason television took so long to become accepted as part of daily life was that it was clearly under government control: ORTF (Office de la Radio et Television Francaise) was a branch of the civil service.

In May 1968, while TV audiences elsewhere were watching the rioting students and workers in the streets of Paris, ORTF was not permitted to broadcast the first few days of the disturbances. The government yielded only when the ORTF staff threatened to strike. A later attempt to reimpose control led to a month-long strike and a virtual blackout of screens.

Australia, with its vast distances for signals to cover, tempered enthusiasm for the new medium with caution. The prime minister, Sir Robert Menzies, set up a Royal Commission in 1953 to advise on the number of television stations and how they should be run. The answer was a mixture of state-run TV and private enterprise. Commercial TV broadcasting began in Victoria in September 1956, and the Australian Broadcasting Control Board laid down strict guidelines that "programs that could be harmful to young people or cause offense to any section should be avoided." Films, for instance, were divided into four categories: unrestricted, not suitable for children, not suitable for broadcasting before 8:30 p.m., and not suitable for TV.

In the democracies, television could make

HISTORY IN THE MAKING A giant TV screen in Trafalgar Square. An estimated 723 million people worldwide watched man's first steps on the Moon.

or break a politician, because it helped voters make a personal assessment of those seeking their support. It helped to break Senator McCarthy, whose wild accusations against so-called communists in high places held America in thrall for almost four years. Veteran broadcaster Ed Morrow exposed McCarthy in a program called *See It Now* in March 1954, and the senator himself added the final touch with the bullying perfor-mance he gave in the televised hearings later that year when he attacked the U.S. army. Richard Nixon used television to save his political life in 1952, when he made his "Checkers" speech. Facing accusations of financial chicanery, Nixon admitted that his family had received a gift—a spaniel named Checkers—and they planned to keep it. But his performance in the 1960 Presidential election campaign was less sure. In a series of TV debates that was watched by more than 115 million Americans, Nixon, who was recovering from illness at the time, looked unimpressive against the energetic, suntanned John F. Kennedy and went on to lose the election. General de Gaulle, who with his passion and monolithic integrity was a natural performer on television, summed up its importance to politicians: "I have two political weapons: TV and TV; TV because I am so good at it; TV because my opponents are so bad." The assassination of President Kennedy, in November 1963, saw television come of age as a news medium. A global audience shared in the shock of the assassination and the murder of the suspected assassin, Lee Harvey Oswald, that followed. And they shared America's grief when television covered Kennedy's funeral. But television could make the news, as well as report it. It brought the Vietnam War into American homes, and its daily portrayal of the carnage helped to build up opposition to the war, and so bring its end nearer.

INTERNATIONAL MOURNING A French family watches President Kennedy's funeral on TV. Through television, people all over the world shared in America's grief.

TIMECHART

1945

APRIL

12 President **Roosevelt dies** and is succeeded by Harry S Truman.

MAY

8 Victory in Europe: **VE Day**.

JUNE

26 Charter of **United Nations** signed in San Francisco.

JULY

26 Winston Churchill loses U.K. election. Attlee's **Labor government** promises nationalization of key industries and a welfare state.

WORKING FOR PEACE
The United Nations set out to abolish the age-old scourge of war.

AUGUST

14 Victory in Japan: **VJ Day**.

15 French Vichy leader Marshal Pétain **condemned to death** (later commuted to life imprisonment).

17 Indonesian nationalists **proclaim independence.**

SEPTEMBER

2 Ho Chi Minh declares **independence of Vietnam.**

---

10 Norwegian politician Vidkun Quisling **sentenced to death** for collaborating with Nazis.

OCTOBER

15 Vichy France's Foreign Minister Pierre Laval **shot for treason**.

17 Juan Perón released from prison after Eva Duarte ("Evita") organizes **mass demonstrations** against his arrest by Argentina's military leaders.

23 In a **referendum and election**, the French vote out the Third Republic and vote in a new National Assembly.

NOVEMBER

13 Charles de Gaulle elected French president.

Ahmed Sukarno becomes president of **Indonesian Republic**.

DECEMBER

27 International Monetary Fund and World Bank established to help postwar economic recovery.

1946

Dr. Benjamin Spock's *Common Sense Book of Baby and Child Care* is published.

JANUARY

2 King Zog of Albania deposed.

3 Lord Haw Haw (British subject William Joyce) hanged for treason in London.

20 De Gaulle resigns as president of France.

FEBRUARY

14 IBM introduces ENIAC (Electronic Numerical Integrator and Computer), the **first electronic calculator.**

22 Dr. Selman Waksam announces **discovery of streptomycin**, an antibiotic used against tuberculosis.

MARCH

5 In Fulton, Missouri, Winston Churchill warns that an **Iron Curtain** has fallen across Europe.

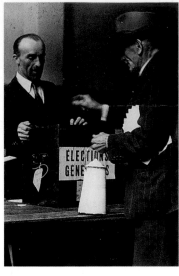

NEW START A Frenchman casts his vote in the combined election and referendum that ended the discredited Third Republic.

APRIL

4 Frenchman Dr. Marcel Petiot sentenced to death for **27 murders**.

18 International Court of Justice opened at The Hague.

JUNE

4 Juan Perón installed as **president of Argentina**.

13 Italian **monarchy abolished** in referendum.

JULY

4 Forty-two Jews killed in **pogrom at Kielce,** Poland.

21 Bread **rationed** in Britain.

---

22 Irgun terrorists blow up Jerusalem's **King David Hotel**, killing 91, in attempt to force Britain to allow unrestricted entry of Jews into Palestine.

AUGUST

16 10,000 casualties in three days of **Hindu-Muslim riots** in Calcutta.

SEPTEMBER

1 Greek **monarchy restored** in plebiscite.

OCTOBER

15 Reichsmarschall Hermann **Göring commits suicide** to escape execution for war crimes.

16 Ten leading Nazi **war criminals hanged** at Nuremberg.

NOVEMBER

3 New **democratic constitution** introduced in Japan: the emperor is no longer divine.

19 Vietminh attack French in Vietnam.

22 World's **first ballpoint pen**, the Biro, goes on sale.

27 Monnet Plan, to modernize French industry and agriculture, introduced.

DECEMBER

21 Earthquake in Japan kills 1,086.

TERROR ATTACK The King David Hotel, Jerusalem, destroyed by a time-bomb planted by Zionist terrorists.

1947

The Diary of Anne Frank is published. It tells the poignant story of a Jewish girl and her family hiding from the Gestapo in wartime Amsterdam.

Marlon Brando becomes a star in Tennessee Williams's play *A Streetcar Named Desire*.

Le Corbusier's Unité d'habitation in Marseilles is built.

JANUARY

Big Freeze continues across Western Europe, blocking roads and railways, and closing factories.

1 Coal industry **nationalized** in Britain.

FEBRUARY

2 Britain's Royal Air Force begins the **evacuation of Britons** from Palestine.

7 Dead Sea Scrolls discovered in caves at Qumran, Jordan. They throw light on early Biblical history.

20 Lord Louis Mountbatten appointed **last Viceroy of India**.

MARCH

12 Truman Doctrine pledges American aid for any country threatened by communism.

APRIL

10 Jackie Robinson joins the Brooklyn Dodgers.

MAY

12 Arabs appeal to the United Nations for an **independent Palestine**.

29 India outlaws **Untouchability**.

JUNE

5 America comes to the aid of Europe with the **Marshall Plan** to rebuild industry and agriculture.

23 Anti-union **Taft-Hartley Act**, passed over President Truman's veto, outlaws the closed shop in the U.S.

24 A flying saucer is reportedly sighted near Mount Rainier in Washington State, the first of many.

JULY

18 Jewish refugee ship *Exodus* impounded by the British and its passengers refused entry to Palestine.

19 Burmese leader **Aung Sang** assassinated.

AUGUST

15 India wins independence, and the **subcontinent is partitioned** between India and Pakistan; widespread massacres as millions of Hindus, Muslims and Sikhs left in the "wrong" country flee to the other.

24 Edinburgh International Festival of music and drama launched, with Rudolf Bing as director.

31 Communists win election in Hungary.

SEPTEMBER

2 American republics sign **Treaty of Mutual Assistance**.

OCTOBER

5 Communist Information Bureau, **the Cominform**, set up to promulgate the party line.

14 Chuck Yeager becomes first man to **break the sound barrier**.

NOVEMBER

1 Benelux Treaty sets up a customs union between Belgium, the Netherlands and Luxembourg.

UNDER NEW MANAGEMENT   On January 1, 1947, day one of coal nationalization in Britain, miners stake a claim with a sign saying their colliery now belongs to the people.

20 Princess Elizabeth marries Philip Mountbatten, Duke of Edinburgh.

29 UN announces plan to **partition Palestine.**

DECEMBER

27 Greek government **dissolves Communist Party**.

29 India-Pakistan **conflict in Kashmir** taken to United Nations.

30 King Michael of Romania **abdicates**.

1948

Cultural purge in U.S.S.R. as Commissar Andrei Zhdanov accuses the composers Shostakovitch, Prokofiev and Khachaturian of writing "formalist" music, above the heads of the masses.

American painter Jackson Pollock introduces **"Action Painting."**

JANUARY

1 Railways **nationalized** in Britain.

4 Burma **wins independence**.

25 Franc devalued, from 120 to 210 to the dollar.

30 Mahatma **Gandhi shot dead** by fanatical Hindu: riots follow.

FEBRUARY

27 Communists come to power in **Czech coup**.

28 Last British **troops leave India**.

MARCH

10 Czech Foreign Minister **Jan Masaryk killed** in mysterious fall from window.

APRIL

9 Jewish terrorists from the Irgun and the Stern Gang carry out **Deir Yassin massacre** at an Arab village.

30 Organization of American States (OAS) created by the U.S. and 20 Latin American countries to foster economic development.

MAY

14 State of Israel proclaimed, with Chaim Weizmann as president and David Ben-Gurion as prime minister. In response, Arab armies mass on borders.

28 Daniel Malan replaces Jan Christian Smuts as prime minister of South Africa and embarks on a **policy of apartheid**—racial separation.

JUNE

Insurrection in Malaya: Chinese communists begin murdering European planters.

7 Eduard **Benes resigns** as president of Czechoslovakia; replaced by communist Klement Gottwald.

18 Deutschmark replaces Reichsmark in German currency reform.

22 The *Empire Windrush* docks at Tilbury with Britain's **first immigrants** from the West Indies.

24 The Soviets, alarmed at currency reform, which they saw as a step toward the formation of West Germany, close the land routes to Berlin in the **Berlin Blockade**. The Western allies respond with the Berlin airlift.

25 Joe Louis knocks out Jersey Joe Walcott, to retain the **world heavyweight** boxing title.

BIRTH OF WEST GERMANY Future Chancellor Konrad Adenauer signing the document that created the Federal Republic of (West) Germany.

JULY

5 National Health Service begins in Britain, with free cradle-to-grave health care for all.

14 Stalin-Tito split comes into the open as Soviet-dominated **Cominform expels Yugoslavia**.

25 Brussels Treaty on Western union comes into force.

26 Englishman Freddie Mills beats American Gus Lesnevich for **world light-heavyweight** boxing crown.

AUGUST

London Olympics: Dutch housewife Fanny Blankers-Koen wins four gold medals.

OCTOBER

12 First **Morris Minor**, a popular small car designed by Alec Issigonis, rolls off assembly line in the U.K.

NOVEMBER

3 Harry S Truman **confounds pollsters and pundits** by winning presidential election.

DECEMBER

1 Transjordan **annexes Arab Palestine**—the West Bank.

23 General Tojo, Japan's former prime minister, is **hanged for war crimes**.

1949

Orson Welles plays Harry Lime in Carol Reed's classic film **The Third Man**, a tale of corruption in postwar Vienna.

George Orwell's **1984** published.

Alec Guinness plays eight parts in the **Ealing comedy** *Kind Hearts and Coronets*.

Rodgers and Hammerstein score a Broadway hit with *South Pacific*.

JANUARY

1 UN imposes **ceasefire in India-Pakistan** quarrel over Kashmir.

13-15 Race **riots in Durban**, South Africa; 106 killed.

FEBRUARY

14 Hungary's Cardinal Mindszenty **sentenced to life** imprisonment on charges of treason, plotting and currency fraud.

MARCH

1 World heavyweight boxing champion **Joe Louis retires** after 25 successful title defenses.

15 Clothes rationing ends in Britain.

APRIL

1 Newfoundland becomes **Canada's 10th province**.

3 Arab nations agree to **armistice with Israel**.

4 12 Western nations sign **North Atlantic Treaty Organization** (NATO) defense alliance.

MAY

12 Soviets lift the **Berlin Blockade**, after the West kept the city supplied by air for nearly a year.

18 Eire becomes the **Republic of Ireland**.

23 The Federal Republic of **(West) Germany** is born.

JULY

10 The frigate HMS *Amethyst*, under Lieutenant-Commander Kerans, makes a 140 mile **dash to freedom** down the Yangtse river, under the fire of communist Chinese guns.

14 Soviet atomic bomb test in central Asia ends the West's monopoly of nuclear weapons.

27 The De Havilland Comet, **the world's first jet airliner,** reaches 500 mph on its first flight.

FALLING POUND In September 1949, Britain devalued the pound by 30 percent to $2.80.

AUGUST

14 Konrad Adenauer becomes **West Germany's first chancellor**.

14 Greek **government troops defeat communist forces** of General Markos in the Vitsi Mountains, effectively ending Greek civil war.

25 America's electronics and broadcasting giant, RCA, announces it has developed **a system for transmitting color television**.

SEPTEMBER

2 The first **Cannes Film Festival**.

18 The pound **devalued** by 30 percent.

LEADER OF THE NEW CHINA Mao Zedong, leader of China's Communists, who came to power after the defeat of Chiang Kai-shek's Nationalist forces.

OCTOBER

1 Communist leader **Mao Zedong** proclaims People's Republic of China, as Chiang Kai-shek's Nationalists flee to Formosa (Taiwan).

6 American-born Iva Ikuko Toguri, (**"Tokyo Rose"**) is jailed for ten years for treason.

7 Democratic Republic of **(East) Germany** proclaimed.

DECEMBER

16 Ahmed Sukarno is elected **first president of Indonesia**.

1950

JANUARY

25 Former U.S. State Department official **Alger Hiss**, accused of having passed secrets to the communists, is sentenced to five years for perjury.

FEBRUARY

9 Senator Joe McCarthy begins his **communist witch hunt** by announcing he has names of 205 card-carrying communists in the State Department.

BACKING MCCARTHY A lapel button pushes support for Senator Joe McCarthy's anti-communist witch hunt to extremes.

14 U.S.S.R. and China sign 30-year **Treaty of Friendship**.

MARCH

6 German-born British scientist Klaus Fuchs jailed for 14 years for **betraying atomic secrets**.

JUNE

25 North Korean troops and tanks invade across 38th parallel: **start of the Korean War**.

28 Shock result in first round of **soccer's World Cup**: England 0— U.S. 1.

SEPTEMBER

16 Inchon landing by UN troops under General MacArthur **drives North Koreans back**.

OCTOBER

21 China **invades Tibet**.

27 First reports of **Chinese troops** fighting UN forces in Korea.

DECEMBER

25 Stone of Scone, the coronation stone for 650 years, vanishes from Westminster Abbey.

1951

J.D. Salinger's *Catcher in the Rye* is published.

JANUARY

27 The Atomic Energy Commission gives no warning before it detonates its **first atomic test bomb** in the Nevada desert.

MARCH

15 Iran nationalizes **Anglo-Iranian Oil Company**.

29 Julius and Ethel Rosenberg sentenced to death for passing atomic secrets to the Soviet Union. This is the first death sentence in the U.S. for peacetime espionage.

APRIL

11 General **MacArthur fired** for public opposition to Truman's policy in Korea.

13 Stone of Scone, taken by Scottish nationalists, is returned to Westminster Abbey.

18 France, West Germany, Italy, Belgium, the Netherlands and Luxembourg set up the **European Coal and Steel Community**, forerunner of the Common Market.

22 Aneurin **Bevan resigns** from British Cabinet in a fight over introduction of charges for NHS-covered false teeth and eyeglasses.

MAY

11 Radio Free Europe begins broadcasting.

14 Voters of mixed race **removed from common electoral roll** in South Africa.

25 British diplomats Guy Burgess and Donald MacLean **flee to Moscow**.

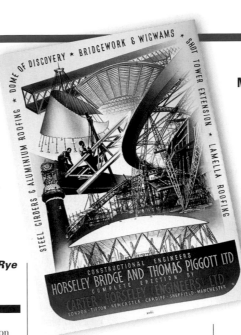

* DOME OF DISCOVERY * BRIDGEWORK & WIGWAMS * SHOT TOWER EXTENSION * LAMELLA ROOFING * STEEL GIRDERS & ALUMINIUM ROOFING *

CONSTRUCTIONAL ENGINEERS
HORSELEY BRIDGE AND THOMAS PIGGOTT LTD
COMPLETE ERECTION BY
CARTER HORSELEY (ENGINEERS) LTD
LONDON · TIPTON · NEWCASTLE · CARDIFF · SHEFFIELD · MANCHESTER

SPONSORING THE FESTIVAL Industry lends support to the Festival of Britain, opened on May 1, 1951, by advertising in the catalogue.

JULY

19 Laos declared Independent.

20 Jordan's **King Abdullah** assassinated.

AUGUST

1 Mau Mau, a terrorist anti-white organization, reported to be administering oaths in Kenya.

DECEMBER

1 Footprints alleged to be those of the **"Abominable Snowman,"** or Yeti, photographed in the Himalayas.

1952

JANUARY

15 Sir Gerald Templer takes charge in **Malayan Emergency**.

25 Forty-six Egyptians die in **British attack** on police station in Ismailia.

26 Riots in Cairo.

FEBRUARY

6 George VI dies. Princess Elizabeth is on safari in Kenya when she hears that she is queen.

21 Identity cards abolished in Britain.

MARCH

8 U.S. doctors announce **first use of an artificial heart**, at Pennsylvania Hospital, Pittsburgh.

21 Kwame Nkrumah becomes the **first black African prime minister**, in the Gold Coast.

APRIL

28 U.S. **ends its occupation** of Japan.

JUNE

11 Non-whites in South Africa combine to launch **defiance campaign** against Apartheid laws.

27 McCarran Act **restricts immigration** to the United States.

JULY

23 General Mohammed Neguib and Colonel Gamal Abdul Nasser **lead coup** against regime of Egypt's playboy King Farouk, who abdicates.

26 "Evita" Perón, heroine of Argentina's "shirtless ones," dies.

AUGUST

11 Harrow-educated Prince Hussein becomes **king of Jordan**.

Helsinki Olympics: Emil Zatopek wins gold medals and sets world records in 5,000 meters, 10,000 meters and marathon.

SEPTEMBER

6 Twenty-six killed as **jet fighter crashes** at an air show in Britain.

10 West Germany announces it will **pay Israel $293 million** compensation for wartime atrocities.

23 Richard Nixon saves his political career with **"Checkers"** broadcast on television.

29 John Cobb, world land speed record-holder, killed in 240 mph boat crash on Loch Ness.

EVITA Eva Perón (background), whose fiery speeches made her popular with the masses, addresses Argentinian voters during the election of October 1951.

OCTOBER

3 Britain tests its **first atom bomb**, in the Monte Bello Islands, off Australia.

21 Jomo **Kenyatta arrested** and charged with being a leader of Kenya's Mau Mau rebellion.

NOVEMBER

4 Dwight D. Eisenhower ("Ike") wins presidential election. He will be the **34th president**.

16 U.S. tests **first hydrogen bomb** at Eniwetok Atoll in the Pacific.

19 Maria **Callas triumphs** in *Norma* at London's Covent Garden.

25 Agatha Christie's ***The Mousetrap*** opens in London.

28 Gatherings of **more than ten "natives"** forbidden in South Africa.

DECEMBER

18 World middleweight champion **Sugar Ray Robinson** retires.

1953

Ian Fleming introduces **007 James Bond** in *Casino Royale*.

JANUARY

13 Nine **Kremlin doctors arrested**, on Stalin's orders.

FEBRUARY

3 **North Sea floods**: more than 1,500 drown in Holland, and more than 300 along Britain's east coast.

13 Roman Catholic Church in Poland brought **under state control**.

MARCH

5 Soviet dictator **Stalin dies**. Georgi Malenkov and Nikita Khrushchev emerge as rivals for the succession.

APRIL

4 **Kremlin doctors** set free.

8 Jomo Kenyatta, **found guilty of leading Mau Mau** in Kenya, sentenced to seven years of hard labor.

KHRUSHCHEV IN CHARGE Nikita Khrushchev won power in the Kremlin after Stalin's death.

25 Cambridge scientists James Watson and Francis Crick unlock the secret of heredity with their proposed **double helix** structure for the DNA molecule.

MAY

2 BOAC's **Comet crashes**: 48 killed.

29 New Zealand climber Edmund Hillary and Nepalese Sherpa Tenzing Norgay conquer the world's highest peak, **Mount Everest**.

JUNE

2 Coronation of **Queen Elizabeth II**.

16 Soviet tanks move in to **crush workers' uprising** in East Berlin.

18 A USAF C124 **Globemaster plane crashes** in Tokyo, killing 129 American servicemen.

19 Julius and Ethel Rosenberg **executed**.

JULY

27 **Korean War ends**, with armistice signed at Panmunjon.

AUGUST

1 **Central African Federation** inaugurated, linking Southern Rhodesia, Northern Rhodesia and Nyasaland.

22 Mohammed Mossadegh, prime minister of Iran who nationalized the Anglo-Iranian Oil Company, **ousted in coup** and jailed.

SEPTEMBER

12 **Nikita Khrushchev** elected First Secretary of Soviet Communist Party.

28 Poland's Roman Catholic primate, **Cardinal Wyszynski**, arrested.

NOVEMBER

21 The **Piltdown Man**, believed to be Europe's earliest man-like creature, is revealed as a hoax.

25 Hungary's soccer team **defeats England** 6-3 at Wembley.

31 British expedition seeking the **Abominable Snowman**, or Yeti, reaches New Delhi.

DECEMBER

23 Lavrenti Beria, feared **head of Stalin's secret police**, is shot for treason.

1954

Tennessee Williams wins the **Pulitzer prize** for *Cat on a Hot Tin Roof*.

3-D movies introduced.

JANUARY

1 **Bantu Education Act** enforced in South Africa.

11 BOAC **grounds Comets** after second fatal crash.

15 **Mau Mau leader** General China captured.

21 Tito dismisses his second-in-command, **Milovan Djilas**.

FEBRUARY

3 First parliament of **Central African Federation** of Northern Rhodesia, Southern Rhodesia and Nyasaland.

26 West German **constitution revised** to permit rearmament.

MARCH

21 British diplomat **Kim Philby** recalled from Washington in "Third Man" spy probe.

22 Crew of Japanese fishing boat *Lucky Dragon* suffers **radiation sickness** after receiving fallout from U.S. nuclear tests at Bikini.

APRIL

12 Virologist Jonas Salk's **vaccine against polio** licensed for tests.

14 Soviet diplomat Vladimir Petrov seeks asylum after **exposing spy ring** in Australia.

17 **Colonel Nasser ousts** General Neguib from power in Egypt.

NASSER TAKES POWER Colonel Abdul Nasser, who plotted with General Neguib to overthrow Egypt's King Farouk, went on to oust Neguib.

17 **Army-McCarthy hearings** begin in Washington.

MAY

6 Medical student Roger Bannister breaks the **four-minute mile** barrier, in a run of 3 minutes, 59.4 seconds.

8 French stronghold of **Dien Bien Phu** falls to General Giap's Vietminh.

24 IBM announces its electronic brain, capable of **10 million calculations** an hour.

JUNE

20 Pierre Mendès-France becomes **French premier**.

ACTIVE SERVICE Camouflaged GIs (background) man a rocket-launcher during the Korean War, which ended on July 27, 1953.

INTO THE JAWS OF HELL French para-troops being dropped into Dien Bien Phu in North Vietnam. The site became a death trap for the French.

21 American Cancer Society says smoking increases the risk of lung cancer.

JULY

3 Food rationing ends in Britain: housewives celebrate by burning their ration books.

20 Delegates at **Vietnam Peace Talks** in Geneva agree to divide the country along the 17th parallel.

31 Mendès-France proposes internal **self-rule for Tunisia**.

AUGUST

12 The UN formally **withdraws from Korea**, ending a four-year police action.

END OF AN ERA This British housewife was one of many who burned their ration books to celebrate the end of food rationing in July 1954.

27 Mendès-France proposes internal **self-rule for Morocco**.

SEPTEMBER

4 Chinese shell **Nationalist-held island** of Quemoy.

8 South East Asia Treaty Organization (**SEATO**) defense pact signed. Eight countries pledge mutual defense against Communist aggression.

OCTOBER

19 Metal fatigue identified as cause of crashes after third Comet jet disaster.

21 French possessions in India, including Pondicherry, ceded to the Indian Republic.

NOVEMBER

1 Nationalist **uprising begins in Algeria**, with terrorist attacks carried out by the FLN, the National Liberation Front.

8 House of Commons approves **Highway Code**.

DECEMBER

2 Red-baiter **Joseph McCarthy** censured by U.S. Senate.

7 Leaders of banned **Muslim Brotherhood** executed in Egypt after failed attempt to kill President Nasser.

18 British troops fire on Enosis (Union with Greece) demonstrators in Cyprus.

1955

JANUARY

10 World-famous contralto Marian Anderson becomes **the first black singer** to perform at New York's Metropolitan Opera.

FEBRUARY

8 Khrushchev **forces the resignation** of his rival Malenkov. Nikolai Bulganin becomes premier of the U.S.S.R.

10 Police in South Africa **evict 60,000 blacks** from Sophiatown after it is declared a white area.

24 Iraq and Turkey form the **Baghdad Pact**, a defensive alliance against communist encroachment.

APRIL

24 Bandung Conference of unaligned African and Asian nations closes with a call to end colonialism and racism.

MAY

2 Mao Zedong launches the **100 Flowers** campaign.

9 West Germany, now a sovereign state, **joins NATO**.

14 Eastern bloc nations **form the Warsaw Pact**.

31 Supreme Court tells Southern States to **end segregation** "soon."

JUNE

2 President Tito and Nikita Khrushchev sign **friendship treaty**, ending split between Yugoslavia and the U.S.S.R.

11 Racing cars crash into grandstand at Le Mans: 80 killed.

JULY

16 Cardinal Mindszenty released from jail in Hungary but placed **under house arrest**.

18 Disneyland opens, at Anaheim, near Los Angeles.

SEPTEMBER

19 President **Juan Perón** ousted by military revolt in Argentina.

22 Commercial television begins in Britain.

OCTOBER

2 France **quits UN General Assembly** in protest over criticism of its policy in Algeria.

31 Princess Margaret, "mindful of the Church's teaching," **decides not to marry** divorced Group Captain Peter Townsend.

NOVEMBER

28 Britain declares **state of emergency** in Cyprus in response to EOKA terror campaign for Enosis (Union with Greece).

DECEMBER

1 Arrest of Rosa Parks for refusing to give up her seat to a white man leads to **black boycott of buses** in Montgomery, Alabama. Parks' action inspires civil rights activists nationwide.

CYPRUS AFLAME Fire leaps from the British Institute in Nicosia in September 1955, as troops move in to disperse anti-British rioters.

1956

FEBRUARY

24-25 Nikita Khrushchev denounces Stalin at the 20th Party Congress.

MARCH

2 Morocco becomes independent.

2 King Hussein sacks **Britain's Glubb Pasha** as head of Jordan's Arab Legion.

9 Archbishop Makarios **exiled from Cyprus** to the Seychelles.

JUNE

13 Last British troops **quit Canal Zone** in Egypt.

28 More than 100 Polish workers killed in **riot in Poznan.**

JULY

26 Egypt's President Gamal Abdel Nasser **nationalizes the Suez Canal.**

OCTOBER

23 Hungarians revolt against Soviet rule.

28 Poland's **Cardinal Wyszynski** released.

29 Israel invades Sinai.

NOVEMBER

5 British and French troops land in Egypt.

PROTEST IN BUDAPEST A photograph of Lenin is burned along with other items looted from a Soviet bookstore by angry Hungarian citizens.

5 Soviet tanks move to **crush Hungarian Revolt.**

7 UN votes to send **peace force** to Canal Zone.

13 U.S. Supreme Court rules that **segregation on buses** violates the Constitution.

DECEMBER

3 Under U.S. and world pressure, Britain and France announce their **withdrawal from the Canal Zone** in Egypt.

1957

Jack Kerouac's **On the Road** published, describing the thoughts and travels of rootless Beatniks.

Albert Camus gives a French view of rootlessness in **The Outsider.**

Work begins on Brazil's new capital city, **Brasília.**

JANUARY

1 Saarland returned to West Germany.

25 Kashmir joins India.

MARCH

15 Egypt **bars Israel** from using newly cleared Suez Canal.

25 France, West Germany, Italy, the Netherlands, Belgium and Luxembourg—the "Six"—sign the **Treaties of Rome**, setting up the Common Market and Euratom.

28 Archbishop **Makarios released from exile** in the Seychelles.

MAY

15 Britain's first **H-bomb tested**, on Christmas Island.

EGYPT WELCOMES THE UN With the Suez crisis over, UN troops are warmly welcomed at Port Said.

JUNE

25 African National Congress (ANC) calls **one-day strike** in South Africa.

26 British Naval Commander "Buster" Crabb's **body found in sea.**

JULY

3 Khrushchev demotes Soviet leadership challengers Molotov, Malenkov and Kaganovich.

15 Franco announces that the **monarchy will be restored** in Spain.

20 British premier Harold Macmillan tells a Tory party rally Britain has **"never had it so good."**

AUGUST

29 Drunkometer tested on drivers in United States.

30 Federation of Malaysia born, with Tunku Abdul Rahman as chief minister and communist terrorists effectively beaten.

SEPTEMBER

4 Wolfenden Report recommends legalization in Britain of homosexual acts between consenting adults in private.

ARMED ESCORT The law was on their side, but black pupils in Arkansas needed the protection of soldiers in 1958. The civil rights movement still had a long way to go.

EXODUS FROM INDONESIA In December 1957, Indonesia expelled Dutch citizens and seized Dutch assets worth $1.5 billion, causing a mass exodus of Europeans and Eurasians.

23 Papa Doc Duvalier wins election in Haiti.

24 U.S. troops, sent in by President Eisenhower, enforce the right of nine black children to **attend a "white" school** at Little Rock, Arkansas.

OCTOBER

4 The U.S.S.R. launches **world's first space satellite**, Sputnik I.

8 Radioactivity escapes during a fire at the Windscale nuclear plant, Cumberland, U.K.

DECEMBER

5 President Sukarno **expels Dutch** from Indonesia.

1958

JANUARY

31 United States launches its first satellite, Explorer, into orbit around the Earth.

FEBRUARY

1 Egypt and Syria combine in **United Arab Republic**.

MAY

5-23 The **Great Leap Forward** launched in China.

8, 13 Anti-American riots in Peru and Venezuela during "goodwill" visit by VP Richard Nixon.

13 *Pieds noirs* French settlers **revolt in Algeria**, and form Committee of Public Safety under General Massu.

JUNE

1 General de Gaulle **recalled to power** in France.

JULY

14 Pro-Western King Faisal of Iraq and Prime Minister Nuri al-Said killed in **Nasser-inspired army coup**.

15 U.S. **Sixth Fleet** called in to support government of Lebanon.

17 British paratroops called in to prevent Syrian army invading Jordan.

30 Race riots in Notting Hill Gate, west London.

SEPTEMBER

2 Britain and Iceland begin the **Cod War** over rights to fish within 12 miles of the Icelandic coast.

25 All of France's **black African territories** apart from Guinea opt for independence within the French Community.

OCTOBER

4 BOAC starts **first Transatlantic passenger jet service**.

DECEMBER

5 Britain's **first highway**, the 8 mile Preston bypass, is opened.

21 De Gaulle elected first president of **France's Fifth Republic**.

31 The drug **thalidomide**, used against morning sickness in pregnancy, is suspected of causing birth defects.

1959

JANUARY

1 Fidel Castro and his **Cuban revolutionaries take over Havana**, toppling the regime of dictator Fulgencia Batista.

25 Pope John XXIII calls Second Vatican Council to **promote Church unity**.

FEBRUARY

19 Archbishop Makarios, Britain and Turkey sign agreement to bring peace and **independence to Cyprus**.

20 Protests against the white-dominated **Central African Federation** begin in Nyasaland, then spread to Southern Rhodesia.

MARCH

3 Eleven **Mau Mau prisoners** beaten to death at Hola camp.

17 Dalai Lama flees Tibet after uprising in Lhasa against Chinese occupation.

JUNE

26 St. Lawrence Seaway officially opened.

AUGUST

21 Hawaii becomes **America's 50th State**.

SEPTEMBER

16 De Gaulle **offers Algeria the choice** of secession, integration or independence in close association with France.

NOVEMBER

1 Congolese nationalist leader **Patrice Lumumba** arrested, after anti-white riots.

10 The **UN General Assembly** condemns South Africa's policy of apartheid.

20 Britain, Norway, Sweden, Denmark, Portugal, Switzerland and Austria—the "Seven"—form the **European Free Trade Association** (EFTA).

DECEMBER

3 Nearly 300 die when **dam bursts** above the French Riviera town of Fréjus.

TATI AS HULOT A German poster for the Oscar-winning French film, *Mon Oncle*. Jacques Tati, France's gift to comedy, played Monsieur Hulot. Background: U.S. marines from the Sixth Fleet land in strife-torn Lebanon in July 1958.

20 World's first **atom-powered ice-breaker**, the Russian ship *Lenin*, begins operations.

1960

JANUARY

10 President Nasser of Egypt lays the foundation stone of **Aswan Dam**.

FEBRUARY

3 British premier Harold Macmillan says a **"wind of change"** is blowing through Africa.

13 France explodes an atomic bomb in the Sahara.

MARCH

21 South African police fire on black demonstrators at **Sharpeville**, killing 69 and injuring 180.

25 All **black political** organizations banned in South Africa.

MAY

1 U.S.S.R. shoots down **U-2 spy plane**, piloted by Francis Gary Powers, over Soviet territory.

5 Israeli agents kidnap **Adolf Eichmann**, former SS officer and organizer of Hitler's "Final Solution."

27 U.S. **cuts off all aid** to Cuba.

JUNE

30 Congo gains independence from Belgium. Patrice Lumumba is first prime minister.

JULY

7 Sirimavo Bandaranaike becomes world's **first woman prime minister**, in Ceylon.

MACMILLAN'S AFRICAN JOURNEY British Prime Minister Harold Macmillan in Swaziland, shortly before making his "wind of change" speech in Cape Town.

16 Soviet-Chinese split comes into the open as U.S.S.R. withdraws its experts from China.

31 Malayan Emergency officially declared over.

AUGUST

16 Cyprus declared independent within Commonwealth, with Archbishop Makarios as president.

SEPTEMBER

10 Organization of Petrol Exporting Countries (**OPEC**) set up in Baghdad.

14 Colonel Joseph **Mobutu seizes power** in the Congo.

OCTOBER

1 Nigeria **becomes independent** within the Commonwealth.

NOVEMBER

2 Jury in **Lady Chatterley** trial at London's Old Bailey rules that D.H. Lawrence's novel is not obscene.

4 John F. Kennedy wins election to become America's 35th president.

DECEMBER

9-13 *Pieds noirs* **riot** as President Charles de Gaulle tours Algeria, promising independence for Arabs.

31 Britain's **last National Servicemen** receive their call-up papers.

1961

Joseph Heller's novel **Catch 22** gives a new phrase to the language.

FEBRUARY

24 Anthropologist Dr. Louis Leakey announces discovery of 1.75 million-year-old remains of **Homo habilis**, a tool-making forerunner of modern man, in Olduvai Gorge, Tanganyika (Tanzania).

APRIL

12 Soviet cosmonaut Yuri Gagarin becomes the **first man in space** when he orbits the Earth in the Vostok spacecraft.

17 U.S.-backed Cuban exiles land at **Bay of Pigs** in attempt to overthrow Castro. They are all killed or captured.

21 Military revolt in Algeria, led by General Salan and other disloyal French army officers. It is crushed in four days.

MAY

31 South Africa becomes a republic and **leaves the Commonwealth**.

AUGUST

13 Walter Ulbricht's communist regime in East Germany begins erecting the **Berlin Wall**.

21 All restrictions lifted on Kenyan nationalist leader **Jomo Kenyatta**.

SEPTEMBER

19 UN Secretary General **Dag Hammarskjold** is killed in an air crash in Northern Rhodesia.

DECEMBER

15 UN General Assembly **votes to admit communist China**.

1962

Alexandir Solzhenitsyn's **One Day in the Life of Ivan Denisovich** is published in the U.S.S.R.

Andy Warhol, Roy Lichtenstein and Claus Oldenburg make **Pop Art** the latest fashion in America.

FEBRUARY

8 Street **fighting** in Paris as the OAS Secret Army tries to topple de Gaulle.

20 Astronaut **John Glenn** becomes first American to orbit Earth.

MAY

31 Adolf **Eichmann hanged**, for crimes against Jews.

BERLIN WALL In August 1961, the East Germans built the wall that became the stark symbol of the Cold War. Background: Kenyans celebrate the release of their leader, Jomo Kenyatta.

JULY

1 Britain **tightens curbs** on immigrants with Commonwealth Immigration Act.

3 De Gaulle signs **declaration of independence** for Algeria, following referendums in France and Algeria.

13 British premier Harold Macmillan **sacks one-third of his Cabinet** in the "night of the long knives."

AUGUST

5 Film star **Marilyn Monroe** found dead in bed, an empty bottle of sleeping tablets nearby.

15 Dutch agree to cede western New Guinea (**Irian Jaya**) to Indonesia.

SEPTEMBER

30 James Meredith becomes the **first black student** to enroll at the University of Mississippi, provoking riots in which two people die.

OCTOBER

2 President Kwame Nkrumah declares Ghana a **one-party state**.

16-28 Cuban missile crisis begins when President Kennedy is informed that the U.S.S.R. is building missile sites on the island. On October 22 he announces that **America will blockade Cuba**. On October 28 Soviet premier Nikita **Khrushchev backs down** and agrees to dismantle the bases.

1963

JANUARY

14 De Gaulle says **"Non" to Britain's application** to join the Common Market.

FEBRUARY

14 Surgeons at Leeds Infirmary in the U.K. reveal they have carried out the **first successful kidney transplant**.

INDEPENDENCE FOR ALGERIA Crowds pour into the streets of Algiers to celebrate independence after nearly eight years of bitter war against France.

MARCH

27 British Railways chairman Dr. Beeching proposes **crushing cuts** in the country's rail network.

JUNE

5 John Profumo, Britain's war secretary, resigns from parliament after lying to the House of Commons in the **Christine Keeler scandal**.

16 Soviet cosmonaut Valentina Tereshkova becomes the **first woman in space**.

26 President Kennedy declares in West Berlin, **"Ich bin ein Berliner."**

JULY

1 British Parliament is told that **Kim Philby** was the "Third Man" who tipped off runaway Foreign Office spies Burgess and Maclean.

AUGUST

5 The U.S., U.K. and U.S.S.R. sign the **Nuclear Test Ban Treaty**.

8 An armed gang gets away with an estimated £2.5 million ($7.5 million) in used banknotes in the **Great Train Robbery** at Cheddington, Buckinghamshire, U.K.

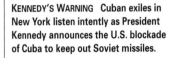

KENNEDY'S WARNING Cuban exiles in New York listen intently as President Kennedy announces the U.S. blockade of Cuba to keep out Soviet missiles.

28 Martin Luther King, Jr., makes his **"I have a dream"** speech at a massive civil rights demonstration in Washington.

NOVEMBER

2 South Vietnam **President Ngo Dinh Diem** is murdered after being overthrown in a military coup.

22 President John F. Kennedy assassinated in Dallas, Texas. Lee Harvey Oswald, accused of being the killer, is shot dead two days later while in police custody.

1964

FEBRUARY

8 America gives a rapturous reception to **The Beatles** when they fly into New York.

12 Fighting flares between **Greek and Turkish Cypriots**: 21 killed.

MARCH

4 UN decides to send **peace-keeping force** to Cyprus.

28 U.K. "Pirate" music station **Radio Caroline** begins broadcasting.

APRIL

3 Soviet leader Nikita Khrushchev publicly attacks **"false and reactionary"** policy of Chinese Communists.

13 Ian Smith is elected prime minister of Southern Rhodesia.

22 Tanganyika and Zanzibar to be united in new State of Tanzania.

JUNE

11 The ANC's Nelson Mandela is **sentenced to life imprisonment** for sabotage and plotting to overthrow the South African government.

14 "Papa Doc" Duvalier declared **president for life** in Haiti.

JULY

2 President Lyndon B. Johnson signs the **Civil Rights Act**, outlawing many forms of racial discrimination.

MAN WITH A VISION Martin Luther King, Jr., leader in America's struggle for civil rights, makes his "I have a dream" speech in Washington.

AUGUST

2 President Johnson acts on reports of North Vietnamese torpedo-boat attacks on U.S. destroyers in Tonkin Gulf to **escalate American action** against the North.

13 Last judicial **hangings** in Britain, at Manchester and Liverpool jails.

SEPTEMBER

7 Congo rebels declare a People's Republic at **Stanleyville**.

25 Frelimo **revolution against Portuguese** begins in Mozambique.

OCTOBER

15 Nikita Khrushchev **ousted from power** in Kremlin coup.

16 China explodes atom bomb.

NOVEMBER

26 Belgian paratroops **rescue whites** in Stanleyville, the Congo.

DECEMBER

12 Kenya **becomes a republic**, with Jomo Kenyatta as president.

1965

JANUARY

4 President Lyndon B. Johnson pledges in his State of the Union address that he will make America a **"Great Society."**

24 Death of **Sir Winston Churchill**.

26 Widespread **riots in India**, following the decision to make Hindi the official language.

FEBRUARY

1 Civil rights leader **Martin Luther King, Jr.,** and 300 supporters arrested in Selma, Alabama.

RACE RIOTS Troops patrol the streets of Watts during the Los Angeles race riots. Background: U.S. infantry on a "Search and Destroy" mission in Vietnam in May 1966.

24 American planes begin **Operation Rolling Thunder**, the sustained bombing of North Vietnam.

APRIL

25 Anti-communist junta seizes power in **Dominican Republic**.

JULY

5 One-party government established in **Tanzania**.

AUGUST

9 Singapore leaves Malaysian Federation.

11-17 Race riots in Watts, Los Angeles.

SEPTEMBER

8 Full-scale **war between India and Pakistan** over Kashmir.

OCTOBER

11 Publication of **Vinland map** is evidence that Vikings landed in North America.

NOVEMBER

11 Ian Smith, prime minister of Rhodesia, makes Unilateral Declaration of Independence (**UDI**). Within days, Britain imposes sanctions.

25 General **Mobutu imposes army** rule in the Congo.

1966

JANUARY

1 Colonel Jean **Bokassa seizes power** in Central African Republic.

ON THEIR OWN Rhodesian Prime Minister Ian Smith, watched by members of his Cabinet, signs Rhodesia's Unilateral Declaration of Independence.

FEBRUARY

22 Milton Obote seizes power in Uganda.

24 Kwame Nkrumah **ousted as president of Ghana** while on a state visit to China.

MARCH

1 De Gaulle announces France's intention to **withdraw from NATO**.

MAY

4-6 Cultural Revolution launched in China.

JUNE

29 U.S. planes bomb oil installations near Hanoi.

JULY

6 Malawi becomes a republic, with **Hastings Banda** as president.

29 Military **coup in Nigeria**: Lt. Col. Yakuba Gowon seizes power.

30 Alf Ramsey's **England wins soccer's World Cup**, beating West Germany 4-2 in the final at Wembley.

SEPTEMBER

6 South Africa's premier, Hendrik Verwoerd, the **"father" of apartheid**, is assassinated.

OCTOBER

21 Sliding coal mine debris buries school and houses in **Aberfan**, Wales, killing 116 children and 28 adults.

NOVEMBER

4 Floods in Italy kill more than 20 and damage art treasures in Florence.

1967

MARCH

6 Stalin's daughter, Svetlana, **requests asylum** at U.S. embassy in Delhi.

APRIL

21 Right-wing army **colonels seize power** in Greece.

MAY

30 Ibo leader Colonel Odumegwu Ojukwe announces that oil-rich Biafra is breaking away from the Nigerian Federation. **Civil war results**.

JUNE

5-10 Israel defeats Egypt, Syria and Jordan in **Six-Day War**.

JULY

24 De Gaulle, on visit to Canada, **encourages separatists** by announcing, *"Vive le Quebec libre!"*

OCTOBER

10 South American revolutionary **Che Guevara** reported dead in Bolivia.

31 70,000 Vietcong launch the **Tet Offensive** against the U.S. and their allies in South Vietnam.

MARCH

11-15 Anti-Soviet riots in Poland.

16 U.S. soldiers carry out **My Lai massacre** in Vietnam.

31 Lyndon B. Johnson calls **partial halt to bombing** of North Vietnam and announces that he will not run again for U.S. presidency.

APRIL

4 U.S. civil rights leader **Martin Luther King, Jr., shot dead** by a white assailant in Memphis, Tennessee. Widespread riots follow.

CROWNING MOMENT David Ben-Gurion, the founding father of Israel, congratulates Israeli troops who have just taken Arab-held Old Jerusalem in the Six-Day War.

27 Abortion Act eases abortion laws in Britain.

NOVEMBER

19 The **pound devalued**, from $2.80 to $2.40.

27 De Gaulle **vetoes Britain's second bid** to join the Common Market.

28 People's Republic of **South Yemen** proclaimed in Aden, ending 128 years of British rule.

DECEMBER

3 Dr. Christiaan Barnard performs **world's first heart transplant**, on Louis Washkansky, at Groote Schuur Hospital, Cape Town, South Africa.

11 Anglo-French Concorde, the **world's first supersonic airliner**, makes its first public flight.

13 King Constantine of Greece flees after failure of coup against military junta.

17 Australian Prime Minister **Harold Holt** drowns while swimming in the sea.

1968

JANUARY

5 Reform-minded **Alexander Dubcek** elected First Secretary of the Czechoslovak Communist Party.

MAYOR DALEY'S RESPONSE When students demonstrated against the Vietnam War at the 1968 Democratic Convention in Chicago, Mayor Richard Daley sent in riot police.

23 Students take over five campus buildings at **Columbia University.**

MAY

Month of the barricades in Paris as students, backed by workers, take to the streets in protest marches.

29 UN imposes mandatory **sanctions on Rhodesia**.

JUNE

5 Presidential candidate **Bobby Kennedy shot dead** by Palestinian Arab Sirhan Sirhan.

JULY

1 U.S., U.S.S.R. and Britain sign Nuclear Non-Proliferation Treaty.

29 Pope Paul reaffirms **Roman Catholic view** that artificial birth control is contrary to divine will.

AUGUST

20 Soviet troops move into Czechoslovakia, **ending the Prague Spring**.

29 Mayor Richard Daley's police use strong-arm tactics against **anti-war demonstrators** outside the Democratic Convention, Chicago.

NOVEMBER

6 Richard Nixon elected 37th president of the United States.

1969

JANUARY

3 Violence in **Londonderry** in Northern Ireland as Catholic civil rights marchers confront the Rev. Ian Paisley and his Protestant supporters.

FEBRUARY

3 Yasser Arafat appointed leader of the **Palestine Liberation Organization** (PLO).

MARCH

18 President Nixon **authorizes secret bombing** of Cambodia.

APRIL

28 President **de Gaulle resigns** after French referendum rejects his plans for constitutional reform.

JUNE

20 Prospecting companies report

discovery of **North Sea oil**.

JULY

20 U.S. astronaut Neil Armstrong becomes the **first man on the Moon**.

22 Franco names **Prince Juan Carlos** as his successor.

AUGUST

15 British troops welcomed in Catholic Bogside area of Londonderry in Northern Ireland.

RESISTANCE LEADER Yasser Arafat, who helped found the Arab resistance movement al-Fatah and became leader of the Palestine Liberation Organization.

SEPTEMBER

1 Muammar Gaddafi **leads army coup** in Libya.

OCTOBER

15 Millions across America **demonstrate against the Vietnam War** on "Moratorium Day."

NOVEMBER

24 Lt. William Calley accused of **My Lai massacre**.

DECEMBER

18 Death penalty abolished in Britain.

INDEX

NOTE: Numbers in *italics* denote illustrations.

Abdullah, King of Jordan 82, 147
Abel, Colonel Rudolf 112
Aberfan disaster 154
Abominable Snowman 147, 148
abortion 136, 155
A Bout de Souffle (film) 34
Abstract Expressionism 142, *142*
Acheson, Dean 107
Aden 84, 155
Adenauer, Konrad 38, 39, 40, 41, 146, *146*
Africa, independence 64-73, *64*
African Nationalist Congress (ANC) 72, 73, 150
Agent Orange 116
airplanes:
    Comet crashes 148, 149
    Concorde 155
    jet 146
Akahito, Crown Prince of Japan 141
Albania:
    aid in Greek civil war 18
    loyalty to U.S.S.R. 17
Aldermaston marches 28
Alexandria summit meeting 84
al-Fatah 85, 86
Algeria:
    anti-colonial riots 74, 149, 151
    French invasion of 74
    independence 36, 76, 76, 152, *153*
    OAS (Organization de l'Armée Secrète) 36, 76, 76
    pieds noirs 35, 74, 75, 75, 76, 151, 152
    war in 35, *35*, 74-76, *74*
Algiers, Battle of 74, 75
Ali, Muhammad 115
Alleg, Henri 75
Allen, Woody 137
al-Said, Nuri 84, 151
Amber Room 13, *13*
Amethyst, HMS 146
Amritsar, Muslims massacred 48
ANC (African Nationalist Congress) 72, 73, 150
And God Created Woman (film) 34, *34*
Angel, Ron 28
Anglo-Iranian Oil Company 147
Angola 66, 73
antibiotics 144
Antonescu, Ion 19
Apprentice Boys' march 31
Arab Legion 78, *79*, 81, 82
Arabs:
    "Catastrophe" 79
    in Palestine 77
    politics 84
    television 141
    unity 84
    war with Israel 78-79, 82, 146
Arafat, Yasser 86, 155, *155*
Arbenz, Jacobo 96, 97
Argentina 96
Armstrong, Neil 95, 155
Arnaz, Desi *137*, 138
Asians, immigrants 29-31
Aswan Dam 82, 152
Attlee, Clement 16, 24, 25, *25*, 47, 48, 108, 110
Australia:
    car industry 57
    immigrants 57, *57*
    in Korean War 107
    Snowy Mountains Hydroelectric Scheme 57
    television 142
    in Vietnam War 115
    welfare state 57
    Woomera rocket range 110
Austria 44
Ayub Khan, General 52
Azikiwe, Nnamdi ("Zik") 65

Bacall, Lauren 89
Badr, Imam 84
Baghdad Pact 149
Balewa, Sir Abubakar Tafawa 65
Balfour Declaration 77
Ball, Lucille 137-8, *137*, 141
Banda, Dr Hastings 70, *70*, 154
Bandaranaike, Mrs Sirimavo 152
Bandung Conference 56, 149
Bao Dai, Emperor of Amman 58, 113
Bardot, Brigitte 34, *34*
Barnard, Dr Christiaan 155
Barnett, Lady 140
Baroda 51

Barry, Jack *138*
Barry, Sir Gerald 26
Baruch, Bernard 20
Basildon 27
Bastien-Thiry, Colonel Jean-Marie 36
Batista, Fulgencia 97, 109, 151
Bay of Pigs invasion 109-10, *109*, 152
BBC 141
Beat the Clock (TV) 141
Beat generation 138
Beatles 128-30, *128-9*, 137, 153
Beatniks 138
Beauvoir, Simone de 133, *133*
Bedouins 82
Beeching, Dr 153
Begin, Menachim 77
Beijing Ballet 123
Belgium:
    colonies in Africa 66-67
    currency devaluation 6
    in ECSC 44
    in EEC 42
    at end of war 6-8
    establishing Benelux 42, 145
    reparations from Germany 12
Belmondo, Jean-Paul 34
Ben Bella, Ahmed 76
Benelux 42, 145
Benes, Edward 145
Bengalis 52
Ben-Gurion, David 78, *78*, 79, 155
Beria, Lavrenti 99, 100, 106, 148
Berkeley Free Speech Movement 132
Berle, Milton 137
Berlin 39, *41*
    airlift to 22-23, *22*, 145
    blockade by Soviets 22, 145, 146
    at end of war 6
    workers' uprising 148
Berlin Wall 40, 111, *111*, 152, *152*
Bernadotte, Count Fulke 78-79
Berry, Chuck 128
Bevan, Aneurin 26, 27, 147
Beveridge Report 26
Bevin, Ernest 20, 25, 78, 80, 110
Bhavnagar, Maharajah of 51
Bhopal 51
Bhutto, Zulfikar Ali 52
Biafra 65, *65*, 154
Bidault, Georges 20
Bihar, India 48
Bing, Rudolf 145
Birmingham, immigrants 29
black market 6, 8, 26, 38
Black Panthers 132
Blankers-Koen, Fanny 146
Bleyer, Sergeant 61
Block, Judge 130
Blunt, Sir Anthony 112
BOAC 148, 151
Bogart, Humphrey 88, 89
Bokassa, Colonel Jean 154
Bolivia 96, 97
Bombay 48
Bonanza (TV) 141
Bormann, Martin 10, 11
Borneo 55
Boumedienne, Colonel Houari 76
Boyd, William 139
Boy Scouts, ban on 19
Bradford, immigrants 29
Bradman, Don 146
brainwashing 109
Brando, Marlon 126, *126*, 145
Brandt, Willi 41
Brasília 150
Breathless (film) 34
Brezhnev, Leonid 105, 112
Britain:
    aid after Second World War 19
    aid in Greek civil war 18-19
    atom bombs 110, 147
    Baghdad Pact 149
    balance of payments crisis 28-29
    celebrating VE Day 24
    colonies in Africa 64-65, 68-71
    cost of food for Germany 9
    death penalty 153, 155
    devaluation of pound 29, 146, *146*, 155
    EC membership 44, 153, 155
    elections 24, *24*, 25, 26, 28, 144
    at end of Second World War 6, 24-25, *24*
    exchange rate 27

exports at end of war 6, 24
granting independence to Malaya 54
housing 27, 27
hydrogen bombs 150
identity cards 147
immigration 29-31, 145, 152
    in India 46-49
industrial unrest 29
and Jewish immigration to Palestine 77, 80
in Korean War 107
loans 25
motorways 151
National Health Service (NHS) 25, 26, 27, 136, 145, 147
nationalization 25, 145
National Plan 28-29
National Service 152
nuclear test-ban treaty 30, 36, 112, 153
overseas debts 24
Palestine problem 77-79, 80
race riots 29, 31, *31*, 151
rationing *24*, 25, 26-27, 144, 146, 148, *149*
shortages 24
"Stop-Go" years 27-28
strikes 25, 29
Suez Crisis 27, 43, 81, *81*, 82-84
television 137, 141-2, 149
in United Nations 43
welfare state 25-26
British Empire 25
Broederbond (Brotherhood) 72
Brooks, Mel 137
Browne, Malcolm 14
Brown, George 28
Brunei 58
Brussels, EEC headquarters *44*
Brussels Treaty 146
B-specials 31
Bucharest 19
Budapest *100-1*, 150
Buddhists:
    in Tibet 121
    in Vietnam 114
Buenos Aires 96
Bulganin, Nikolai 99, 149
Bulgaria, destruction in Second World War 13
Bundy, McGeorge 92
Burgess, Guy 112, *112*, 147, 153
Burma, independence 25, 145
Burroughs, William 138, *138*
Busby, Matt 151
Butler, R.A. ("Rab") 27-28

Caen, Herb 138
Caesar, Sid 137
Cairo:
    riots 147
    summit meeting 84
calculators, electronic 144
Calcutta *46*
    riots 48
Callas, Maria 148
Calley, Lt. William 116, 155
Calwell, Arthur 57
Cambodia 58, 59, 155
Campaign for Nuclear Disarmament (CND) 28
Camus, Albert 150
Canada:
    economic boom 94
    French Canadian separatists 94, 154
    immigrants 94
    in Korean War 107
    loan to Britain 25
    Newfoundland 146
    St Lawrence Seaway 94, *94*, 151
    ties with U.S. 94
Canal Zone 150
Cannes Film Festival 146
capitalism 19
capital punishment 136
Carmichael, Stokely 134
Carnegie, Mrs Dale 133
cars:
    Beetle *40*
    Morris Minor 146
Carson, Johnny 137
Casino Royale (Fleming) 148
Castries, Colonel de 61
Castro, Fidel 96, 97, *97*, 109-10, 151
Castro, Raul 97
Catcher in the Rye (Salinger) 147
Catch 22 (Heller) 152
Cat on a Hot Tin Roof (Williams) 148

Cavern Club, Liverpool 129
CBS 138
Central African Federation 70, 148, 151
Central African Republic 154
Cerdan, Marcel 33
Chambers, Whittaker 89
Chamoun, Camille 84
Chechens 99, 102-3
Cheng Ping 55
Cheyenne (TV) 141
Chiang Kai-shek 43, 89, 118, 120, 146
Chifley, Ben 57
Chile 96
China 118-24
    aid from U.S.S.R. 118, 147
    aid to Vietminh 60
    atom bomb 124, 154
    communism in 118-24
    conformity 119
    Cultural Revolution 121, 122-4, *122*, *123*, 141-2, 154
    "Five Antis" campaign 119
    five-year plan 120
    foreign affairs 124
    Great Leap Forward 120-1, 151
    Hundred Flowers campaign 120, 149
    invasion of India 51-52
    invasion of Tibet 121, *121*, 124, 147
    in Korean War 108-9, 124
    Land Reform Laws 118-19
    peasants 118, 119, 121
    population 118
    rebellion in Malaya 54, 55, 55
    Red Guards 122-4, *122*, *124*
    refusal to sign test-ban treaty 112
    relationship with India 51-52, 124
    relationship with U.S.S.R. 104, 120-2, 124, 152
    revolution 118-22, *119*, *120*
    television 141-2
    "Thought Reform" 119
    "Three Antis" campaign 119
    in United Nations 43, 51, 152
    women 118-19, *119*, *120*, 121
China, General 149
China, Nationalist, in United Nations 43
Christian Democrats 39, 41
Christie, Agatha 148
Churchill, Winston 17, 82, 102, 112
    agreements with U.S.S.R. 18
    death 154
    election defeat 24
    and European unity 42
    "Iron Curtain" speech 17, 144
    as Prime Minister 26-27
    retirement 27
    in Second World War 6, 24, 25
CIA 109, 114
cinema 28
    drive-in movies 92, *92*
    French 34, *34*, 35
    New Wave 34
    for teenagers 126-7, *126*
    3-D movies 148
Clay, General Lucius D. 22
Cleave, Maureen 129
CND (Campaign for Nuclear Disarmament) 28
Cobb, John 147
Coca, Imogen 137
Cocteau, Jean 33
Cod War 151
Cohn, Roy 90, *90*
Cohn-Bendit, Daniel 36
Cold War 17-18, 19-23, 39, 52, 57, 59, 107
    spies 112, *112*
    symbol of 111
    U.S. fear of communism 88-90
Colombey-les-deux-Eglises, France 33
Columbia University protest *132*, 132
Cominform (Communist Information Bureau) 21, 145
Common Market *see* European Economic Community
Commonwealth Immigration Acts 29-31
communism 87
    appeal of 19
    in China 118-24
    defections to 109
    in Eastern Europe 17, 18-20
    in Indonesia 58
    in Malaya 54, 55, *55*
    in Philippines 53
    in Singapore 54-55

U.S.A. and 42
    U.S. witch hunts 88-90, 147, *147*
    in Western Europe 20, 33-34
    Western view of 19
    writings against 23
    see also Cold War; Korean War; Vietnam War
Comoros 66
Compton, Denis 145
Condon, Richard, *The Manchurian Candidate* 109
Congo 66-68, *66-67*, 152, 153, 154
    UN in 43
Connally, John 95
Conservatives:
    election victories 26
    government 26-28
    Profumo scandal 30
Constantine, King of Greece 155
Conte, Richard 89
contraception:
    Pill 134, 136, *136*
    Roman Catholic view 155
Convention on Human Rights 42
Cooper, Gary 88
Council of Europe 42
Crabb, "Buster" 150
Crawley 27
Crick, Francis 148
Cripps, Stafford 25, 47
Crockett, Davy 139
Crosby, John 131
Cuba 96, 97, 109-10, 151, 152, 153
Cyprus:
    Greek/Turkish clashes 84, 149, *149*, 153
    independence 84, 151, 152
    UN in 43, 153
Czechoslovakia:
    communists in 19-20, 145
    coup in 21
    at end of Second World War 13
    expelling Germans 9
    Prague Spring 105-6, *105*, *106*, 155
    sending military aid to Egypt 81-82

Dalai Lama 121, 151
Daley, Richard 115, 155, *155*
Danzig 9
Dayan, Moshe 85
Dead Sea Scrolls 145
Dean, James 126-7, *126*
Deir Yassin 78, 145
de Kooning, Willem 142
Deng Xiaoping 122, 123
Denmark:
    EC membership 44
    in EFTA 44
    at end of war 6
Devlin, Bernadette 31, 155
Diary of Anne Frank 145
Dick Barton, Special Agent (radio) 142
Diem, Ngo Dinh 62, 113, 114, 153
Dien Bien Phu, battle of 60-61, *60-61*, 113, 148, *149*
Diner's Club 90
Dior, Christian 134
Disney, Walt 88
Disneyland 149
displaced persons *see* refugees
Divorce Reform Act 136
Djibouti 66
Djilas, Milovan 148
DNA 148
Dominican Republic 154
Dong, Pham Van 61, 114
Dönitz, Grand Admiral K. 6
Douglas-Home, Alec 30
Dragnet (TV) 141
drugs:
    antibiotics 144
    illegal 130
    thalidomide 151
Dubcek, Alexander 105, *105*, 106, 155
Dulles, Alan 109
Dulles, John Foster 82-83
Durban, South Africa 146
Dutch East Indies 56
Dutch New Guinea 58
Duval, General 74
Duvalier, Papa Doc 150, 153
Dylan, Bob 130, *130*

EAM (National Liberation Front) 18

East Kilbride 27
East Prussia 9
Eden, Anthony 27, 81, 82-83, 84
EDES (National Republican Greek League) 18
Edinburgh International Festival 145
Edwards, Duncan 151
EEC see European Economic Community
EFTA (European Free Trade Association) 44, 151
Egypt:
    aid from Soviet bloc 81-82
    aid from West 79, 81-82
    attack on Israel 78
    defeat by Israel 79
    nationalises Suez Canal 27, 150
    Six-Day War 85-86, 86
    in Suez Crisis 43, 81, 81, 82-84
    in UAR 84, 151
    union with Syria 84
Eichmann, Adolf 11, 79, 152
Eisenhower, Dwight D. 83-84, 90-91, 90, 112, 113, 148
Eisenhower Doctrine 84
ELAS 18, 19
Elizabeth II, Queen:
    coronation 28, 28, 140, 148
    marriage 145
Ellis, Ruth 149
Emmett, Roland 26
Empire Windrush (ship) 145
Eniwetok Atoll 148
EOKA 84
Epstein, Brian 129
Erhard, Professor Ludwig 38, 39, 40-41
Essen, Germany 12
    Krupps' factory 39
Estonia, annexation by U.S.S.R. 14, 17
Euratom (European Atomic Energy Community) 44, 150
European Coal and Steel Community (ECSC) 35, 39, 44, 147
European Community (EC) 44
European Court of Human Rights 44
European Court of Justice 44
European Economic Community (EEC) 35, 36, 39, 42-44
    African associate members 66
    original members 42, 44, 150
European Free Trade Association (EFTA) 44, 151
European Recovery Program see Marshall Plan
Evening Standard 129
Everest, Mount 147
Exodus (ship) 80, 80, 145

Faisal, King of Iraq 82, 84, 151
Farnborough Air Show 147
Farouk, King of Egypt 79, 147
fashion:
    teenage 131-2
    women's 134, 134
Fearless, HMS 70, 71
Female Eunuch (Greer) 134
Feminine Mystique (Friedan) 133
Festival of Britain 26, 147, 147
    catalogue 26
Final Solution 11
Finland, land taken by U.S.S.R. 14
Fleming, Ian 148
FLN (Front de Libération Nationale) 74, 75
Florence, Italy, flood damage 154
Flower Children 130, 131, 132
flying saucers 145
food:
    rationing 8, 12, 25, 26-27, 144, 148
    shortages 6, 6-7, 8-9, 8, 9, 9
Ford, John 34
Formosa (Taiwan) 43, 124, 146
France 32-37
    aid to Africa 66
    Algerian war 35, 35, 36, 74-76, 74
    alliance with Germany 35, 39, 42-44
    atom bombs 36, 152
    collaborators punished 32-33
    colonies in Africa 65-66
    communism in 33-34
    dam bursts 151
    devaluation 145
    during Second World War 32
    in EEC 42
    election system 34
    at end of war 8
    exports 35

Fifth Republic 35-37
Fourth Republic 33-34, 75
    in Korean War 107
    Liberation 32
    loans from U.S.A. 35
    miners 35
    nationalization 34, 34
    National Plan 34-35, 44
    nuclear tests 36
    OAS (Organization de l'Armée Secrète) 36, 76
    ordering U.S. troops out 36
    postwar recovery 34-35
    referendum paper 32
    refusal to sign test-ban treaty 112
    reparations from Germany 12
    Resistance 32-33
    student riots 36-37, 36-37, 155
    Suez Crisis 27, 43, 83-84
    television 141, 142
    Third Force 34
    Third Republic ends 32, 33, 144, 144
    in United Nations 43
    use of torture 74, 75
    war in Indochina 58-59, 58
    withdrawal from NATO 154
Franco, General Francisco 150, 155
Fraser, Robert 130
Frederick William I 13
Freed, Johnny 127
Friedan, Betty 133, 134, 134
Frost, David 140
Fuchs, Klaus 112, 147
Fulani people 64
Fulbright, Senator 115
Fürstenau 12

Gaddafi, Muammar 155
Gagarin, Yuri 94, 104, 152
Gandhi, Indira 51, 52, 52
Gandhi, Mohandas Karamchand (Mahatma) 46, 47, 49, 49, 145
Garland, Judy 88
Gasperi, Alcide de 42
Gassion, Jean 33
Gatow airfield 23
GATT (General Agreement on Tariffs and Trade) 43
Gaulle, General Charles de 8, 32-33, 34, 143
    and African colonies 65-66
    and Algeria 36, 65, 75-76, 151, 152
    attempts on life 36, 36, 152
    attitude to Britain 39, 44, 155
    and EEC 44, 155
    elected President 35, 37, 44, 144, 151
    in Fifth Republic 35-36, 37
    and Germany 49
    head of Provisional Government 32-33
    and nuclear weapons 35-36
    and Quebec 94
    resignations 37, 44, 144, 155
Geneva Summit conference 112
George II, King of Greece 18
George VI 24, 147
Germany:
    aid from Allies 12, 39
    British aid after Second World War 19
    destruction in war 12
    at end of war 9, 38
    food shortages 9
    occupation zones 9, 9
    refugees in 9
    reparations made after war 9, 12, 38, 99, 147
    slave laborers in 9, 12
    television 137
    territorial changes 9, 38
    see also Germany, East; Germany, West
Germany, East:
    Democratic Republic created 23, 146
    television 141
    under communists 100
Germany, West:
    alliance with France 35, 39, 42-44
    Bundestag 23
    creation 146, 146
    currency reform 21-22, 38, 145
    in EEC 42
    exports 40, 40
    Federal Republic created 23, 39
    guest workers 40
    merging of zones 21
    in NATO 149
    Ostpolitik (Eastern policy) 41

postwar recovery 21, 38-41
    rearmament 148
    refugees from East Germany 40
    television 141, 142
    unemployment 40
Ghana 64, 153, 154
Giap, General Vo Nguyen 59, 60, 61
GI brides 8
Gleason, Jackie 137
Glenn, John 152
Glubb, General John ("Glubb Pasha") 78, 79, 81, 82, 150
Godard, Jean-Luc 34
Godse, Nathuram 49
Gold Coast 64
Gomulka, Wladyslaw 100
Gorton, John 57
Gottwald, Klement 21, 21, 145
Gowon, Lt. Col. Yakuba 65, 154
Gracey, General Douglas 58-59
Great Train Robbery 153
Greece:
    civil war 13, 14, 18-19, 18, 146
    colonels seize power 154
    communists in 145
    currency 13
    at end of Second World War 13
    fight for union of Cyprus with 84
    monarchy 144
Greer, Germaine 134
Grivas, Colonel George 84, 84
Guatemala 96
Guevara, Ernesto "Che" 97, 97, 154
Guinea 66, 151
Guinea-Bissau 66
Guinness, Alec 146
Gujrat, massacre in 48
Gulag Archipelago (Solzhenitsyn) 104
Gurney, Sir Hugh 55
Gwalior, Maharajah of 51

Haganah (Israeli army) 78
Haiti 150, 153
    television 140
Haldemann, H.R. 117
Haley, Bill 128, 128
Hammarskjöld, Dag 43, 67, 152
Harding, Gilbert 140
Harrison, George 129
Hasad, Hafiz 85
Hatfield New Town 27
Hausa people 64, 65
Haw Haw, Lord 144
Hawaii 151
Háy, Julius 101
Heath, Edward 31
Hecht, Ben 77
Heller, Joseph 152
Hell's Angels 131
Helsinki Olympics 147
Hertzog, Albert 140
Hess, Rudolf 10, 11
Highway Code 149
Hillary, Edmund 148
Hindus:
    anti-Muslim riots in India 48, 144
    fleeing Pakistan 46-47
    fleeing Punjab 48
hippies 130-1, 131, 132
Hirohito, Emperor of Japan 62
Hiroshima 62, 110
Hiss, Alger 88-89, 147
Hitchcock, Alfred 34
Hitler, Adolf 10, 13, 16, 39, 40
Ho Chi Minh 58-59, 58-59, 61, 113, 113, 117, 124, 144
Holly, Buddy 128
Hollywood, communist witch hunts in 88
Holt, Harold 57, 155
Homo habilis 152
homosexuality 135, 136
Honeymooners (TV) 137, 141
Hoover, Herbert 14
Hoover, John Edgar 98
Hopalong Cassidy 139
Hopkinson, Henry 84
Horne, Donald 57
Houphouet-Boigny, Félix 65
housing:
    Levitt instant homes 92
    prefabs 27, 27

Hukbalahaps (Huks) 53
Hungary:
    communism 19, 100-2, 145
    destruction in Second World War 13
    revolt in 150, 150
Husák, Gustav 106
Hussein, King of Jordan 81, 81, 82, 82, 147, 150
Hyderabad 50, 51
Hyderabad, Nizam of 51

IBM 144, 148
Ibo people 64-65, 65
Iceland, Cod War 151
I.G. Farben 9
I Love Lucy (TV) 137-8, 137, 141
IMF (International Monetary Fund) 43, 144
immigrants:
    to Australia 57, 57
    to Britain 29-31, 145, 152
    to Canada 94
    to Israel 78
    to Palestine 77, 80, 145
Imperialism 19
India:
    caste system 49, 145
    foreign policy 50-51
    French possessions 149
    independence 25, 46-52, 145
    Kashmir conflict 50, 50, 52, 145, 146, 154
    life expectancy 49
    modernization 49-50
    Muslim riots 48
    official language 154
    Partition 46-47, 145
    Princely States 50, 51
    relationship with China 51-52, 124
    Untouchables 49, 145
Indochina, war in 34, 36, 58-62, 58, 60-61
Indonesia:
    aid from U.S.S.R. 56
    declaration of Republic 56
    exodus of Europeans 151, 151
    guided economy 58
    independence 56-58, 144
    rebellion 56
    UN in 43
Ingush 99
International Court of Justice 144
International Monetary Fund (IMF) 43, 144
Iran 147
    Baghdad Pact 149
    U.S.S.R. troops in 18
Iraq:
    aid from U.S.A. 84
    attack on Israel 78
    Baghdad Pact 149
Ireland 146
    EC membership 44
Ireland, Northern, violence 31, 31
Irgun Zv'ei Leumi 77, 78, 144, 145
Irian Jaya 58, 152
Iron Curtain 15, 17-18, 39, 110-12, 144
Israel:
    Arab attacks 78-79
    army (Haganah) 78
    birth 78-79, 145
    boundaries 85, 86
    ceasefire 79, 81, 146
    diverting River Jordan 84
    Occupied Territories 86
    reparation payments from Germany 147
    Six-Day War 82, 85-86, 86, 154
    Suez War 82-83, 83, 84
Issigonis, Alec 146
Italy:
    in ECSC 44
    in EEC 42
    end of monarchy 144
    at end of war 8-9
    floods 154
Ivanov, Eugene 30
Ivory Coast 65

Jagger, Mick 130, 130
Jaipur, Maharajah of 51
Japan:
    against communism 62
    American occupation 62-63, 63, 147
    company songs 62
    corruption 63
    defense costs 63
    democracy in 62
    earthquake 144
    economic recovery 62-64

exports 62, 63
    GDP 63
    guerrilla war against 53
    industry 62, 63
    shipbuilding 63, 63
    trade unions 63
    victories 47, 53
    war criminals executed 62
Jerusalem 78, 144, 144
Jews:
    creating national home 77-79
    illegal immigrants into Palestine 77, 80, 145
    immigrants into Israel 78
    laws against 10
    persecution 12-13
    pogroms 12, 99-100, 144
    in Poland 12
    protests 77
    retaliation by 12
    Zionism 77
Jiang Qing 123
Jinnah, Mohammad Ali 47-48, 49, 52
Johnson, Lady Bird 98
Johnson, Lyndon Baines 154
    becomes President 98, 98
    Civil Rights Acts 93, 134, 153
    policy 98
    talks with U.S.S.R. 112
    Vietnam War 98, 114-15, 117, 155
John XXIII, Pope 151
Jordan 81, 82, 85, 86
Jour de Fête (film) 34
Joyce, William 144
Juan Carlos, Prince 155
Junagadh 50, 51
Junagadh, Nawab of 51

Kadar, Janos 102
Kaganovich, Lazar 102, 150
Kalmucks 99, 102-3
Kaltenbrunner, Ernst 10, 10-11, 11
KANU (Kenya African National Union) 69, 70
Karachi 48
Kasavubu, Joseph 67
Kashmir, conflict in 50, 50, 52, 145, 146, 154
Katanga 67
Kaunda, Kenneth 70
Kaye, Danny 88, 89
Kazakhstan 103
Keeler, Christine 30, 30, 153
Keitel, Field Marshal Wilhelm 10, 11
Kelly, Gene 88
Kennan, George 17
Kennedy, Jackie 92, 92, 95, 98
Kennedy, John Fitzgerald 92, 94-95
    advisers 92
    assassination 95, 95, 98, 143, 153
    becomes President 91, 152
    and Berlin 111-12
    and Cuba 109, 110, 153, 153
    funeral 143, 143
    inaugural address 91-92
    and Latin America 96
    policy 94-95, 98
    on TV 143
    and Vietnam War 113-115
    and women's rights 133
Kennedy, Robert 79, 155
Kenya:
    Asian immigrants from 29-31
    becomes republic 154
    Mau Mau rebellion 68-69, 68, 147
Kenya African National Union (KANU) 69, 70
Kenyatta, Jomo 68-70, 69, 148, 152, 154
Kerans, Lt-Cmdr 146
Kerouac, Jack 138, 138, 150
Keynes, Lord John Maynard 25
Khan, General Ayub 52
Khan, Liaquat Ali 52
Khan, Yahya 52
Khrushchev, Nikita 56, 91, 99, 102, 150
    argument with Nixon 91
    becomes Premier 149
    and Berlin Wall 111
    and China 104, 120
    and Cuban missile crisis 110, 153
    denounces Stalin 100, 102, 106
    de-Stalinization 102-3
    and Eastern bloc 149
    elected Party Secretary 100, 148
    and Hungary 102
    "peaceful co-existence" talks 112
    and Poland 100

removed from power 154
retirement 105
and Suez 102
Virgin Lands scheme 103-4
Kielce, Poland 12, 144
Kikuyu tribesmen 66
Kimathi, "Field Marshal" Dedan 69
Kim Il Sung 107, *107*, 109
Kind Hearts and Coronets (film) 146
King, Martin Luther 93, *93*, 115, 153, *153*, 154, 155
Kinsey, Alfred 134-5
Kinshasa 66
Kissinger, Henry 117
Klement, Ricardo 79
Koch, Erich 13
Köningsberg 13
Korean War 39, 63, 107-9, *107*, 108, 147, *148*
brainwashing in 109
China in 108-9
end 60, 109, 148
outbreak 27, 43, 62, 147
Kosygin, Alexei 105
Krokodil (magazine) *42*
Krupps 9
Kutchuk, Dr Fazil 84
Ky, Air Vice Marshal Nguyen Cao 115

Labor Party:
against Europe 42
election victories 24, 25, 28, 144
government 25-26, 27, 28-31, 47, 144
Lady Chatterley's Lover (Lawrence) 135, *135*, 152
Lahore, riots 52
Lang, Michael *131*
Laos 58-59, 147
Lardner, Ring, Jnr 88
Lasky, Meyer 91
Last Year at Marienbad (film) 34
Las Vegas 91, *91*
Latin America 96-97
television 141
Latvia, annexation by U.S.S.R. 14, 17
Laval, Pierre 32-33, 144
Lawrence, D.H. 135, 152
League of Nations 43
Leakey, Dr Louis 152
Leary, Professor Timothy 130
Lebanon:
aid from U.S.A. 84
attack on Israel 78
pro-Western regime 84
UN in 43
Leclerc, General Jacques 59
Le Corbusier 145
Lee Kuan Yew 55
Lemay, General Curtis 22
Lend-Lease system 14, 24-25
Lenin, Vladimir *102*, 106
Lenin (ice-breaker) 151
Lennon, John 129, 131
Lennox-Boyd, Alan 68
Lesnevich, Gus 146
Levitt, Arthur 92
Levitt, Bill 92
Lewis, Jerry Lee 128
Lewis, John L. 88
Ley, Robert 10
Liaquat Ali Khan 52
Libya 155
Lichtenstein, Roy 152
Lie, Trygve 43
Lin Piao 122, 124
Literary Currents (journal) 122
Lithuania, annexation by U.S.S.R. 14, 17
Little Richard 128
Liu Shao-chi 121-2
Liverpool, Cavern Club 129
London:
immigrants 29
Olympics 146
race riots 29, *31*, 151
"Swinging" 131, 132
Londonderry, violence in 31, *31*, 155
Louis, Joe 145, 146
Lower Silesia 9
Lumumba, Patrice 66-67, *67*, 97, 151, 152
Luthuli, Chief Albert 72
Luxembourg:
in ECSC 44
in EEC 42
establishing Benelux 42, 145

Lysenko, Trofim Denisovich 103, *103*, 104
Lyttleton, Oliver 54

MacArthur, General Douglas 62, *62*, 107-8, 109, 124, 147
McCarthy, Eugene 115
McCarthy, Joseph 89-90, *90*, 143, 147, 149
McCartney, Paul 129
Maclean, Donald 112, *112*, 147, 153
Macmillan, Harold 152
becomes Prime Minister 27, 84
and EEC 44
"never had it so good" speech 28, 150
and Profumo affair 30
"Wind of Change" speech 70, 151, 152
McNamara, Robert 92, 116
Magsaysay, Ramon 53-54
Makarios, Archbishop 84, 150, 151, 152
Malan, Daniel 72, 145
Malawi 70, 73, 154
Malaya:
communist Emergency 54, 55, *55*, 145, 147, 152
independence 54
Malaysia, Federation of 55, 150
Malenkov, Georgi 100, 102, 149, 150
Manchester United, air crash 151
Mandela, Nelson 71, *72*, 73, 153
Man in the Gray Flannel Suit (film) 92
Manson, Charles 155
Mao Zedong 43, 51, 62, 99, 104, 118-24, *118*, *146*, 149
Little Red Book 124
Marcos, Ferdinand 54, *54*
Marcos, Imelda 54, *54*
Margaret, Princess 149
Marker, Russell E. 136
Markos, General 18, 19, 146
Marshall, General George C. 20, 90
Marshall Plan/Aid 14, 15, 20-22, *20-21*, 35, 39, 42, 145
Martin, Corporal Matt 114
Martin, George 129
Marxism 17
Marxist-Leninists 19
Masaryk, Jan 21, *21*, 145
Massu, General Jacques 37, 74, 75
Matsu 124
Matsushita Electric 62
Mau Mau *66*, 68-69, 147, 151
Maverick (TV) 141
May, Dr Allan Nunn 112
medicine:
artificial heart 147
heart transplant 155
kidney transplants 153
polio vaccine 148
see also drugs
Medina, Captain Ernest 116
Mendès-France, Pierre 33, 34, 148, 149
Menon, Krishna 51
Menzies, Robert 57, 142
Meredith, James 153
Michael, King of Romania 19
abdication 19, 145
Middle East 77-86
Mills, Freddie 146
Mindszenty, Cardinal 146, 149
Mirza, General Iskander 52
Missouri, USS *108*
Mitsubishi 62
Mitsui company 62
Mobutu, Joseph 67-68, 152, 154
Molotov, Vyacheslav 18, 20, 99, 102, 150
Monnet, Jean 34, 35, 44, 144
Mon Oncle (film) *151*
Monroe, Marilyn 153
Monroe Doctrine 96
Monsieur Hulot's Holiday (film) 34
Montand, Yves 33, 34
Montgomery, Field Marshal Bernard 9
Moon, first man on 94-95
Moore, Henry 26
Moorfields Eye Hospital, London 26
Morgenthau, Henry 12
Morocco 74, 149, 150
Morrow, Ed 111, 143
Mossadegh, Mohammed 148
Mountbatten, Edwina *48*
Mountbatten, Lord Louis 48, *48*, 50, 59, 145
Mousetrap (play) 148
Mozambique 66, 73, 154
Mujibar Rahman, Sheikh 52

Munich *41*
air crash 151
music, rock'n'roll 127-30, 131
Muslim Brotherhood 149
Muslims:
fleeing Punjab 48
in India 48
massacred in Punjab 48
remaining in India 49
riots in India 48, 144
My Lai massacre 116, 155
Mysore 51
Mysore, Maharajah of *51*

Nagasaki 62, 110
Nagy, Imre 100-1, 102
Naked Lunch (Burroughs) 138
Namibia 66
Nasser, Colonel Gamal Abdul 79-83, *81*, 84-85, 86, 147, 148, *148*, 149, 150
National Guard *132*
National Health Service (NHS) 25, 26, 27, 136, 145, 147
National Liberation Front (EAM) (Greece) 18
National Liberation Front (FLN) (Algeria) 149
National Liberation Front (NLF) (Vietnam) 113
National Organization for Women (NOW) 134
National People's Congress 118
National Republican Greek League (EDES) 18
NATO (North Atlantic Treaty Organization) 23, 23, 25, 39, 40, 146, 149, 154
Navarre, General Henri 60-61
Nazis 12
war criminals 10-11, *10-11*, 79
NBC 138
Neguib, General Mohammed 79, 147, 148
Nehru, Jawaharlal 46, 49, 50-52, *51*
Netherlands:
in ECSC 44
in EEC 42
at end of war 8
establishing Benelux 42, 145
flooding by Germans 8
Newfoundland 146
New Towns 27, *27*
New York Times 109
New Zealand, in Korean War 107
Nhu, Madame 113
Nhu, Ngo Dhin 113
Nicaragua 97
Nicosia *149*
Nigeria 64-65, 152, 154
television *140*
Nixon, Richard Milhous *90*, 98, 115, 116, 151
becomes President 98, 155
loses election 91
on television 91, 143, 147
as Vice-President 91
and Vietnam War 117
Nkrumah, Kwame 64, *64-65*, 147, 153, 154
Nobusuke, Kishi 63
Nordhoff, Dr Heinz 40
North Atlantic Treaty Organization (NATO) 23, 23, 25, 39, 40, 146, 149, 154
North Sea, oil finds 155
Norway:
currency devaluation 6
in EFTA 44
at end of war 6
merchant navy 6
Nottingham, race riots 29
Novotny, Antonin 105
nuclear power, atom-powered ice-breaker 151
nuclear weapons:
atom bombs 23, 62, 89, 110, 124, 146, 147
British tests 110
French tests 36, 152
marches against 28
Non-Proliferation Treaty 112, 155
radiation sickness 148
SALT talks 112
spies 112, 147, 148
test-ban treaty 30, 36, 112, 153
U.S. tests 110, 148
Nuremberg:
rallies 10
war trials 10-11, *10-11*, 144
Nuremberg Laws 10
Nutting, Anthony 81
Nyasaland 70, 151
Nyerere, President 140

OAS (Organization of American States) 145

OAS (Organization de l'Armée Secrète) 36, 76, *76*
oath-taking, Mau Mau 68
Obote, Milton 154
Obscene Publications Act 135
OEEC (Organization for European Cooperation) 42
Ojukwo, Colonel Odumegwu 65, 154
Oldenburg, Claus 152
Olympics 146, 147
One Day in the Life of Ivan Denisovich (Solzhenitsyn) 103, 152
On the Road (Kerouac) 138, 150
OPEC (Organization of Petrol Exporting Countries) 152
Operation Barbarossa 13
Operation Rolling Thunder 115, 154
Organization of American States (OAS) 145
Organization for European Cooperation (OEEC) 42
Organization of Petrol Exporting Countries (OPEC) 152
Orwell, George 23
Oswald, Lee Harvey 95, 98, 143, 153
Outsider (Camus) 150

Paar, Jack 137
Paisley, Rev. Ian 155
Pakistan:
aid from U.S.A. 52
anti-communism 52
Baghdad Pact 149
education 52
exports 52
independence 25, 46-52
Kashmir conflict *50*, 50, 52, 145, 146, 154
Partition 46-47, 48-49
problems as nation 52
Pakistan People's Party 52
Palach, Jan 106
Palermo, Sicily, at end of war 8
Palestine:
Arab refugees from 82
British aid after Second World War 19
end of British mandate in 80
Jews and Arabs in 77-79
partition 145
Palestine Liberation Organization (PLO) 82, 84-85, 86
Pan African Congress (PAC) 73
Panchen Lama 121
Panmunjon 109, 148
Paris:
at end of war 8
fashions 134, *134*
student riots 36-37, *36-37*, 155
Paris Conference 20
Parks, Rosa 93, 149
Parlophone 129
Patiala, Maharajah of *51*
Peace Corps 92
Pearl Harbor 83, 62
Peck, Gregory 92
Peng Dehui 122
Perón, Colonel Juan 96, 97, 144, 149
Perón, Eva (Evita) Duarte de 96, *97*, 144, 147, *147*
Peru 151
Pétain, Marshal H.P. 32-33, 144
Peter the Great, Tsar 13
Peterlee 27
Petiot, Dr Marcel 144
Petrov, Vladimir 148
Philby, Harold "Kim" 112, 148, 153
Philip, Duke of Edinburgh 145
Philippines, independence 53-54, *53*
Phillips, Sam 127
Piaf, Edith 33, 33
Pill 134, 136, *136*
Piltdown Man 148
Pincus, Gregory 136
Piper, John 26
Piroth, Colonel 61
PLO (Palestine Liberation Organization) 82, 84-85, 86
Podgorny, Nikolai 105
Poland:
borders 9, 13, 38
Church in 148
deaths during war 13
Jews in 12-13
land taken by U.S.S.R. 14
riots 150

slave laborers in Germany 9, 12
under communism 100
U.S.S.R. control in 19
Polish Home Army 19
Pollock, Jackson 142, 145
Pomerania 9
Pompidou, Georges 37
Pondicherry 149
pop art 142
Porsche, Ferdinand 40
Port Said *81*, *150*
Portugal, in EFTA 44
Potsdam Conference *16*
Powell, Enoch 31
Powers, Francis Gary 112, 152
Prague Spring 105-6, *105*, *106*, 155
President Garfield (ship) 80
Presley, Elvis 127-8, *127*, 137
Price is Right (TV) 141
Profumo, John 30, *30*, 153
Punjab, massacres in 48

Quang Doc, Thich 114
Quant, Mary 132
Les Quatre Cents Coups (film) 34
Quemoy 124, 149
Quisling, Vidkun 144

Race Relations Act 31
race riots:
in Britain 29, *31*, 151
in South Africa 146, 152
in U.S.A. 93, 149, 153, 154, *154*
Radcliffe, Sir Cyril 48
radio 142, 153
RAF, Berlin airlift 23
Rahman, Sheikh Mujibar 52
Rahman, Tunku Abdul 54, 55, 150
Rajk, Laszlo 100
Rákosi, Mátyás 100-1
Ramadier, Paul 33-34
Rampur, Nawab of 51
Ramsey, Alf 154
Rauff, Walter 79
Rawalpindi, India 48
Ray, James Earl 93
RCA 127, 146
Reagan, Ronald 130
Rebel Without a Cause (film) 126-7
Red Army 16
Red Cross 13
Red Guards 122-4, *122*, *124*
refugees, at end of Second World War 9, *9*, 40, 82, 86
Renison, Sir Patrick 69
Resnais, Alain 34
Reuter, Ernst 23
Rhee, Syngman 107, *107*, 109
Rhodesia 70-71, 151, 154, 155
Ribbentrop, Joachim von 10, 11
Richards, Keith 130, *130*
Robben Island 73
Robinson, Sugar Ray 148
Rock, John 136
Rock Around the Clock (film) 128
rock'n'roll 127-30, 131
Rodgers and Hammerstein 146
Rolling Stones 130, 131
Romania:
communists in 19
destruction in Second World War 13
land taken by U.S.S.R. 14
Rome, Treaties of 42, *42*, 150
Rommel, Field Marshal Erwin 10
Roosevelt, Franklin D. 88, 144
Rosenburg, Ethel and Julius 112, *112*, 148
Rothko, Mark 142
RPF (Rassemblement du Peuple Français) 34
Ruby, Jack 95, 98
Rusk, Dean 92, 110

Saarland 150
Sabah 55
St Lawrence Seaway 94, *94*, 151
St Petersburg, Winter Palace 13
Salan, General Raoul 75, 152
Salinger, J.D. 147
Salk, Jonas 148
SALT (Strategic Arms Limitation Talks) 112
Sang, Aung 145
Sarapo, Theo 33
Sarawak 55
Sardinistas 97

Sartre, Jean-Paul 133
Saudi Arabia, aid from U.S.A. 84
Schine, David 90, 90
Schuman, Robert 35, 44, 44
SEATO (Southeast Asia Treaty Organization) 52, 54, 149
Second Sex (Le Deuxième Sexe) (de Beauvoir) 133
Seeger, Pete 130
See It Now (TV) 143
Senegal 65
Senghor, Léopold 65
77 Sunset Strip (TV) 141
Sexual Behavior in the Female (Kinsey) 134-5
Sexual Behavior in the Male (Kinsey) 134-5
sexual conduct:
    homosexuality 135
    reports on 134-5
Sharpeville massacre 73, 73, 152
Shastri, Lal Bahadur 52
Sherrin, Ned 140
Shigeru, Yoshida 63
Shinwell, Emmanuel 26
shipbuilding, in Japan 63, 63
Show of Shows (TV) 137
Siberia 99, 103
Siegel, Benjamin "Bugsy" 91
Siemens 12
Sikhs 48
Simon, Neil 137
Simpson, Howard R. 61
Singapore:
    communists in 54-55
    fall 47
    Malay/Chinese problems 55, 55
    separation from Malaysia 55, 154
Sirhan, Sirhan 155
Six-Day War 82, 85-86, 86, 154
$64,000 Question (TV) 138, 141
Smith, Ian 70, 71, 153, 154, 154
smoking 151
Smuts, Jan 72, 145
Solanas, Valerie 142
Solzhenitsyn, Alexandr 103, 104, 152
sound barrier, breaking 145
Soustelle, Jacques 74
South Africa:
    apartheid 71-72, 145, 147, 148, 149, 152
    protests against 72-73, 72-73
    Bantu Education Act 148
    becomes republic 152
    boycott 73
    Group Areas Act 72
    homelands 72
    Immorality Act 72
    Mixed Marriages Act 72
    Pass Laws 72-73, 73
    Population Registration Act 72
    race riots 146, 152
    racial discrimination 70-72
    Suppression of Communism Act 72
    television 140
Southeast Asia Treaty Organization (SEATO) 52, 54, 149
South Pacific (musical) 146
Spaak, Paul-Henri 42, 44
space exploration:
    Soviet 94, 104, 151, 152, 153
    U.S. 94-95, 143, 151, 152, 155
Spain, monarchy restored 150
Spanish Civil War 23
Speer, Albert 10, 11
spies 112, 112, 147, 148, 153
"spivs" 26
Spock, Dr Benjamin 144
Sri Lanka, television 140-1
Stalin, Josef 16, 99, 146
    control in East Europe 16-17, 19
    death 148
    denounced by Khrushchev 102, 106
    fears about West Germany 21
    personality cult 106
    prison camps 104
    purges 104
    reign of terror 99-100, 148
    rejecting Marshall Plan 20-21
    scorched earth policy 99
    statues 99, 100-1
    Yalta conference agreements 18
Stangl, Franz 79
Starr, Ringo 129
Stempel, Herbert 138
Stern Gang 77, 78, 79, 145
Stevenage New Town 27, 27

Strachey, John 26
Streetcar Named Desire (Williams) 145
Streicher, Julius 10, 11
Strijdom, Johannes 72
strikes 25, 29, 88
students:
    Black Panther founders 132
    Berkeley Free Speech Movement 132
    rebellion in Columbia 132
    role in feminist movement 134
    uprising in France 36-37, 36-37, 155
Sudetenland 9
Suez Canal 78
Suez Crisis 27, 43, 63, 81, 81, 82-84
Suharto, General 58
Sukarno, Dr Ahmed 56-58, 56, 144, 146, 151
Sullivan, Ed 128, 137
Sun Records 127
Sutherland, Graham 26
Sweden, in EFTA 44
Switzerland, in EFTA 44
Syria:
    attack on Israel 78
    military aid from U.S.S.R. 84
    refugees in 86
    Six-Day War 85-86
    threats to Israel 85
    in UAR 84, 151

Taft-Hartley Act 88, 145
Tagore, Rabindranath 46
Taiwan (Formosa) 43, 124, 146
Talal, King of Jordan 82
Tanganyike 153
Tanzania 153, 154
television 140
Tartars 99
Tashkent Declaration 50
Tate, Sharon 155
Tati, Jacques 34, 34, 151
Teddy Boys 128, 128
teenagers 126-32
television 137-43, 146
    in Britain 137, 141-2, 149
    commercial 28, 137, 138, 142, 149
    ownership of sets 28, 28, 137
    politicians on 143
    spread round world 140-2
    translations of U.S. programs 141
    in U.S.A. 137-8
Tempelhof airfield 23
Templer, Sir Gerald 54, 55, 147
Tensing Norgay, Sherpa 148
Tereshkova, Valentina 153
Texaco Star Theater (TV) 137
That Was the Week That Was (TW3) (TV) 140
Thieu, General Nguyen Van 115
Thompson, Warrant Officer Hugh 116, 116
Thorez, Maurice 33
Thozo, Colonel Jean "Leathernose" 76, 76
Tibet:
    Chinese invasion 121, 121, 124, 147
    uprising 151
Tiger, HMS 70
Time magazine 131, 132
Times 130
Tin, Colonel Bui 61
Tito, Marshal 13, 17, 19, 146, 148, 149
Toast of the Town (TV) 137
Toguri, Iva Ikuko ("Tokyo Rose") 146
Tojo, General 62, 146
Tokyo Rose 146
Tonight (TV) 137
torture 74, 75
totalitarianism 23
Touré, Ahmed Sekou 66
Townsend, Group Captain Peter 149
trade unions, strikes 25, 29, 88
transcendental meditation (TM) 130
Transjordan 78, 81, 146
Trudeau, Pierre 94
Truffaut, François 34
Truman, Harry S 14, 16, 18, 19, 21, 77, 88, 146
    and Korean War 107, 108
Truman Doctrine 19, 145
Trumbo, Dalton 88
Tshombe, Moïse 67, 68
Tunisia 74, 149
Tupamaros 97
Turkey:
    Baghdad Pact 149
    British aid after Second World War 19
    in Korean War 107

Twenty-One (TV) 138

Uganda 154
Ulbricht, Walter 100, 111, 152
UNESCO 43
United Arab Republic 84, 151
United Fruit Company 96
United Nations 43, 107, 109, 144, 144, 151
    agencies 43
    members 43, 51, 152
    peace-keeping forces 43, 67, 85, 150, 153
    powers 43
    role 43
    Secretariat 43
UNRRA (United Nations Relief and Rehabilitation Administration) 14, 43
Uruguay 97
U.S. 88-98
    aid from 14, 20-22, 24-25
    American dream 92, 92
    attitudes to colonialism 59-60
    attitudes towards U.S.S.R. 18
    Baghdad Pact 149
    boom years 90-91
    civil rights 93, 98, 134, 150, 150, 153
    and communism 42, 107-9, 145
    communist witch hunts 88-90, 147, 147
    Cuban missile crisis 109-10
    defense costs 63
    demobilization of troops 17
    drive-in movies 92, 92
    Drunkometer 150
    Economic Opportunity Act 98
    at end of Second World War 6-7
    Fair Deal program 88
    gangsters 91
    gay sub-culture 136
    GI Bill of Rights 88
    GI brides 8
    GNP 90
    granting independence to Philippines 53-54, 53
    in Greek civil war 19
    "hot line" to Moscow 112
    India's attitude to 50, 52
    inflation 88
    isolationism 6, 19
    Jews in 77
    in Korean War 107-9, 108
    Levittowns 92
    loans to Britain 25
    loans to France 35
    McCarran Act 147
    McMahon Act 110
    nuclear test-ban treaty 30, 153
    nuclear weapons 110, 148
    occupation of Japan 62-63, 63, 147
    population 90
    race riots 93, 149, 153, 154, 154
    space exploration 94-95, 143, 151, 152, 155
    spy planes 112
    states 151
    strikes 88
    suburbia 92, 92
    Taft-Hartley Act 88, 145
    teenagers 126-7
    television 137-8, 141
    trade unions 88
    Treaty of Mutual Assistance 145
    troops in Britain 8
    UnAmerican Activities Committee 88-90
    in United Nations 43
U.S. Air Force:
    Berlin airlift 22-23
    stationed in Britain 23
U.S.S.R. 99-106
    in Africa 67
    agriculture 99, 103-4
    aid to China 118, 147
    anti-Semitism 99-100
    art treasures stolen by Germans 13
    atom bombs 23, 89, 110, 146
    blockade of West Berlin 22
    broken agreements 18
    China's split from 104, 152
    cultural purge 145
    deaths in Second World War 14
    demobilization of troops 17
    Eastern European satellite countries 16-17
    ethnic minorities rehabilitated 102-3
    ethnic minorities resettled 99
    five-year plans 99
    gulags 103, 104, 104

"hot line" to Washington 112
    nuclear test-ban treaty 30, 36, 112, 153
    in Poland 19
    relationship with China 104, 120-2, 124
    reparation payments from Germany 9, 38, 99
    scorched earth policy 99
    size 14
    slave laborers in Germany 12
    space exploration 94, 104, 151, 152, 153
    television 141, 141
    territories 14, 17
    in United Nations 43
    Virgin Lands scheme 103-4
Ustachi 14

Vadim, Roger 34
Van Doren, Charles 138, 138
Vassall, John 112
Venezuela 151
Verwoerd, Hendrik 72, 154
Vietcong 113, 115, 116, 116, 144
Vietminh 59-60, 61
Vietnam 113
    ARVN (Army of the Republic of Vietnam) 115
    French in 58-62, 144
    independence 144
    partition 61-62, 149
Vietnam War 55, 98, 113-17, 114, 116, 117, 124, 154, 154
    behavior of U.S. troops 116
    demonstrations against 36, 115, 115, 131, 132, 155, 155
    Gulf of Tonkin Resolution 115
    My Lai massacre 116, 155
    Operation Rolling Thunder 115, 154
    on television 43
    Tet offensive 116, 155
    U.S. body counts 114, 116
    use of Agent Orange 116
Volkswagen (VW) 40
    Beetle 40
Vorster, Johannes Balthazar 72

The Wages of Fear (film) 34
Waksam, Dr Selman 144
Walcott, Jersey Joe 145
Warhol, Andy 142, 142
War, Indochina 34, 36, 58-62, 58, 60-61
War, Korean see Korean War
War, Second World:
    aftermath 6-14
    cost 6
    end 6, 24
    U.S. and Soviet link up 16
    VE Day 24, 144
    VJ Day 25, 144
War, Six-Day 82, 85-86, 86, 154
War, Vietnam see Vietnam War
Ward, Dr Stephen 30, 30
Warhol, Andy 152
Warren, Earl 93, 98
Warsaw Pact 149
Watson, James 148
Wavell, Lord Archibald 48
Weekend Telegraph 131
Weizmann, Chaim 145
Welensky, Sir Roy 70
Welles, Orson 146
Werewolves (Nazis) 12
Western Sahara 66
Western Wall 85
West Indians, immigrants 29, 29
Westmoreland, General William 114, 116
The Who 130
WHO (World Health Organization) 43
Wiesenthal, Simon 79, 79
Wild One (film) 126, 126
Wilhelm Gustloff (cruise ship) 13
Williams, Tennessee 148
Wilson, Harold 28, 44, 70, 71, 134
Wilson, Sloan 92
Windscale, Cumberland 151
Winfield, Pamela 8
Wolfenden Report 150
Wolfsburg, Germany, VW plant 40
women 133-6
    in China 118-19, 119, 120, 121
    discrimination against 133-4
    doing men's work 133
    fight for equality 133, 134-5
    and Pill 134
Women's Lib 134

working 133
Woodstock festival 131, 131
World Cup (football) 154
Wyszynski, Cardinal 100, 148, 150

Yahya Khan 52
Yalta conference 18, 33
Yasgur, Max 131
Yeager, Chuck 145
Yemen 84, 155
Yogi, Maharishi Mahesh 130
Yoruba people 64
youth rebellion 126-32
Yugoslavia:
    aid in Greek civil war 18
    at end of Second World War 13
    loyalty to U.S.S.R. 17, 149
    Second World War enemies 13-14

Zambia 70
Zanzibar 140, 153
Zatopek, Emil 147
Zen Buddhism 130
Zhdanov, Andrei 100, 122, 145
Zhou Enlai 118, 123
Zilliacus, Konni 25
Zimbabwe 66
Zionism 77
Zog, King of Albania 144

ACKNOWLEDGMENTS

Abbreviations:
T=top; M= middle; B= bottom;
L= left; R= right.

3 Kobal Collection, L; AKG, ML; Topham Picturepoint MR; Jean-Loup Charmet, R. 6 Topham Picturepoint, BL. 6-7 The Mariners' Museum/ Corbis, M. 8 Popperfoto, TR; AKG, B. 9 AKG, TL, BR. 10 AKG, BL. 10-11 Ullstein Bilderdienst, M. 11 Popperfoto, TR. 12 Popperfoto, TL; AKG, BR. 13 Novosti, TM; Topham Picturepoint, BR. 14 Popperfoto, TL; UPI/Corbis-Bettmann, BR. 15 AKG, Background; Popperfoto, L; AKG, LM; Popperfoto, RM; Topham Picturepoint, R. 16 Hulton-Getty, B. 17 AKG, TL; Topham-Picturepoint, BR. 18 Hulton-Getty, TR; Topham Picturepoint, B. 19 Topham Picturepoint, BR. 20 Topham Picturepoint, BM. 20-21 Popperfoto, TM. 21 Hulton-Getty, BM; AKG, RM. 22 Topham Picturepoint, TR; Ullstein Bilderdienst, B. 23 AKG, TM, BR. 24 Topham Picturepoint, TR; Hulton-Getty, B. 25 Hulton-Getty, BR. 26 Topham Picturepoint, TR, BM. 27 Topham Picturepoint, BL, MR. 28 Science and Society Picture Library, TR; Hulton-Getty, BR. 29 Topham Picturepoint, T; Popperfoto, MR. 30 Hulton-Getty, TM; Popperfoto, BL; Topham Picturepoint, BR. 31 Popperfoto, TM; Popperfoto, B. 32 Roger-Viollet, BL. 32-33 Popperfoto, BM. 33 Jean-Loup Charmet, TR. 34 Roger-Viollet, TR; AKG, BL; Jean-Loup Charmet, BR. 35 Jean-Loup Charmet, TM; AKG, B. 36 Popperfoto, TM; AKG, BL. 36-37 Ullstein Bilderdienst, BR. 37 Popperfoto, TL. 38 AKG, B. 39 Ullstein Bilderdienst, TL; Topham Picturepoint, BL; Topham Picturepoint, MR. 40 AKG, TL, MR; Ullstein Bilderdienst, BL. 41 AKG, TR; Suddeutscher Verlag, B. 42 Topham Picturepoint, TR, BL. 43 Jean-Loup Charmet, TM; Popperfoto, BL. 44 Hulton-Getty, TR; Suddeutscher Verlag, BL. 45 Magnum Photos, Background; Corbis/Bettman/UPI, L; Jean-Loup Charmet, ML; Topham Picturepoint, MR; AKG, R. 46 Hulton-Getty, BL. 46-47 Magnum Photos, M. 47 AKG, BR. 48 Corbis/Bettman/UPI, TR; Topham Picturepoint, BL. 49 Hulton-Getty, BL. 50 Magnum Photos, T. Suddeutscher Verlag, BR. 51 Topham Picturepoint, ML, BR; Hulton-Getty, TR. 52 Magnum Photos, TL; AKG, BR. 53 Jean-Loup Charmet, TR; Topham Picturepoint, BL. 54 Corbis/ Bettman/UPI, BL. 54-55 Popperfoto, TM. 55 Popperfoto, TR; Suddeutscher Verlag, BM. 56 Corbis/UPI, TL; Popperfoto, B. 57 Suddeutscher Verlag, TR; Topham Picturepoint, BL. 58 Roger-Viollet, BL. 58-59 Corbis/Bettman/UPI, TM. 59 Roger-Viollet, BL. 60 Corbis/ Bettman/UPI, B. 60-61 Suddeutscher

Verlag, TM. 61 Roger-Viollet, BL; Jean-Loup Charmet, TM. 62 Topham Picturepoint, TR; Corbis/UPI, BL. 63 Magnum Photos, TL, BR. 64 Jean-Loup Charmet, BL. 64-65 Magnum Photos, TM. 65 Popperfoto, BR. 66 Jean-Loup Charmet, TL. 66-67 Magnum Photos, B. 67 Hulton-Getty, MR. 68 Topham Picturepoint, BL. 68-69 Popperfoto, T. 69 Magnum Photos, BR. 70 Topham Picturepoint, TR; Suddeutscher Verlag, BL. 71 Hulton-Getty, T; Topham Picturepoint, BR. 72 Topham Picturepoint, BM; Magnum Photos, BR. 72-73 Magnum Photos, TM. 73 Corbis/Bettman/UPI, TR; Topham Picturepoint, BR. 74 AKG, BL. 74-75 Magnum Photos, TR. 76 Roger-Viollet, ML; AKG, TR; Hulton-Getty, BR. 77 Hulton-Getty, TR; AKG, BL. 78 Corbis/Bettman/ UPI, T, BR. 79 Corbis/UPI, ML; AKG, BR. 80 Popperfoto, TR; Corbis/ Bettman/UPI, BL. 81 Suddeutscher Verlag, TL; Suddeutscher Verlag, B. 82 Popperfoto, BL. 82-83 Magnum Photos, BR. 84 Popperfoto, ML; Suddeutscher Verlag, TR. 85 Bettman/Corbis, B. 86 Hulton-Getty, T; Magnum Photos, BR. 87 Network, Background; Roger-Viollet, L; David King Collection, ML; Corbis/UPI, MR; Topham Picturepoint, R. 88 Popperfoto, BL. 89 Corbis/ Bettman/UPI, T; 90 Magnum Photos, TL; E.T. Archive, BR. 91 Corbis/ Bettman/UPI, TR, BR; Advertising Archives, ML. 92 Advertising Archives, TL; Rex Features, MR; Corbis/Bettman/UPI, BL. 93 Corbis/ Bettman/UPI, TR, BM. 94 Topham Picturepoint, TL; Magnum Photos/ Henri Cartier-Bresson, BM. 94-95 AKG, T. 95 Topham Picturepoint, MR; David King Collection, BR. 96 Corbis/Bettman, BL. 96-97 Topham Picturepoint, B. 97 Magnum Photos, TR. 98 Corbis/ Bettman/UPI, TL; David King Collection, BR. 99 Sygma, B. 100 Hulton-Getty, M. 100-101 Corbis/Bettman/UPI, T. 101 Hulton-Getty, BM. 102 Roger-Viollet, BL; Topham Picturepoint, TR. 103 Corbis/Bettman/UPI, TR; Magnum Photos, B. 104 David King Collection, TM; Network, BL. 105 Sygma, T, MR. 106 Sygma, B. 107 Jean-Loup Charmet, TR; Corbis/UPI, BL. 108 Corbis/UPI, TL; Hulton-Getty, B. 109 Hulton-Getty, BR. 110 Topham Picturepoint, BL. 111 Corbis/Bettman/UPI, TL; Topham Picturepoint, TR. 112 Corbis/Bettman/UPI, TM. Hulton-Getty, BL, BM. 113 Topham Picturepoint, BL; Bradbury & Williams, TR. 114 Topham Picturepoint, T; Sygma, BL. 115 Corbis/Bettman/UPI, BR. 116 Corbis/Bettman/UPI, TM. Topham Picturepoint, BR. 117 Corbis/Bettman/UPI, TR. 118 E.T. Archive, BL; Magnum

Photos, TR. 119 Sygma, T; Mary Evans Picture Library, BR. 120 Mary Evans Picture Library, TL; Magnum Photos/Rene Burri, B. 121 Topham Picturepoint, BR. 122 Sygma, TL; Network, BR. 123 David King Collection, T, MR. 124 David King Collection, TR; Network, B. 125 Hulton-Getty, Background; David King Collection, L; Roger-Viollet, ML; Topham Picturepoint, MR; Corbis/Bettman/UPI, R. 126 Magnum Photos, BL; Kobal Collection, BR. 127 Corbis/Bettman/ UPI, TL, R. 128 Hulton-Getty, TL; Sygma, BL. 128-9 Hulton-Getty, M. 129 Popperfoto, TR; National Trust Photo Library, M. 130 Hulton-Getty, TL; Rex Features, BR. 131 Corbis/Bettman/UPI, TL; Henry Diltz/Corbis, LM; Bettman/Corbis, RM. 132 Bettman/Corbis, TM; Bettman/Corbis, BR. 133 Hulton-Getty, BL. 134 Jean-Loup Charmet, TM; Hulton-Getty, BR. 135 Hulton-Getty, TR; Topham Picturepoint, B. 136 Roger-Viollet, TM; David King Collection, BR. 137 Topham Picturepoint, TR; Hulton-Deutsch Collection/Corbis, BL. 138 Magnum Photos, TR, M; Topham Picturepoint, BL. 139 Topham Picturepoint, T; Bettman/Corbis, ML, BR. 140 Corbis/ Bettman/UPI, TL; Mark Edwards/ Still Pictures, B. 141 Roger-Viollet, TR; David King Collection, M; Hulton-Getty, BM. 142 Francis G. Mayer/Corbis, M; Bettman/Corbis, BL. 143 Popperfoto, TL; Corbis/Bettman/ UPI, B. 144 Topham Picturepoint, ML, Roger-Viollet, TR; Hulton-Getty, BR. 145 Popperfoto, TM. 146 Popperfoto, TM, RM; Topham Picturepoint, BL. 147 Topham Picturepoint, TR; David King Collection, ML; Hulton-Getty, Background. 148 Roger-Viollet, TM; Magnum Photos, MR; Hulton-Getty, Background. 149 Hulton-Getty, TM, ML; Corbis/Bettman/UPI, BR. 150 Corbis/Bettman/UPI, TL; Popperfoto, MR; Magnum Photos, BR. 151 Magnum Photos, TL; AKG, MR; Suddeutscher Verlag, Background. 152 Topham Picturepoint, TL, MR; Magnum Photos, Background. 153 Corbis/ Bettman/UPI, TM; Sygma, MR; Magnum Photos, BL. 154 Suddeutscher Verlag, TR; Magnum Photos, BL; Topham Picturepoint, Background. 155 Magnum Photos, TL, M; Suddeutscher Verlag, MR.

Front cover: Sygma, T; Topham Picturepoint, M; Kobal Collection, B.

Back cover: Photo Researchers,Inc., T; Roger-Viollet, M; AKG, B.

The editors are grateful to the following individuals and publishers for their kind permission to quote passages from the publications listed below:

Brassey's Inc, from *Dien Bien Phu: The Epic Battle America Forgot*, by Howard R. Simpson & Stanley Karnow, 1994.
Calder, from *La Question*, by Henri Alleg, 1958.
Constable, from *Sentimental Journey: The Story of the GI Brides*, by Pamela Winfield, 1984.
The Evening Standard, from an interview by Maureen Cleave, 1966.
Fontana, from *The Gulag Archipelago*, by Alexander Solzhenitsyn, 1995.
Little, Brown & Company, from *Khrushchev Remembers*, Jerrold L. Schecter, Vyacheslav V. Luchkov & Strobe Talbott, 1990.
Methuen, from *Too Much*, by Robert Hewison, 1988.
Pavilion Books, from *In the Sixties*, by Ray Connolly, 1995.
The Times, 1967.
Vintage, from *The Second Sex*, by Simone de Beauvoir, 1997.
Weidenfeld & Nicolson from *Justice, Not Vengeance*, by Simon Wiesenthal, 1989.
The editors would also like to thank Ron Angel for his permission to quote his reminiscences.